MARRIAGES
of
SUMNER COUNTY,
TENNESSEE

1787–1838

MARRIAGES
of
SUMNER COUNTY,
TENNESSEE

1787-1838

Compiled by
EDYTHE RUCKER WHITLEY

With an Index by Gary Parks

CLEARFIELD

Reprinted for
Clearfield Company, Inc. by
Genealogical Publishing Co., Inc.
Baltimore, Maryland
1999, 2005

Copyright © 1981
Genealogical Publishing Co., Inc.
Baltimore, Maryland
All Rights Reserved
Library of Congress Catalogue Card Number 80-84317
International Standard Book Number 0-8063-0922-9
Made in the United States of America

Introduction

UMNER COUNTY, Tennessee was erected on November 17, 1786 by an act of the Legislature of North Carolina. It was formed from a part of Davidson County and was named in honor of General Jethro Sumner. The first court of Sumner County was held on the first Monday in March of 1787 at the house of John Hamilton at Station Camp Creek, about five miles from the present town of Gallatin, which became the county seat.

For some unknown reason the Clerk of Sumner County did not record the early marriages in a book or ledger, as was the custom. The marriages listed here derive instead from original marriage bonds and unrecorded licenses found amongst loose papers in the courthouse in Gallatin. Some original bonds had been lost or were taken from the courthouse before I made my original transcriptions in 1937.

The reader should note the following: (1) Marriage bonds were frequently issued the same day as licenses, but the marriage itself was usually—though not always—solemnized at a later date. If no date of marrriage, or solemnization, is given, then the single date provided refers to the date of issue of either the bond or the license; (2) Persons named in the bonds and licenses, other than brides and grooms, of course, when not identified by abbreviations such as BM or M.G., are most probably either bondsmen or witnesses; (3) Abbreviations other than J.P. (Justice of the Peace), BM (bondsman), and M.G. (Minister of the Gospel) usually refer to clergymen of various denominations, both lay and ordained.

Edythe Rucker Whitley
Nashville, Tennessee
May 1980

SUMNER COUNTY, TENNESSEE:

Marriages, 1787-1838

Joseph Crabtree & Hannah Carr, Sep. 10, 1787. James Frazier, BM.
Thomas Hampton & Susannah Arrington, June 19, 1787. Anthony Bled-
soe, BM.
George Blackmore & Sally Thompson, Sep. 10, 1787. Geo. D. Black-
more.
William Clay & Tilley Hays, Oct. 9, 1787. Peter Looney, BM.
Thomas Conyers & Jane Wills, Sep. 10, 1787. James Frazier, BM.
Henry Houndshell & Isbell Snoddy, Oct. 9, 1787. Peter Looney, BM.
George Ridley & Thankful Hall (Junr), Oct. 10, 1787. William Nee-
ly, BM.
James Wilson & Mary Wilson, Sep. 7, 1787. John Wilson, BM.
Stephen Byrns & Mary Thompson, April 14, 1788. James Byrns, BM.
Edward Jones & Magdaleen Rule, Feb. 4, 1788. John Rule, BM.
Thomas McMullin & _____(?), Oct. 14, 1788. Charles Harring-
ton, BM.
Thomas Williamson & Polly Bell, Aug. 5, 1788. Samuel Bell, BM.
King Carr & Anne Hamilton, Jan. 24, 1789. Richard Carr, BM.
James Clendening & Betsy Bledsoe, June 10, 1789. William Neely, BM.
Joseph Desha & Peggy Bledsoe, Dec. 29, 1789. _____(?), BM.
Joseph Dixon & Catherine Lovin, Aug. 6, 1789. James Ruse, BM.
William Frazer & Jenny Hambleton, Jan. 31, 1789. James Frazer, BM.
Thomas Lemartis & A. McDonald, Sep. 22, 1789. William Baldwin, BM.
William McFadden & Rachael Hendricks, Oct. 18, 1789. Edward Bogin,
BM.
James McDonald & Jerusy Jones, Nov. 24, 1789. Stephen Jones, BM.
Jeremiah Morgan & Mary Morgan, Nov. 28, 1789. Armistead Morgan, BM.
William Neely & Rachel Bledsoe, June 10, 1789. James Clendening,
BM.
John Payton & Peggy Hamilton, Dec. 24, 1789. Ephraim Payton, BM.
James Reese & Polly Desha, Sep. 18, 1789. James Desha, BM.
Alexander Walker & Sibella Whitsetts, Dec. 15, 1789. James Whit-
setts, BM.
George Wills & Nancy Mains, Nov. 18, 1789. Thomas Conyers, BM.
William Allen & Elon Harmon, Aug. 31, 1790. James Hays, BM.
Uriah Anderson & Milly Jones, March 9, 1790. Robert Jones, BM.
Charles Brantley & Dicy Anderson, Nov. 24, 1790. Robert Jones, BM.
Wilson Coats & Caty Rule, Feb. 8, 1790. John Cravins, BM.
Zachariah Cross & Esther Johnson, Aug. 11, 1790. John Frederick
Morgan, BM.
Robert Erspy & Curry Cribbins, Feb. 1, 1790. Thomas Mastin, BM.
Thomas Hendricks & Sarah Lynn, Oct. 16, 1790. William Totwine, BM.
Harry Hicks & Ann Ramsey, March 12, 1790. David Wilson, BM.
Robert Jones & Agnes Anderson, Nov. 24, 1790. Charles Brantley, BM.
Thomas Lemartis & Jenny Dyal, March 22, 1790. Hugh Crawford, BM.

1

SUMNER COUNTY MARRIAGES

William Marshall & Ann Bell, Oct. 30, 1790. George Williamson, BM.
William Penny & Suckey Bledsoe, March 12, 1790. David Wilson, BM.
Robert Shannon & Rebeccah Buchanon, April 14, 1790. James Buchanon, BM.
James Sheppard & Elizabeth Bickert, March 16, 1790. Alexander Whittaker, BM.
Zacheus Wilson & Elizabeth Wilson, Nov. 24, 1790. David Wilson, BM.
William Anderson & Betsey Jones, Nov. 23, 1791. Stephen Anderson, BM.
John Carr & Sally Cage, Nov. 23, 1791. James Frazer, BM. King Carr.
James Carson & Nancy S. Stuart, Dec. 19, 1791. Joseph Waller, BM.
Thomas Cartwright & Agnes Christian, Jan. 22, 1791. Thomas Masten, BM.
John Cotton & Fanny Hamilton, Jan. 4, 1791. Lazrus Cotton, BM. Ephraim Payton.
Reubin Douglass & Betsy Edwards, Jan. 25, 1791. Edward Douglass, BM.
William Fisher & Faithy Hix, May 17, 1791. Robert Looney.
Basil Fry & Jane Mansker, March 8, 1791. John Dawson, BM.
John Gathier & Elender Buck, March 26, 1791. John Payton, BM.
David Hainey & Sarah Campbell, Oct. 19, 1791. John Roberts, BM.
John Hannah & Mary Pryor, Jan. 20, 1791. William Pryor, BM.
Martin Harpole & Betsey Rule, Aug. 16, 1791. William Reed, BM.
Cornelius Herndon & Polly Harrison, Sep. 26, 1791. James Adams, BM.
Jacob Sanders & Sarah Hardin, May 31, 1791. Richard Hogin, BM.
John Lawrence & Betsy Hynes, Feb. 4, 1791. William Lawrence, BM.
Charles Myars & Betsey Biter (or Bitner), May 23, 1791. Jacob Turner (or Tupner).
John Neely & Masey Harrison, April 6, 1791. Roger Gibson, BM.
Thomas Payton & Alia Gilbert, Nov. 16, 1791. Samuel Gilbert, BM.
Nathaniel Parker & Mary Bledsoe, Dec. 4, 1791. James Douglas, BM.
William Reed & Peggy Rule, Aug. 16, 1791. Martin Harpool, BM.
John Roberts & Nancy Ferguson, Oct. 19, 1791. David Hainey, BM.
Elias Smith & Esther Barr, April 16, 1791. John Boyd, BM.
William Smith & Elsy McDonald, March 25, 1791. Richard Hogin, BM.
Amos West & Frances Herndon, April 7, 1791. Richard Hogin, BM.
Edward Williams & Darkness Edwards, Dec. 12, 1791. John Williams, BM.
Elisha Burk & Mary Robinson, Aug. 25, 1792. William Miller, BM.
William Cage & Nancy Morgan, June 19, 1792. David Shelby, BM.
Thomas Edwards & Elizabeth Turner, Feb. 7, 1792. Edward Williams, BM.
William Gibson & Polly Brigance, June 27, 1792. Wm. Brigance, BM.
Francis Glasser & Molly Benas, Aug. 29, 1792. Gabriel Black, BM.
Joshua Haskin & Susannah Bone, Jan. 2, 1792. James Bone, BM.
William Haynes & Polly Lawrence, Jan. 7, 1792. Peter Turney, BM.
Josiah Hunter & Rachael Hannah, Aug. 20, 1792. Robert McCrory, BM.
John Lawrence & Lydia Malone, Aug. 29, 1792. Saml. Pharr, BM.
Isaac Lowell & Sarah McAdams, June 20 (21), 1792. James Franklin, BM.
John Nancarro & Celia Slade, Jan. 24, 1792. Thos. Smith, BM.
Thos. Perry & Catherine McAdams, July 24, 1792. Isaac Lowell, BM.
John Rule & Polly Bird, March 17, 1792. Valentine Shoat, BM. Date

SUMNER COUNTY MARRIAGES

Performed.
Joseph Steele & Darcus Wilson, Nov. 19, 1792. Wm. Snoddy, BM.
John Benton & Jane Kendrick, March 18, 1793. _____(?), BM.
Robert Campbell & Martha Hamilton, March 29, 1793. John Hamilton, BM.
Elijah Clary & Polly Barnes, Feb. 20, 1793. Peter Looney, BM.
Richard Freeman & Sally Haynes, June 6, 1793. Sion Perry, BM.
James Farr & Polly King, March 13, 1793. Richard King, BM.
Joseph Griggs & Sally Cowan, Feb. 28, 1793. Jas. McKinzy, BM.
Jacob Houndeshell & Elizabeth Wilson, June 27, 1793. James Wilson, BM.
Ezekiel Lindsey & Nancey Green, Sep. 21, 1793. Isaac Lindsey, BM.
William Maxey & Sarah Emily Allen, Feb. 11, 1793. Edw. Maxey, BM.
Robert McKinley & Sally Cowan, Dec. 10, 1793. Reason Bowyer, BM.
Flower McGreggor & Polly Payne, Oct. 5, 1793. Henry Bradford, BM.
Joseph Morgan & Peggy Maxwell, Sep. 28, 1793. Jeremiah Morgan, BM.
Robert Patterson & Betsey Lanier, Dec. 16, 1793. John Roberson, BM.
Thomas Walker & Betsey Cathey, Sep. 21, 1793. John Laurence, BM.
William Walker & Priscilla Hannah, April 2, 1793. Josiah Hunter, BM.
William Wilson & Sally Brevard, Nov. 10, 1793. David Wilson.
James Womack & Elizabeth Dillard, Jan. 10, 1793. Elmore Douglass, BM.
William Clary & Nancy Mercer, April 3, 1793. Peter Looney, BM.
George Fairly & Jenny Pryor, Feb. 14, 1794. Wm. Pryor, BM.
Richard Freeman & Nelly Yates, March 10, 1794. Rich. King, BM.
John Hamilton & Isabel Houndeshell, March 13, 1794. Thos. Patton, BM.
Samuel Hollis & Nancy Strother, Sep. 22, 1794. Richard Strother, BM. Edwd. Douglass.
Richard King & Rachel Blythe, July 1, 1794. Andrew Blythe, BM.
Rhubin Martin & Jenny Kuykendall, Jan. 5, 1794. Date performed, Jan. 20, 1794. Sion Perry, BM.
William McCorkle & Martha Purviance, Dec. 25, 1794. Samuel King, BM.
Nathaniel Parker & Sally Ramsey, Dec. 10, 1794. Wm. Neely, BM.
William Reed & Polly Bledsoe, Nov. 27, 1794. Peter Fisher, BM.
Thomas Reese & Margaret Thompson, April 5, 1794. Andrew Patterson, BM.
Anthony Sharp & Peggy Nelson, Feb. 3, 1794. Abraham Landers (or Sanders), BM.
James Wilson & Rachel Harrington, March 10, 1794. Charles Harrington, BM.
Joseph Worthington & Betsey Hughes, Sep. 9, 1794. Matthew Kuykendall, BM.
Thomas Waller & Elizabeth Pierce, March 13, 1794. Isaac Pierce, BM.
Orman Allen & Betsey Beard, April 20, 1795. Adam Beard, BM.
Isham Baird & Clarissa Bushrod, Oct. 21, 1795. Griswold Latimer, BM.
Adam Beard & Caty Barkley, March 10, 1795. Orman Allen, BM.
William Brazil & Sarah Sebastan, Sep.___, 1795. Thomas Edwards, BM.
Dennis Bryan (or O'Bryan) & Anny Hamilton, June 16, 1795. John Hamilton, BM.
William Burk & Rachel Cooper, Dec. 31, 1795. William Parmer, BM.

SUMNER COUNTY MARRIAGES

Isaac Caldwell & Betsey Hart (or Hurt), Dec. 14, 1795. Absolum Hart (or Hurt), BM.
Joseph Crabtree & Sally Holdman, April 10, 1795. Nathan Holdman, BM.
Thomas George & Polly Bird, Aug. 25, 1795. Wilson Cage, BM.
Samuel Gibson & Sally Bledsoe, March 9, 1795. William Neely, BM.
William Harrington (or Haffington) & Nancy Crabtree, Sep. 15, 1795. Wm. Bird, BM.
John Harrod & Caty Roberson, Nov. 2, 1795. Simon Kuykendall, BM.
Sam'l King & Anny Dixon, Aug. 25, 1795. James Farr, BM.
Walter Maxey & Sarah Allen, Sep. 26, 1795. Henry Morris, BM.
Isreal Moore & Betsey Wallace, May 15, 1795. Joseph Steel, BM.
John Moore & Caty Hammond, Sep. 20, 1795. Jonathan Pearce, BM.
Henry Morris & Christiana Zeigler, Aug. 24, 1795. Henry Loving, BM.
John Savley & Martha Moore, April 28, 1795. Thomas Strain, BM.
Samuel Scott & Caty Morrison, March 25, 1795. William Morrison, BM.
Isaac Stanley & Betsey Pankey, Nov. 16, 1795. John Pankey, BM.
James Strain & Catharine McAdams, Jan. 21, 1795. Isaac Lowell, BM.
David White & Anne Caldwell, June 16, 1795. Abraham Landers, BM.
James Wright & Elizabeth Rutherford, July 27, 1795. James Wilson, BM.
Benj. Wood & Betsey Winters, April 15, 1795. Lewis Crane, BM.
Wilson Cage & Mary Dalton, Feb. 29, 1796. Ezekiel Douglass, BM.
John Barns & Mary Turney, Dec. 27, 1796. Elisha Clary, BM.
Samuel Barns & Sally Jewel, Sep. 28, 1796. William Snoddfeald, BM.
Gabriel Black & Jenny McKain, March 15, 1796. Pearce Wall, BM.
Robert Dougan & Elizabeth Scoby, Oct. 7, 1796. Wilson Cage, BM.
Archibald Effitor (Haffington) & Martha Lemon, Oct. 6, 1796. Peter Lemon, BM.
George Evans & Sally Morrison, June 7, 1796. Sam'l Rice, BM.
Nathaniel Farrier & Agnes Patterson, March 4, 1796. Andrew Patterson, BM.
John Farrier & Anne Thompson, Oct. 1, 1796. Andrew Robinson, BM.
George Flynn & Sally Baynes, March 26, 1796. Jacob Thomas, BM.
Jesse Glasgow & Peggy Lefavor, July 13, 1796. William Walton, BM.
Jonathan Hannum & Ann Neely, April 16, 1796. Wm. Neely, BM.
Henry Harrison & Polly Howell, Oct. 26, 1796. James Williams, BM.
Elijah Hedgcock & Rhody Jones, March 8, 1796. James Jones, BM.
Samuel Hog & Rebecka Beard, May 30, 1796. William Green, BM.
Leonard Jones & Nancy Jenkins, Oct. 21, 1796. John Jenkins, BM.
Thomas Jones & Milly Wilkins, Jan. __, 1796. Stephen Anderson, BM.
Dempsey Kennedy (or Canedy) & Patsey Barnes, Jan. 19, 1796. John Kennedy (or Canedy), BM.
William McGee & Ann King, May 30, 1796. Samuel King, BM.
John McMillen & Susannah Beson, March 8, 1796. James Givens, BM.
James Morgan & Betsey Dyer, July 14, 1796. Wm. Morgan, BM.
John Found & Anne Dobbins, Dec. 31, 1796. Robert Dobbins, BM.
John Reed & Sarah Dixon, May 7, 1796. Thomas Masten, BM.
Thomas Robinson & Betsey Blackwell, Sep. 17, 1796. Andrew Robinson, BM.
John Searcy & Patty Claybrook, Oct. 7, 1796. Thos. Masten, BM.
Michael Shannon & Margaret Hopkins, Oct. 18, 1796. John Stockard, BM.
John Tinnon & Betsey Moore, July 22, 1796. Joseph Moore, BM.

4

SUMNER COUNTY MARRIAGES

James White & Jane Cathey, April 5, 1796. Abraham Landers, BM.
Samuel White & Polly Braton, April 19, 1796. Thomas Kellon, BM.
James William & Massey Neely, Oct. 3, 1796. Edward Williams, BM.

NO RECORD FOR YEAR 1797

NO RECORD FOR YEAR 1798

NO RECORD FOR YEAR 1799

Moses Adams & Hastey Bass, July 23, 1800. James Vinson, BM.
John Allen & Lastitia Sanders, Dec. 21, 1800. John F. Gillespie,
BM.
James Ball & Biddy Brezeal, Sep. 4, 1800. James Orr, BM.
David Beard & Jenny Wallace, March 24, 1800. James Wallace, BM.
Peter Bellew & Mary Casselberry, July 22, 1800. George Cummings,
BM.

John Benton
                To David Shelby Esq.,
                Dear Sir:
                    The bearer John Benton having given me Satisfactory
                Security for his true performance of his article of
                covenent with me. I have no objections to his commit-
                ting matrimony.
                I am sir with respect and Esteem.
                            Yr. Most Aft. Serv.
                            G. Winchester.

Joseph Bishop & Sally Norris, Sep. 16, 1800. James Norris, BM.
William Bradshaw & Betsey Espy, Nov. 11, 1800. John Hodge, BM.
Lazarus Brown & Peggy McCarty, Aug. 5, 1800. Benjamine Davis, BM.
Stephen Brown & Milley Rhodes, Oct. 21, 1800. Edwin L. Moore, BM.
Reuben Cage & Polly Morgan, Jan. 7, 1800. Wilson Cage, BM.
James Carothers & Jane Irwin, Jan. 29, 1800. Hugh Carothers, BM.
Jonathan Clampel & Priscella Rogers, Sep. 17, 1800. King Carr, BM.
James Clark & Leah Gilleland, Sep. 24, 1800. William Morrison, BM.
Thomas Clark & Sally Diggins, March 27, 1800. James Trousdale, BM.
    Vachel Clark.
William Temple Cole & Mary Brown, Sep. 19, 1800. James Bentley, BM.
Charnel Corbin & Celia Barns, Oct. 30, 1800. Elisha Clary, BM.
William Corkle (or McCorkle) & Jenny Graham, June 9, 1800. Griffeth
    Rutherford, BM.
John Cotton & Jennet Crafford, Nov. 22, 1800. Moore Cotton, BM.
Mathew Cowen & Katy Trousdale, March 8, 1800. Edward Hogin, BM.
Edmund Crutcher & Jenny Allcorn, Sep. 23, 1800. William Gillespie,
BM.
Isaac Donoho & Cretia Totwine, Aug. 27, 1800. John Donoho, BM.
Leonard Dugger & Elizabeth Taylor, Nov. 27, 1800. Whitehead Join-
er, BM.
Luke Dugger & Isbel Gibs, April 26, 1800. Isaac Lowell, BM.
James Edwards & Patsey Cartwright, June 19, 1800. William Hankins,
BM.
Abraham Ellis & Prudence Lindsey, April 24, 1800. Ezekiel Lind-

5

sey, BM.

Cloudsberry Greenhaw & _____ (?), Aug. 15, 1800. Champ Madding, BM.

John Hail & Peggy Carr, July 7, 1800. John Carr, BM.

Jeremiah Hale & Sarah Carr, July 30, 1800. James Carr, BM.

Richard Hankins & Sally Cartwright, Feb. 7, 1800. Wm. Hankins, BM.

Daniel Harpole & Rachael Reiley, April 24, 1800. John Reiley, BM.

John Harrison & Ann Story, Aug. 13, 1800. Jonah E. Giles, BM.

James Hodges & Hannah Wilson, Sep. 16, 1800. James Wilson, BM.

Isaac Hooks & Sally Douglas, May 21, 1800. Joshua Chambers, BM.

William Jenkins & Savory Witcher, April 26, 1800. Roderick Jenkins, BM.

George Johnson & Molly Berry, April 15, 1800. Asa Hassell, BM.

William Lambuth & Elizabeth Greenhaw, Sep. 13, 1800. Vloudsberry Greenhaw, BM.

George Logan & Peggy Alexander, May 27, 1800. Silas Alexander, BM.

Edwin S. Moore & Polly Watson, Oct. 21, 1800. Stephen Brown, BM.

William Morrison & Elenor Wilson, Aug. 27, 1800. James Clark, BM.

David Ormond & Betsey Patton, Jan. 24, 1800. John Hamilton, BM.

David Orr & Jenny McElarath, Feb. 21, 1800. Joseph McElarath, BM.

John Orr & Telitha Cotton, March 21, 1800. David Orr, BM.

Isaac Phillips & Charlotte House, Jan. 8, 1800. Henry Bunn, BM.

John Ragan & Nancey Null (or Neill), Jan. 22, 1800.

John Reason & Sally Impson, Sep. 13, 1800. Ezekiel Douglas, BM.

Edward Sanders & Sukey (Locky) Trigg, April 26, 1800. Will Trigg, BM.

Joseph Sebastan & Polly Summers, March 24, 1800. William Brazel, BM.

David Shelby, Esq. (See John Benton).

William Sheppard & Elizabeth Enox, Oct. 3, 1800. William Shelton, BM.

Joseph Sloan & Polly Hamilton, Sep. 22, 1800. John Hamilton, BM.

Benjamine Smith & Keziah Dixon, June 10, 1800. John Dawson, BM.

George Stout & Jenny Cooper, Nov. 25, 1800. Benjamine Dickerson, BM.

James Stuart & Jane Anderson, July 22, 1800. John Gandy, BM.

Monoah Taylor & Elizabeth Taylor, Dec. 6, 1800. Robert Taylor, BM.

William Thompson & Polly Parker, May 3, 1800. Nichl. Boyce, BM.

Joseph Weatherly & Kezina Anderson, Aug. 6, 1800. William Crawford, BM.

Richard Waller & Sally Harrison, Oct. 10, 1800. Richard Boyer, BM.

G. Winchester (See John Benton).

Robert Wynne & Cynthia Harrison, Jan. 6, 1800. Thomas Harrison, BM.

NO RECORD FOR YEAR 1801 (Lost)

NO RECORD FOR YEAR 1802 (Lost)

Thomas Barret & Charlotte Reason, July 18, 1803. John Reason, BM.

Joseph Biggs & Patsey Kelly, Jan. 29, 1803. Elijah Riggs, BM.

David Bradley & Nancy Taylor, Aug. 29, 1803. John Taylor, BM.

William Bradshaw & Betsey Stubblefield, Aug. 19, 1803. Daniel Trigg, BM.

Griffith Cathey & Susannah Cathey, March 15, 1803. Griffith

SUMNER COUNTY MARRIAGES

W. Rutherford, BM.
Archibald Davis & Elizabeth McBride, Aug. 26, 1803. David Stuart, BM.
George Dempsy & Polly Brigance, Oct. 6, 1803. James Brigance, BM.
Wire Dickerson & Polly Etherly, Aug. 24, 1803. Zacheus Wilson, BM.
James Elder & Polly Watwood, Sep. 21, 1803. James Suiter, BM.
William Espey & Susanna Suiter, Dec. 26, 1803. Benjamine Suiter, BM.
James Franklin, Jr. & Prudy McKain, Feb. 19, 1803. James McKain, BM.
John Garret & Jenny McMurtry, Aug. 4, 1803. Henry McMurtry, BM.
Josiah Hammond & Polly Jones, May 2, 1803. Richard Jones, BM.
Enos Hannah & Sally Harris, Dec. 10, 1803. Drury Milan, BM.
Moses Hardin & Orphy Hassel, June 16, 1803. Jesse Hassel, BM.
Richard Harrell & Nancy Reason, Feb. 24, 1803. Jeremiah Doxey, BM.
Blair Harris & Rachel Gardner, Aug. 1, 1803. Joshua Bradley, BM.
John Hoover & Lydia Waller, Feb. 12, 1803. Saml. Donelson, BM.
George Johnson & Penny Seat, Feb. 3, 1803. William Crawford, BM.
Samuel S. Kennedy & Rebeccah Simpson, April 12, 1803. Wm. Kennedy, BM.
James Latimer & Jinny Hamilton, July 16, 1803. John Hutson, BM.
James Locke & Peggy Cathey, May 19, 1803. Jos. M. Crewan, BM.
John McBride & Fanny Clark, March 19, 1803. James Clark, BM.
Nathaniel McBride & Elizabeth Davidson, March 19, 1803. James Clark, BM.
Jacob McKee & Elizabeth Hamilton, Aug. 4, 1803. James Latimer, BM.
Robert Moffit & Patsey Simpson, March 7, 1803. Charles Simpson, BM.
Jeremiah Murphy & Sally Gwin, June 14, 1803. Earnest Watson, BM.
Jacob Null & Elizabeth Graham, Aug. 30, 1803. James A. Wilson, BM.
William Ogles & Peggy Orr, July 15, 1803. John Orr, BM.
William Palmer & Sally Rankins, July 6, 1803. Samuel Gibson, BM.
John Parks & Hannah Latimer, June 15, 1803. James Latimer, BM.
Thomas Reid & Susannah Shaw, April 8, 1803. Robert Shaw, BM.
William Reid & Polly Turner, Feb. 11, 1803. John Turner, BM.
Bartlett Renfro & Cloe Parker, Nov. 14, 1803. John Parker, BM.
William Ring & Polly Cunningham, April 27, 1803. Isaac M. Bledsoe, BM.
William Robinson & Patty Melton, Dec. 10, 1803. William Melton, BM.
Armstead Rogers & Bridia Whitsett, Sep. 27, 1803. Laurence Whitsett, BM.
Goldsberry Sanders & Susannah Granger, July 2, 1803. Henry Palmer, BM.
John Sedgley & Mary Willis, Feb. 26, 1803. Nathaniel Willcomb, BM.
Thomas Silliman & Sally Wilkins, July 18, 1803. Thos. Anderson, BM.
Nathan Stiner & Hartey Womack, Dec. 31, 1803. Barnabas Stiner, BM.
Stephen Stone & Polly Loving, Dec. 24, 1803. Eusebius Stone, BM.
Robert Strother & Polly Gambling, June 18, 1803. David Brigance, BM.
William Stuart & Delilah Vinson, _____, 1803. John Stuart, BM.
James Sullinger & Levatha Cravatt, Aug. 5, 1803. Thos. Farmer, BM.
Will Trigg, Jr. & Maryann Burton, Dec. 10, 1803. Daniel Trigg, BM.
James Turner & Nancy Goodrum, Feb. 11, 1803. John Goodrum, BM.
Bental Vinson & Jane Patton, Nov. 14, 1803. William McCall, BM.
James Wallace & Lydia Gillespie, Feb. 11, 1803. Jacob Gillespie, BM.

7

Lewis West & Margaret Cowan, June 29, 1803. Wm. Bell, BM.
Thomas Willis & Milly Edwards, June 11, 1803. William Phipps, Jr.,
    BM.
James A. Wilson & Perry Graham, July 5, 1803. John Shelby, BM.
Daniel Woods & Flavia Reese, Nov. 5, 1803. James Reese, BM.

Wm. Daniel Woods

> To David Shelby, Esq.,   Nov. 4, 1803
> Sir:
> The Bearer Wm. Daniel Woods wishing to obtain a
> License for marriage with my Daughter Flavia, it
> being not convenient for me to attend with him at
> this time will inform that he has my aprobation
> but if for the sake of form. Security is nec-
> essary you may either assign my son Georges or my
> name or let it lye over till we can Either of us
> do it with convenience or compliance. Will
> oblige yours.
>   James Reese

William Wright & Nancy Cochran, Sep. 8, 1803. Wm. Hubbard, BM.
Wm. Dill & Eve Houck, Sep. 18, 1804. Philip Kiser, BM.
George Crosner & Catey Houck, Nov. 26, 1804. George Grimes, BM.
Henry Allen & Polly Barns, Dec. 18, 1804. Solomon Shoulders, BM.
James L. Armstrong & Sophia W. Smith, Sep. 27, 1804. _____(?),
    BM.
Adam Atchison & Maryan Jones, Aug. 13, 1804. John Barnett, BM.
Nathan Atchison & Nelly Bearnard, May 24, 1804. Jacob Bearnard, BM.
John Billings & Rebecca Barns, Feb. 2, 1804. Michael Robertson, BM.
Isaac W. Bledsoe & Nancy Lockette, April 23, 1804. James Black-
    more, BM.
Web Bloodworth & Mary Benthall, Dec. 18, 1804. David Allen, BM.
Lewis Booth & Winnie Richardson, July 23, 1804. Robt. Wildure, BM.
John Bradshaw & Oney Henry, Sep. 4, 1804. Hugh Henry, BM.
Walter Bruce & Polly Smith, Oct. 10, 1804. D. Dugger, BM.
Aron Butler & Rosannah Bracken, Feb. 11, 1804. Wm. Bracken, BM.
Thomas Carothers & Sally Holland, Oct. 23, 1804. James Carothers,
    BM.
Kinchin Carter & Mary Benthall, Feb. 25, 1804. James Haynes, BM.
Thomas Campbell & Fanny McHenry, March 26, 1804. Wm. King, BM.
James Clark & Edy Lowry, Aug. 18, 1804. David Stuart, BM.
William Cloar & Polly Hubbard, March 27, 1804. Isaac Bledsoe, BM.
John Dailwood & Nancy Reed, July 30, 1804. William Reed, BM.
Matthew Dixon & Polly Hill, Sep. 18, 1804. Jas. Reason, BM.
Walter Donoho & Caty Haines, Nov. 22, 1804. William Haines, BM.
James Dugger & Kesiah Smith, July 28, 1804. Dred Dugger, BM.
John Elliss & Nancy Britton, Aug. 11, 1804. Wm. Garrett, BM.
Francis Eury & Peggy Espy, Aug. 14, 1804. J. Yowell, BM.
Hezekiah Gardner & Elizabeth Lauderdale, Jan. 16, 1804. James Lau-
    derdale, BM.
Francis Garrett & Ellenor Blair, Oct. 15, 1804. Peter Blair, BM.
John Giles & Eliza Morrison, Oct. 17, 1804. Josiah Morrison, BM.
Thomas Granger & Margaret Lilley, March 10, 1804. Robert Lilley,
    BM.

SUMNER COUNTY MARRIAGES

William Hall & Polly Alexander, Sep. 25, 1804. Edward Bradley, BM.
James Harden & Elizabeth Pitt, May 12, 1804. James Brigance, BM.
William T. Henderson & Eliza J. Smith, Aug. 6, 1804. Jas. L. Armstrong, BM.
David Hobbs & Cloe Hunt, Dec. 21, 1804. Littleberry White, BM.
Zachariah Hogan & Catherine Bunckley, April 25, 1804. Cerban Hall, BM.
Isaac Hurt & Salley Boothe, Dec. 28, 1804. Chas. Boothe, BM.
John Hutson & Elizabeth Dorris, Sep. 15, 1804. Thomas Hamilton, BM.
John Johns & Juliet Trigg, June 19, 1804. Edward Sanders, BM.
Richard Jones & Elizabeth Caviatt, Jan. 26, 1804. Wandy Jones, BM.
Abraham King & Penelope Todd, Feb. 8, 1804. Julias Jones, BM.
James Kirkham & Elizabeth Kirkham, Oct. 4, 1804. Wm. Gready, BM.
Anthony Levit & Hannah Groom, Oct. 2, 1804. Jeremiah Claxton, BM.
William Lilley & Elizabeth Martin, March 10, 1804. Robert Lilley, BM.
Elisha Looney & Polly Lenix (or Lenox), Jan. 2, 1804. Israel Ambers, BM.
James Looney & Polly Smith, Aug. 17, 1804. Isreal Ambers, BM.
Michael Looney & Caroline Latimer, April 4, 1804. Joseph Scobey, BM.
Peter Looney & Polly Bonds, Nov. 7, 1804. Isreal Ambers, BM.
John Marlow & Aney Faulk, March 7, 1804. Wm. Faulk, BM.
Obediah Martin & Sarah Abbott, ____ 7, 1804. Robert Lilley, BM.
Samuel McAdams & Margaret Robinson, June 2, 1804. William Sample, BM.
John McConnell & Betsey Strother, Aug. 1, 1804. Joseph Conn, BM.
John McDaniel & Bathshelia Senter, June 16, 1804. Wm. Senter, BM.
Francis McDonald & Rebeckah Suiter, July 6, 1804. Benjamine Suiter, BM.
Samuel McReynolds & Melberry Dement, Oct. 8, 1804. John Pendergrass, BM.
Joseph Norman & Hannah Jones, Sep. 25, 1804. Samuel Moore, BM.
Shadrack Nye & Elizabeth Latimer, March 20, 1804. Sam'l Donelson, BM.
Daniel Oglesby & Mary White, Sep. 3, 1804. King Carr, BM.
Shadrack Olivis & Nancy Hall, Oct. 21, 1804. A. Edwards, BM.
Sterling Osbrooks & Polly Barker, Aug. 11, 1804. Leonard Brown, BM.
Henry Parmer & Patsey Angle, May 22, 1804. James White, BM.
Henry Powell & Courtney Brasil, July 24, 1804. Laurence Whitsett, BM.
James Reasons & Charlotte Bryant, April 11, 1804. John Reasons, BM.
John Reasons & Anny Herefore, May 1, 1804. Thos. Barrett, BM.
Richard Sanders & Sally Storey, Jan. 7, 1804. Wm. Cathey, BM.
John Lemmons & Priscilla Abbitt, Sep. 3, 1804. Wm. Bracken, BM.
Thomas Shackleford & Agnes Closter, July 21, 1804. Wm. Pittman, BM.
John Simpson & Celia King, Sep. 18, 1804. L. Todd, BM.
Vatchel Stevens & Jinny Jones, Oct. 29, 1804. Isiah Hammond, BM.
Nathan Stiner & Harty Womack, Jan. 12, 1804. Richard Wilson, BM.
Samuel Sullivan & Betsey James, Nov. 12, 1804. James James, BM.
Thomas Summers & Celia Summers, Dec. 3, 1804. Wm. Summers, BM.
William Thomas & Petsey Hashlock, Oct. 22, 1804. Thomas McGuire, BM.
Burrell Thompson & Celia Powell, Dec. 28, 1804. John Hatfield, BM.

9

SUMNER COUNTY MARRIAGES

Cornelius Tinsley & Fanny Stone, Jan. 16, 1804. James Duke, BM.
Asa Todd & Polly Jones, July 17, 1804. Samuel Todd, BM.
Robert Trousdale & Siney Wynham, Jan. 28, 1804. James Trousdale, BM.
Frederick Turner & Catherine Grimes, Aug. 28, 1804. George Crosner, BM.
Edmond Turpin & Charity McBride, May 26, 1804. David Stuart, BM.
Joseph Waller & Elizabeth Railey, Nov. 21, 1804. Samuel Moore, BM.
James Ward & Sally Henson, June 9, 1804. George Morris, BM.
James Watwood & Jenny Williams, Oct. 3, 1804. Thos. Cook, BM.
Daniel Webster & Elizabeth Lloyd, April 30, 1804. Joel Childress, BM.
Ephraim Wells & Nancy Hodge, Oct. 5, 1804. Wm. Trigg, BM.
Stephen White & Jane Bell, Jan. 24, 1804. John D. Hodge, BM.
Job Williams & Nancy Campbell, Oct. 10, 1804. Thomas Cook, BM.
Cabel Willis & Sarah Cantrell, Nov. 9, 1804. Merrell Willis, BM.
Henry Richard Willis & Caty Brigance, Dec. 31, 1804. Daniel Willis, BM.
Merrell Willis & Perry Cherry, Dec. 8, 1804. Sam'l Scott, BM.
David Wilson & Jinny Carothers, May 9, 1804. James Carothers, BM.
Elijah Adams & Elizabeth Miller, Sep. 23, 1805. James Oglesby, BM.
Francis Boren & Edy Wimberly, March 30, 1805. John Boren, BM.
Abraham Bledsoe & Milly Weathered, May 4, 1805. Jas. Rawlings, BM.
Henry Bledsoe & Nancy Gillespie, May 22, 1805. Thos. Gillespie, BM.
William Brackin & Penelope Searcy, Nov. 20, 1805. Howard Douglass, BM.
James Bratton & Betsy Wilson, Dec. 14, 1805. James Wilson, BM.
John Bridgers & Dicy Hunt, Feb. 8, 1805. Edmund Bridgers, BM.
John Brisley & Rosey Clendening, June 10, 1805. Robt. Campbell, BM.
James Brown & Sylva Break, April 1, 1805. James McKain, BM.
John Brown & Elizabeth Ball, July 29, 1805. Abner Ball, BM.
James Burns & Anny White, Dec. 24, 1805. Stephen Cantrell, BM.
Loftain Cage & Naomi Gillespie, Sep. 30, 1805. Jesse Cage, BM.
William Cathey & Elizabeth Cathey, Feb. 5, 1805. Wm. Cathey, BM.
John Cloar & Sally Turner, Oct. 19, 1805. John Hubert, BM.
John Comar & Peggy McCarty, March 18, 1805. Elijah Pruett, BM.
William Crutchfield & Hannah Mabry, March 4, 1805. John Jarratt, BM.
David Dement & Elizabeth Kirkpatrick, Nov. 5, 1805. Thomas Dement, BM.
William Dinning & Betsey Roney, Dec. 16, 1805. Sam'l Roney, BM.
Henry Dorr & Eve Grimes, Aug. 6, 1805. Frederick Miller, BM.
Shadrack Dunn & Polly Pankey, May 30, 1805. John Pankey, BM.
Stephen Evans & Susannah Claxton, May 7, 1805. Thos. Higgombotham, BM.
Arthur Exum & Sarah Davidson, Sep. 12, 1805. Robert Bell, BM.
John Gambill & Hanna Snodgrass, Nov. 11, 1805. Henry Gambill, BM.
James Gamblin & Nelly Noel, Feb. 12, 1805. Reubin Noel, BM.
Summers Harper & Katurah Peairs (Pearce), Jan. 8, 1805. James Charlton, BM.
John Hatfield & Sally Thompson, Jan. 26, 1805. Wm. Shoulders, BM.
Benjamine Hudson & Sarah Hudson, Nov. 28, 1805. Dawsey Hudson, BM.
Marmaduke Ingram & Peggy McConnell, July 24, 1805. M. McConnell, BM.

Nathaniel Irwin & Polly Irwin, July 24, 1805. Wm. McWhirter, BM.
Stephen Jackson & Elizabeth Giles, Nov. 16, 1805. John Giles, BM.
Isaac Jones & Polly Oglesby, Oct. 14, 1805. P. Cuffman, BM.
Allen Josey & Nancy McKinsey, Jan. 22, 1805. James McKinsey, BM.
Sam'l Kerr & Cynthia Wynne, July 31, 1805. Richard Taylor, BM.
John Mauton & Elizabeth White, Aug. 2, 1805. Page Rock, BM.
William Marlin & Eliza Hollis, Dec. 21, 1805. Jesse Hollis, BM.
John McCarthney (McCartney) & Polly Thomas, March 7, 1805. Sam'l.
    Kilbrough, BM.
Robert Marshall & Sally Dobbins, Feb. 26, 1805. Carson Dobbins, BM.
Adam Milam & Jenny Short, Oct. 5, 1805. Drury Milan, BM.
Daniel Minor & Elizabeth Briley, Oct. 24, 1805. James Brigance, BM.
Samuel Moore & Betsy Peares (Pearse), March 5, 1805. Thos. Kirk-
    ham, BM.
William Moore & Polly Badgett, Dec. 24, 1805. John Johnson, BM.
John Moss & Polly Stevenson, Aug. 31, 1805. Josiah Stevenson, BM.
Robert Neeley & Margaret Young, Jan. 18, 1805. James Richardson,
    BM.
Andrew Norwood & Anny Chambers, Nov. 25, 1805. John Dawson, BM.
Randel Owens & Hannah Oglesby, June 11, 1805. Jonathan Wilson, BM.
Bartholemeu Osburn & Betsy Abbott, April 30, 1805. Samuel Roney,
    BM.
Andrew Parker & Elizabeth Noble, April 22, 1805. Reuben Ross, BM.
Duncan Patton & Polly Gwin, April 29, 1805. Sam'l Watson, BM.
William Pitman & Mary Ragsdale, Dec. 28, 1805. Abraham Douglass,
    BM.
William Pittman & Tabitha Burton, Jan. 7, 1805. Abram Trigg, Jr.,
    BM.
Ambrose Porter & Rebecca Snoddy, March 9, 1805. Thos. Marquis, BM.
James Reed & Elender Crawford, Nov. 2, 1805. Elijah Simpson, BM.
Joel Reese & Sarah Ramsey, Aug. 14, 1805. Joshua Ramsey, BM.
Adam Reeves & Polly Nipper, June 27, 1805. Wm. McAdams, BM.
James Roberts & Patsey Evans, May 8, 1805. James Harten, BM.
Jacob Robertson & Elizabeth Cherry, July 6, 1805. Wm. White, BM.
William Robertson & Fanny Harris, Sep. 16, 1805. Robt. Harris, BM.
Barnet Rork & Stasy Heaspeth, June 10, 1805. Robt. Allen, BM.
Abraham Rutledge & Nancy Wills, Oct. 16, 1805. Wyat Wills, BM.
Abraham Rutledge & Mary Ragsdale, Dec. 28, 1805. Jas. Cryer, BM.
Joseph Seawell & Prudence Bleason (Bledsoe), April 1, 1805. John
    Lyon, BM.
Daniel Shaver & Josa Chaddock, Sep. 18, 1805. Wm. Pervience, BM.
William Shoulders & Clarissa Dement, Aug. 10, 1805. Abner Should-
    ers, BM.
Charles Simpson & Sally C. Harris, Aug. 2, 1805. Robt. Hanes, BM.
Joshua Smith & Nancy Pankey, July 4, 1805. John Pankey, BM.
Joseph Stevenson & Polly Pitt, Jan. 22, 1805. John Donoho, BM.
William Stuart & Sally Cougher, Sep. 20, 1805. Wm. Sample, BM.
Fletcher Sullivan & Betsey Crane, Feb. 13, 1805. Lewis Crane, BM.
Francis Tinsley & Polly Cary, May 7, 1805. James Cary, BM.
John Thompson & Mary Young, Aug. 30, 1805. Wm. Caldwell, BM.
Daniel Trigg & Nancy Hodge, June 3, 1805. James Cage, BM.
James Trousdale & Milindy May, Feb. 13, 1805. Robert Trousdale, BM.
William White & Jinny Burton, Oct. 24, 1805. Jesse McClendon, BM.
Thomas Whitford & Polly Henderson, March 27, 1805. Abraham Hollins-

worth, BM.

Henry Williams & Elsy Ridley, Aug. 26, 1805. Isaac Towell, BM.

Robert Williams & Polly Barnes, July 3, 1805. John Billings, BM.

William Wyles & Nancy McKee, April 18, 1805. John Wyles, BM.

Hugh Torrence Dunn & Susannah Clark, July 13, 1805. James Clark, BM.

William Clark & Abagail Gardner, July 13, 1805. Hugh T. Dunn, BM. James Clark.

Sam'l P. Black & Fanny Sanders, Dec. 23, 1805. James Cage, BM.

James Allen & Peggy Franklin, March 3, 1806. Jas. Franklin, BM.

Isreal Ambrose & Gilly Wright, Feb. 11, 1806. John Wright, BM.

Kinchen Barnes & Elizabeth Braswell, July 22, 1806. Ruffin De-loeeh, BM.

William Barnet & Casander Barnet, Sep. 25, 1806. Nathan Atcheson, BM.

Thomas Barnett & Henry Noble, Jan. 27, 1806. Jeremiah Claxton, BM.

Elsworth Baynes & Peggy White, Aug. 28, 1806. Jacob Seaves, BM.

John Bentley & Rachel Brown, Feb. 5, 1806. John L. Swaney, BM.

Henry Bloodworth & Dolly Griffin, May 28, 1806. Miles Anderson, BM.

Joseph Bowman & Peggy Hamilton, May 14, 1806. J. W. Hamilton, BM.

David Bradley & Rebecah Granger, Oct. 18, 1806. John Taylor, BM.

George Browning & Sally McIntosh, Jan. 27, 1806. Reuben Nowell, BM.

William Burchett & Sally Doyal, May 28, 1806. John Doyal, BM.

George Bush & Elizabeth Marlin, Nov. 27, 1806. Archibald Marlin, BM.

William Cage & Fanny Street, March 12, 1806. James Winchester, BM.

David Campbell & Catherine Bowen, April 10, 1806. Jas. Desha, BM.

Alexander Cartwright & Patsey P. Rawlings, Dec. 24, 1806. James Rutherford, BM.

Alex Cathey & Mary Malone, April 8, 1806. Thos. Malone, BM.

William Cathey & Betsey Gale, April 2, 1806. Alex. Cathey.

William Caveness & Polly Bruce, Dec. 16, 1806. John Chapman, BM.

Joseph Christopher & Rebecka Coleman, Nov. 1, 1806. Thomas Groves, BM.

Richard Cocke & Elenor Desha, July 1, 1806. Thomas Cocke, BM.

William Coventon & Priscilla Bloodworth, Feb. 28, 1806. Webb Bloodworth, BM.

William Davis & Nancy Cotton, Nov. 15, 1806. James Sryer, BM.

Isaac Dillon & Polly Kilbrath, Sep. 19, 1806. Tarlton Boren, BM.

Andrew Dinning & Polly Groves, Sep. 15, 1806. Thomas Groves, BM.

John Dinning & Elizabeth Whitworth, Aug. 11, 1806 by Thomas Groves, Jr., J.P., Aug. 21, 1806. Joseph McGlothin, BM.

Josiah Dixon & Dusty Williams, April 29, 1806. David Stafford, BM.

John Dobbins & Elizabeth Shaw, May 24, 1806. Jonathan Trousdale, BM.

Marcus Dodd & Polly Wilson, Dec. 22, 1806. Laurence Owen, BM.

William Edwards, Jr. & Peggy Hassel, Sep. 13, 1806. Richard Ed-wards, BM.

Everard Elliss & Polly Calvin, Sep. 17, 1806. William Rainey, BM.

Levi Fawke (Fowke) & Nancy White, Dec. 29, 1806. Littleberry White, BM.

Thomas Ferrell & Betsy Shaw, Jan. 27, 1806. Joshua Smith, BM.

George Farrier & Sally Mooney, April 19, 1806. John Mooney, BM.

Robert Fleming & Nancy Mitchell, June 16, 1806. John Mitchell, BM.

SUMNER COUNTY MARRIAGES

David Foster & Anny Beard, June 29, 1806. David Beard, Sr., BM.
John Freeland & Catherine McKee, Feb. 18, 1806. William McKee, BM.
Burwell Fulke & Patsey Locke, Feb. 1, 1806. Thos. White, BM.
Moses Gaines & Elizabeth Marshall, Nov. 20, 1806. William Capps.
Thomas Gordon & Rebeccah Womack, Dec. 13, 1806. Hiram Womack, BM.
Benjamine Grainger & Lilly Groves, Nov. 8, 1806. William Grainger,
    BM.
Edmund Green & Rhody Harris, Oct. 4, 1806. Thomas Edwards, BM.
Allen Groves & Polley Uzzell, Feb. 10, 1806. Thomas Groves, Jr.,
    BM.
Charles Hereford & Polly Herring, Nov. 3, 1806. Jesse Hereford, BM.
James Hamilton & Susannah Vinson, April 8, 1806. John Hamilton, BM.
Wm. Hamilton & Fanny Latimer, Aug. 15, 1806. Daniel Latimer, BM.
William Hammond & Jane McMurtry, Aug. 4, 1806. John McMurtry, BM.
Jesse Hereford & Polly Turner, Jan. 1, 1806. Adam Turner, BM.
Jesse Hollis & Phoebe Gambling, Dec. 3, 1806. William Marlin, BM.
Henry Hunt & Darcus Giles, Jan. 31, 1806. Josiah E. Giles, BM.
John Hutchings & Susannah Youree, Jan. 13, 1806. Patrick Youree,
    BM.
Chestly Jackson & Sally Lilley, Jan. 9, 1806. Jacob Lilley, BM.
John Jones & Hannah Oglesby, March 31, 1806. Daniel Oglesby, BM.
Thomas Kirkham & Betsey Prevett, May 23, 1806. William Grady, BM.
Daniel Latimer & Elizabeth Gwin, Sep. 23, 1806. John Pendergrast,
    BM.
William Lemmons & Patsey Gipson, Feb. 17, 1806. Peter Lemmons, BM.
John Lindsey & Nancy Smothers, Dec. 20, 1806. James Carr, BM.
James Love & Salley Watwood, Jan. 4, 1806. Samuel Roney, BM.
Walter Loving & Dolly Stone, April 23, 1806. Eusebius Stone, BM.
John Lyon & Agnes Keese, April 21, 1806. William Henry, BM.
William Lyon & Rebeccah Steel, Jan. 8, 1806. Robert Steel, Jr., BM.
Thomas Malone & Hannah Cathey, March 1, 1806. John Lyon, BM.
Thomas Marlin & Polly Rice, Oct. 1, 1806. Archibald Marlin, BM.
Lewis Martin & Anny Clendening, Feb. 13, 1806. John Brisby, BM.
Edward Maxey & Polly Chance, Jan. 21, 1806. Wm. Maxey, BM.
Samuel McAdow & Hannah Coop, July 24, 1806. Wm. Hodge, BM.
Alexander McElroy & Polly Elliss, Jan. 6, 1806. William Davis, BM.
James McCollaster (McAllister) & Elizabeth Asque, March 26, 1806.
    John F. Mingion, BM.
John McGee & Elizabeth Rogers, Dec. 22, 1806. James Rogers, BM.
John McLin & Rebeccah Anderson, Feb. 3, 1806. Robert Anderson, BM.
John Mitchell & Sally Garnder, Oct. 3, 1806. Benjamine Rawlings,
    BM.
William Moody & Rebeccah Trible (or Tribble), Feb. 3, 1806. Abra-
    ham Trible, BM.
Richard Moore & Elizabeth Johnson, March 6, 1806. James Johnson,
    BM.
Robert Moore & Nancy Green, March 3, 1806. John Trice, BM.
William Newton & Polly Tire, April 17, 1806. Henry Allen, BM.
Greenberry Orr & Aramintha Juliett Harris, May 28, 1806. Wm. Alder-
    son, BM.
Robert Parks & Nancy Gwin, March 18, 1806. Jacob Parks, BM.
William Payton & Barbara Rogers, Nov. 26, 1806. Wm. Novell, BM.
Allen Purvis & Peggy Franklin, Dec. 27, 1806. Henry Vinson, BM.
William Rainey & Sibella Elliss, Sep. 16, 1806. Edward Elliss, BM.

SUMNER COUNTY MARRIAGES

Moses Rhodes & Polly Norris, Dec. 22, 1806. James Rogan, BM.
Samuel Roulston & Elizabeth Shaw, Jan. 28, 1805. Hugh McBride, BM.
James Sanders & Molley Donelson, Feb. 26, 1806. Edward Sanders, BM.
Robert Sanders & Jane Keesee, July 16, 1806. Wm. Henry, BM.
Herod Seat & Jinny Merell, Dec. 6, 1806. Thos. Barrot, BM.
Abner Shoulders & Elizabeth Combs, March 26, 1806. Isaac Baker, BM.
Edwin Smith & Susannah Thomas, Sep. 20, 1806. Jacob Smith, BM.
Jeremiah Smith & Fanny Ashlock, April 1, 1806. Peter Fisher, BM.
Vardiman Smith & Polly Gaines, Oct. 6, 1806. Jas. McKain, BM.
John Spradling & Susannah Bradley, Jan. 16, 1806. George Stallcup, BM.
Joseph Spradlin & Nancy Bradley, Feb. 19, 1806. John Bradley, BM.
James Summers & Polly Hood, July 21, 1806. Sam'l Watson, BM.
John L. Swaney & Anny Belote, Feb. 5, 1806. John Bentley, BM.
Benjamine Tarver & Sally Odom, Aug. 18, 1806. George Elliott, BM.
John Taylor & Barbary Bason, May 26, 1806. David Bradley, BM.
Goolsby Thurman & Patsey Stoval, July 14, 1806. Thomas Stovall, BM.
Abram Tribble & Polly Nelson, Sep. 17, 1806. William Moody, BM.
Jonathan Trousdale & Sally Josey, May 21, 1806. Wm. Murrell, BM.
Joseph Underwood & Betsy Young, July 25, 1806. Amos Gowen, BM.
Millinton Wall & Sally Ellis, Sep. 13, 1806. Simeon Ellis, BM.
Adam Wallace & Salley Stuart, Jan. 7, 1806. Sam'l Stuart, BM.
Hardy Warren & Sally King, Feb. 11, 1806. William King, BM.
Wm. Weathers & Dicy Trible, Feb. 18, 1806. Jesse Keen, BM.
John Weaver & Elizabeth Cross, Sep. 4, 1806. John Bailey, BM.
William West & Polly Taylor, Oct. 18, 1806. David Bradley, BM.
Littleberry White & Nancy Dillard, Sep. 16, 1806. Bernard Ferrell, BM.
Robert Williamson & Keriah Whitsett, Sep. 10, 1806. Laurence Whitsett, BM.
John Willis & Jinny Kirkpatrick, Feb. 26, 1806. Wallie Kirkpatrick, BM.
Meshack Willis & Nancy Pritchet, Oct. 25, 1806. Joseph Clark, BM.

NO RECORD FOR THE YEAR 1807 (all lost)

James Bell & Betsy Easbery, June 9, 1808. Frederick Brown, BM.
John Black & Cena Blackamore, May 5, 1808. Robert White, BM.
Thomas Bloodworth & Aly White, Oct. 13, 1808, by S. Hunt, J.P., Oct. 13, 1808. Serrel White, BM.
Nathan Boon & Betsey Thorn, Dec. 29, 1808. Robert Lytle, BM.
Henry Boyer & Mary Gambell, Jan. 2, 1808. John Gambell, BM.
David Bruce & Lucy Bruce, Dec. 24, 1808. James McKain, BM.
Andrew Buckham & Charlotte Taylor, July 15, 1808. Joe Parrish, BM. William McNutt.
Wiley Carrel & Elizabeth G. Gilpin, July 30, 1808. James G. Sloan, BM.
Richard Center & Betsey Hunt, July 9, 1808. Moses Bains, BM.
Pleasant Crews & Elizabeth Lavender, March 21, 1808. John Jones, BM.
Pavatt Cufman & Jinny Gunsaw, Feb. 15, 1808. Geo. G. Chapman, BM.
Thomas Davis & Clounda Eckols, Aug. 4, 1808. John Pendergast, BM.
William Davis & Polly Sebastan, Jan. 6, 1808. John Davis, BM.
William Durham & Frances Marshall, July 15, 1808. _____(?), BM.

14

Joseph Easley & Betsey Wethers, April 19, 1808. Rhodam Allen, BM.
Simon Edwards & Elizabeth Hail, March 6, 1808. Adonyah Edwards,
    BM.
Simeon Ellis & Delilas Smith, Nov. 25, 1808. Abraham _____, BM.
James Ervin & Polly Bates, March 30, 1808. Samuel Patterson, BM.
Garrard Ethridge & Polly Murnan, Dec. 25, 1808. Benj. Dickerson,
    BM.
Birrom Ferrell & Sally Clor, March 15, 1808. James Douglas, BM.
John Finix & Polly Sloane, March 15, 1808. Richard Ball, BM.
Daniel Frailey & Milley Miller, Feb. 22, 1808. Henry Marrick, BM.
Alexander Frazor & Elizabeth Harper, April 8, 1808. William Harp-
    er, BM.
Martin Gambill & Susanna Shaddis, Sep. 11, 1808. John Gambill, BM.
John Gaines & Charlotte Pruett, May 9, 1808. Josephus Conn, BM.
Mason Garrison & Betsey Harten, Aug. 19, 1808. James Harten, BM.
David Groves & Susanna Roney, Dec. 19, 1808. Thomas Groves, BM.
John Gourley & Prudence Wilson, Dec. 15, 1808. William Kirkpat-
    rick, BM.
John Hall & Patsey Douglas, Oct. 4, 1808. W. H. Douglas, BM.
George Harpole & Sally Chapman, May 23, 1808. Pavatt Cufman, BM.
Jacob Hicks & Polly Lewis, Dec. 6, 1808. John Hicks, BM.
John Hicks & Philpeny Holt, Nov. 10, 1808. John Chapman, BM.
Samuel Holloway & Hiddy Hassel, April 2, 1808. Edmund Hogan, BM.
John Huberts & Sally Bough, April 25, 1808. Humphreys Bates, BM.
John Hudson & Betsey Ellis, Jan. 20, 1808. Dawsey Hudson, BM.
Needham Hunter & Polly Parnell, Dec. 15, 1808. Joshua Rice, BM.
Shadrick Finn & Rebecca Henderson, Oct. 31, 1808. Porter Allen,
    BM. Thos. Keif.
James Jackson & Lucresia Boyers (or Rogers), July 9, 1808. Will
    Trigg, Jr., BM.
Larkin Jackson & Anna Parker, Dec. 26, 1808. James Cathey, BM.
James Job & Catherine Pitt, Sep. 10, 1808. Robert Pitt, BM.
Archibald Johnson & Elizabeth Gilmore, July 12, 1808. Abner Gil-
    more, BM.
Robert Johnson & Patsey Goodrum, Aug. 31, 1808. Lemuel Stubble-
    field, BM.
Hezekiah Jones & Lina Oglesby, Aug. 16, 1808. Isaac Simpson, BM.
William Jones & Polly Haw, July 25, 1808. Joseph Clark, BM.
Samuel Kennedy & Judith Pruett, Dec. 31, 1808. Thomas T. Rawlings,
    BM.
Davis King & Sally Joiner, Jan. 27, 1808. John Pendergast, BM.
David King & Sarah Pike, Sep. 10, 1808. John F. Gillespie, BM.
William M. King & Prescilla Hassell, Dec. 8, 1808. John Pender-
    gast, BM.
James Kirkman & Milley Anderson, May 19, 1808. _____(?), BM.
Griswold Latimer & Celia Gardner, Sep. 17, 1808. Peter Looney, BM.
Lynde Latimer & Polly Hamilton, May 26, 1808. Shadrack Nye, BM.
Stark Lewis & Phanny Paradice, Nov. 17, 1808. William Paradice, BM.
Daniel Liggett & Sally Garrison, Nov. 18, 1808. John McMurtry, BM.
Jarrot Loyd & Rebeckah Stuart, Feb. 16, 1808. Wm. T. Lindsey, BM.
James Mabry & Susanna Bernard, Aug. 15, 1808. William Atchinson,
    BM.
John Mabry & Peggy Trago, Dec. 9, 1808. John W. Byrn, BM.
Oliver Martin & Polly Hicks, Aug. 23, 1808. John Hicks, BM.

15

William McCarty & Polly Chappell, Dec. 31, 1808. Dickie Chappell, BM.
John McElwrath & Oliver (Olive) Deloach, Nov. 23, 1808. James Orr, BM.
Henry Miller & Nancy Garrison, May 27, 1808. William McMinn, BM.
David Mitchell & Elizabeth Clary, Jan. 1, 1808. Peter Luma, BM.
John Mitchell & Fanny Busby, July 23, 1808. Hugh Findley, BM.
William Mitchener & Elizabeth Corcle, March 14, 1808. Samuel Watson, BM.
Moe Jones &_____(?), June 27, 1808. Bond not filled out. Signed and dated as above on back.
Richard Moore & Elizabeth Cowen, March 21, 1808. Isarael Moore, BM.
Mathew Neel & Sally Trousdale, March 1, 1808. John Pendergast, BM.
Henry M. Newlin & Polly N. Sims, April 16, 1808. _____(?), BM.
Reuben Norman & Oina Brackin, Sep. 16, 1808. Wm. Brackin, BM.
William Paradice & Elizabeth Stuart, Nov. 17, 1808, by S. Hunt, J.P., Nov. 17, 1808. Stork Sims, BM.
Noah Parker & Rhoda Parker, Jan. 30, 1808. James Fisher, BM.
Robert Parker & Patsey Martin, May 27, 1808. Thomas Parker, BM.
John Parson & Sally Wilson, Oct. 31, 1808. Rolls Perry, BM.
Hugh Patterson & Synthia Murray, Oct. 17, 1808. James Grayham, BM.
John Payton & Sally Rogers, Dec. 24, 1808. Joseph Campbell, BM.
James Ragen & Betty Simpson, Sep. 7, 1808. John Simpson, BM.
John Pitt & Susannah Strother, March 12, 1808. John C. Hamilton, BM.
_____Reeves & Hannah Cooper, Dec. 28, 1808. John Cooper, BM.
Philip Reyman & Susannah White, Jan. 30, 1808. Julius Sims, BM.
Samuel Rooney & Patsey Haune, Jan. 19, 1808. Reuben Norman, BM.
William Roney & Leah Groves, Aug. 3, 1808. David Groves, BM.
John Scott & Betsey Bradshaw, Nov. 1, 1808. John Bradshaw, BM.
Joseph Short & Rebeccah Abbott, Sep. 1, 1808. John Copland, BM.
Richard Smith & Peggy Dinning, Feb. 6, 1808. George Steel, BM.
Nicholas Stone & Betsey Lovin, Feb. 24, 1808. Eusebues Stone, BM.
William Stone & Sally Gains, Jan. 11, 1808. Moses Gains, BM.
James Story & Nancy Watson, Sep. 29, 1808. Sandy P. Duncan, BM.
Sterling Tinsley & Kesiah Wynn, June 16, 1808. James Edwards, BM.
Abraham Trigg & Martha Sanders, Aug. 29, 1808. Will Trigg, BM.
William Taylor & Nancy Edwards, Jan. 5, 1808. Robert Lytle, BM.
John Turner & Anny Bauldright, Jan. 27, 1808. Samuel E. Blythe, BM.
James Whitworth & Anne Harding, Aug. 12, 1808. Thomas Stark, BM.
Green Williford & Lucy Alley, Sep. 12, 1808. John Pendergast, BM.
Ebenezer Wilson & Rebeckah Pearson, June 30, 1808. James C. Wilson, BM.
Abraham Young & Peggy Cavatt, Jan. 9, 1808. James Roney, Jr., BM.
John Allen & Nancy Wells, July 14, 1809. John D. Hodge, BM.
Thomas Anderson & Elizabeth McKorkle, March 13, 1809. John H. Bowen, BM.
Nathan Atchison & Lucusia Barnard, Jan. 2, 1809. John Chapman, BM.
William Atchison & Darcus Barnard, Jan. 2, 1809. John Chapman, BM.
John Atherly & Nancy Joiner, Nov. 6, 1809. Leaborn Pruett, BM.
Harris Avent & Dolly Trice, Feb. 10, 1809. Robt. Trousdale, BM.
Martin Baker & Polly Ellis, May 31, 1809. Simeon Ellis, BM.
Isreal Barker & Polly Brackin, March 14, 1809. _____(?), BM.
Silas Barr & Hannah White, Feb. 2, 1809. John Barr, BM.

James Barry & Polly Sanders, Dec. 6, 1809. William H. Douglass, BM.
Samuel K. Blythe & Dotia Trigg, Oct. 25, 1809. P. W. Trigg, BM.
Jeremiah Bowers & Margaret Easten, Sep. 4, 1809. Nathan Parker, Jr., BM.
Samuel Brown & Susannah Benthal, Sep. 20, 1809. Robert Patton, BM.
Peter Bryson & June Gillespie, Aug. 1, 1809. George Gillespie, BM.
James Caldwell & Polly Davis, Dec. 16, 1809. Abram Trigg, BM.
William Campbell & Jenny Pentecost, May 15, 1809. John Farley, BM.
John Carr, Jr. & Hannah Carr, May 10, 1809. King Carr, BM.
Alexander Carter & Rhody Benthal, April 23, 1809. Webb Bloodworth, BM.
Harry Clark & Rhody Vinson, Sep. 11, 1809. James McKain, BM.
Elijah Cloe & Betsey Cloe, Jan. 5, 1809. William Cloe, BM.
Abner Collier & Elerna Milam, Feb. 17, 1809. L. Sims, BM.
Yerby Cook & Elinor Morris, Jan. 4, 1809. Mathias Mouch, BM.
Houston Cooper & Peggy Snoddy, Sep. 23, 1809. David Snoddy, BM.
William Cowden & Elizabeth Sulivan, March 20, 1809. Robert Simpson, BM.
William Creenshaw & Polly Edwards, Dec. 31, 1809. David Edwards, BM.
John Davis & Betsey Shaw, June 25, 1809. Robt. Shaw, BM.
John Davis & Sally Goodin, June 21, 1809. Wallace Kirkpatrick, BM.
Solomon Frail & Nancy Duren, Oct. 24, 1809. George Duren, BM.
Ephraim Garrison & Caty Haw, Jan. 14, 1809. Joseph Clark, BM.
John Garrison, Jr. & Polly Brown, Jan. 11, 1809. John McMurtry, Jr., BM.
Eli Giles & Polly Alvis, April 11, 1809. _____ (?), BM.
Jacob Graves & Caty Black, Nov. 17, 1809. George Richmond, BM.
Edmund Green & Polly Marcum, Dec. 19, 1809. M. Green, BM.
Cage Hail & Rebeccah Rankin, Nov. 1, 1809. Jonathan Badgett, BM.
Enos Halbert & Rebecca Harper, Sep. 15, 1809. Andrew Harper.
Daniel Hays & Priscilla Dobbins, Jan. 22, 1809. Carson Dobbins, BM.
Joseph Hickman & Patsey Johnson, Dec. 28, 1809. Robt. Johnson, BM.
Henry Hover & Melberry Railey, June 8, 1809. John Mitchell, BM.
Henry Jacobs & Rhoda Clark, Dec. 20, 1809. Levi Winnberry, BM.
John King & Winny Atkins, March 11, 1809. Isaac Atkins, BM.
James Leath & Sally Murphy, Dec. 26, 1809. Jacob Thomson, BM.
Peter Lemons & Dicy Atkins, Oct. 24, 1809. Arthur Hicks, BM.
Cyrus Loving & Betsey McDowell, June 20, 1809. Colston Loving, BM.
John McDowell & Dolly Flood, Oct. 26, 1809. William Short, BM.
Archibald McKenny & Sally Moody, Nov. 29, 1809. Colston Lovel, BM.
Robert McKisick & Elenor McMurry, Dec. 25, 1809. Arch McKissick, BM.
Robert Mitchell & Nancy Latimer, July 5, 1809. John Leak, BM.
Robert Moore & Sally Hale, April 7, 1809. Abraham Bledsoe, BM.
Jonathan Morton & China Thompson, Nov. 24, 1809. Samuel Tinnon, BM.
John Moss & Annah (Amah) Laurence, May 24, 1809. Abraham Trigg, BM.
William Murphey & Nancy Melton, Nov. 24, 1809. John Robinson, BM.
William Orr & Annie Smith, Aug. 2, 1809. William King, BM.
Thomas Ozborn & Polly Abbott, April 20, 1809. John Lemmons, BM.
Dan'l Patton & Mariah Overton, Aug. 10, 1809. Shadrack Nye, BM.
Samuel Patton & Elenor Wilson, Nov. 8, 1809. Joseph Wilson, BM.
Samuel Patton & Cynthia Wells, March 16, 1809. Zack Wilson, BM.

SUMNER COUNTY MARRIAGES

Henry Pinson & Betsey Hamilton, Feb. 13, 1809. Robt. Shaw, BM.
Stephen Pitt & Nancy Gamblin, Jan. 11, 1809. Wm. Neal, BM.
John Pitt & Sarah Stovall, Nov. 11, 1809. William Stovall, BM.
Oliver Porter & Jane Bracken, Feb. 20, 1809. Wm. Brackin, BM.
William Reese & Frankey Ruyle, March 29, 1809. Henry Ruyle, BM.
James Reynolds & Nancy Wilkins, Nov. 20, 1809. William Exum, BM.
Joseph Robb & Anna Motheral, Dec. 21, 1809. John Hodge, BM.
Ezekiel Ross & Polly Pentecost, April 20, 1809. Edmund Holloway,
  BM.
Moses Ruyle & Elizabeth Ruyle, May 19, 1809. John Ruyle, BM.
William Smothers & Sarah Smothers, Sep. 13, 1809. John Lindsey, BM.
James G. Sloan & Anna Lauderdale, Dec. 18, 1809. Robert Gardner,
  BM.
John Sloan & Betsey Carroll, Aug. 20, 1809. James Gardner, BM.
William Stevens & Ann Beasly, Aug. 28, 1809. Henry Wright, BM.
Joseph Taylor & Anny Blackmore, Nov. 21, 1809. John Blackmore, BM.
Mabry Walton & Martha Exum, Feb. 23, 1809. Arthur Exum, BM.
Daniel Willis & Betsey Smith, Dec. 14, 1809. Harvey R. Willis, BM.
Levi Wimberly & Polly Laurey, Dec. 9, 1809. John McMurtry, BM.
Joseph D. Wood & Ann Franklin, June __, 1809. Robt. Trousdale, BM.
William Woodruff & Tildy Ferguson, Dec. 19, 1809. William Hall,
  BM.
John Yandle & Judith Pitts, March 13, 1809. Wilson Yandle, BM.
Joseph Young & Elizabeth Hale, March 6, 1809. Robert Moore, BM.
Allen Askew & Betsey Phipps, March 6, 1810. D. Dement, BM.
Willis Atkinson & Nancy Barnard, Dec. 18, 1810. James Jones, BM.
John Banton & Polly Bruce, April 21, 1810. Robt. Bruce, BM.
Alvan Bingham & Jane Baldridge, Dec. 25, 1810. John Turner, BM.
Edmund Boaz & Nancy Nowlin, March 28, 1810. John Reeves, BM.
John D. Bradley & Patsey Trice, May 22, 1810. Wm. H. Douglass, BM.
John Brooks & Sally Parker, Sep. 11, 1810. Noah Parker, BM.
James Brown & Patsey Chappel, Aug. 21, 1810. Patrick Youree, BM.
Stephen Busby & Sally Hale, May 12, 1810. John Mitchell, BM.
Ota Cantrell & Sally Nolen, Feb. 14, 1810. _____(?), BM.
Robert Cartwright & Elizabeth Vinson, Dec. 2, 1810. Charles
  Thompson, BM.
Joshua Claxton & Susannah Rice, Oct. 3, 1810. James Claxton, BM.
Absalom Cloar & Ann Cockran, July 18, 1810. John Hubert, BM.
John Crawford & Betsy Payne, Nov. 10, 1810. Hugh Finley, BM.
Nathaniel Crenshaw & Harriett Rice, Sep. 10, 1810. John Edwards,
  BM.
Robert Davis & Priscilla Sebastain, Oct. 9, 1810. Robert Shaw, BM.
William H. Douglass & Sally Edwards, Jan. 21, 1810. John D.
  Gillespie, BM.
James Dosit & Elizabeth Donoho, Aug. 14, 1810. Isaac Forrest, BM.
Flood Dugger & Polly Bruce, Aug. 29, 1810. Jesse Skeen, BM.
Micajah Dunning & Tabitha Murphey, Aug. 14, 1810. Aaron Butler, BM.
Thomas Dyer & Celia Crabb, Nov. 13, 1810. Henry Shelby, BM.
Haxin Dyer & Lucretia Bryant, Dec. 22, 1810. William Gwin, BM.
Isaac Earthman & Catharine Garrett, Dec. 4, 1810. George Garrett,
  BM.
Joel Echols & Susannah Weir, Oct. 13, 1810. Jesse Cage, BM.
Thomas Edwards & Priscilla Edwards, May 4, 1810. William White, BM.
Isaac Ellis & Polly Hudson, March 19, 1810. John Hudson, BM.

18

SUMNER COUNTY MARRIAGES

Smelling Ellis & Peggy Hudson, Nov. 14, 1810. Benj. Hudson, BM.

William Evans & Kidey Freeman, March 26, 1810. Hugh Elliott, BM.

John Galbreath & Susanna Ferrell, Sep. 19, 1810. Greenberry Randell, BM.

John Granger & Peggy Norvel, Nov. 22, 1810. William Norvel, BM.

Daniel Green & Nancy Sharp, Jan. 18, 1810. Isaac Gregory, BM.

Isaac Grim & Sally Allslack, Nov. 22, 1810. Mathew Neal, BM.

Fielding Grimsely (Grimsley) & Penelope Hunt, July 2, 1810. Jesse Cage, BM.

John Hale & Tabitha Badgett, Dec. 6, 1810. Jno Byrn, BM.

William Hargue & Sally Roper, July 21, 1810. Wm. McAdams, BM.

Joseph Harper & Betsy Conger, Sep. 19, 1810. Simon Shoecraft, BM.

Bright Harris & Sally Walton, Oct. 15, 1810. Martin Smith, BM.

Ambrose Helban & Peggy Moody, Nov. 19, 1810. Robt. Moody, BM.

John Helms & Janny Meadows, June 30, 1810. Joseph Helms, BM.

Bennett H. Henderson & Lucinda Shelby, June 23, 1810. Jno. Shelby, BM.

Daniel Henderson & Margie Holmes, Dec. 20, 1810. Abram Byrd, BM.

Henry Hendricks & Peggy Barnett, May 28, 1810. Abram Hendricks, BM.

Samuel Higgerson & Polly Richardson, May 29, 1810. Goalsberry Thurman, BM.

Samuel Hinton & Rebecca Hendricks, Nov. 10, 1810. Albert Hendricks, BM.

James Howard & Willa (Willia) Rawlings, Feb. 20, 1810. A. K. Shaifer, BM.

John Hunt & Patsey Easley, Aug. 11, 1810. John Robertson, BM.

William Jackson & Betsey Summers, March 20, 1810. Thomas Summers, BM.

John Jennings & Nancy Parker, Sep. 18, 1810. Peter Parker, BM.

Charles Kelly & Elizabeth Lafferty, June 11, 1810. Philip Howell, BM.

John Kennedy & Margaret Parks, Jan. 24, 1810. Jacob Parks, BM.

Henry Kensey & Susannah Pitt, June 2, 1810. James Johnson, BM.

William Lavender & Prudence Reeves, June 1, 1810. William Reeves, BM.

George Logan & Esther Carrothers, Jan. 10, 1810. William Carrothers, BM.

Jarrot Loyd & Charity Corder, Oct. 10, 1810. William Bruce, BM.

John Mandrell & Catherine Sarver, Dec. 4, 1810. Daniel Melton, BM.

John Moore & Sally Barnes, Oct. 31, 1810. Jacob Mayo, BM.

Robert Moody & Margaret Murphy, Dec. 28, 1810. William Murphy, BM.

George Nelson & Polly Vallentine, July 18, 1810. Isaac Valentine, BM.

Holly Organ & Nancy Ferrell, Aug. 11, 1810, by S. Hunt, J.P. Reuben Cage, BM.

John Ozburn & Henrietta Noble, Sep. 11, 1810, by Jacob B. Seuter, J.P.

William Patton & Anne Presley, Nov. 28, 1810. _____(?), BM.

William Proctor & Harriett Beardon, Feb. 6, 1810. Hazel Butt, BM.

Greenberry Randall & Betsey Adams, Sep. 19, 1810. John Galbreath, BM.

James Rankin & Catherine Pennington, June 25, 1810. Henry Young, BM.

Gardner Reed & Rebecca Morrow, Feb. 26, 1810. William Morrow, BM.
Samuel Reed & Louise Overby, Aug. 27, 1810. Joseph Reed, BM.
Nathaniel Richard & Betsey Knight, May 12, 1810. Thomas Knight, BM.
Samuel Robb & Hannah Stewart, July 6, 1810. Adam Wallace, BM.
John Robertson & Abagail Collins, April 19, 1810. William Robert-
son, BM.
Jonathan Rogers & Ruth Holloway, May 10, 1810. Samuel Rogers, BM.
George Sarver & Rachel Stalcup, Jan. 23, 1810. Jeremiah Sarver,
BM.
Jeremiah Sarver & Peggy Ozburn, Nov. 7, 1810. William Graves, BM.
John Scoby & Elizabeth Howell, Oct. 6, 1810. Matthew Scoby, BM.
Abner Scott & Patsey Duty, April 1, 1810. John Mitchell, BM.
Thomas Scurry & Caty Bledsoe, Jan. 4, 1810. John F. Gillespie, BM.
Archibald Skipper & Betsey Collier, Aug. 23, 1810. John Hodge, BM.
Peter Smart & Polly Cavitt, July 7, 1810. Samuel Piper, BM.
John Spencer & Elizabeth Reed, April 21, 1810. Andrew Robinson,
BM.
George Steel & Martha J. Baskerville, Aug. 6, 1810. John McKis-
sack, BM.
William Stevens & Janny Crouder, Aug. 20, 1810. John Curry, BM.
James Street & Elizabeth Carey, July 27, 1810. Henry Hart, BM.
Peter Sulivan & Nancy Stubblefield, Dec. 12, 1810. Abraham Ellis,
BM.
Thomas Swann & Elizabeth Johnson, July 20, 1810. James Barry, BM.
George Taylor & Edna Spradling, Aug. 20, 1810. Jesse Spradling, BM.
Lemuel Tinnon & Elizabeth Walton, Oct. 16, 1810. Martin Smith, BM.
Moses Tinsley & Sally Patterson, Nov. 15, 1810. John Gregory, BM.
Arioch Thomas & Sally Leath, Feb. 3, 1810. James Leath, BM.
Adam Turner & Polly Riley, Oct. 13, 1810. Frederick Miller, BM.
Martin Turner & Elizabeth Martin, Oct. 10, 1810. Isaac Baker, BM.
Nicholas Thompson & Elizabeth Marshall, Dec. 24, 1810. John Gran-
ger, BM.
Archibald Wallace & Rottey McRunnel, Dec. 20, 1810. Samuel Clenney,
BM.
William Watwood & Euridice Farrier, April 14, 1810. Ezekiel Nor-
man, BM.
Robert White & Betsey Duty, Feb. 28, 1810. Wm. Bledsoe, BM.
John Webb & Abagail Davis, April 23, 1810. James Caldwell, BM.
John West & Susanna Freeland, Aug. 9, 1810. Edmund Browning, BM.
Charles White & Laverne Hunt, Nov. 30, 1810. Thos. Hunt, BM.
John Williams & Lidia Stalcup, Dec. 27, 1810. George Sarver, BM.
Moses Wilson & Elizabeth Martin, Sep. 12, 1810. Robert Parker, BM.
Peter Winn & Patsey Hunley, July 7, 1810. Amos Gowan, BM.
Daniel Womberdurf & Anne Freeman, May 17, 1810. Solomon Shoulers,
BM.
Christopher Woodall & Lydia Roney, Dec. 24, 1810. Thos. Nicholson,
BM.
George Abbutt & Nancy Noble, March 21, 1811. James Abbutt, BM.
David Alexander & Rebeccah McElwrath, Oct. 16, 1811. Thos.
Brookshires, BM.
Samuel Anderson & Jan Bellmay, Oct. 31, 1811. Albert Holmes, BM.
John Baker & Julia Strong, Aug. 14, 1811. Abram Trigg, BM.
James Bale & Evaline Barry, Feb. 2, 1811.
James Barnett & Peggy Abbott, Oct. 25, 1811. George Abbott, BM.

David Barrott & Nancy Hales, Feb. 9, 1811. Solomon Barnes, BM.
John Batcheldor & Hannah McGloughlin, May 25, 1811. Moses Morris,
    BM.
John C. Beeler & Elizabeth Parker, Sep. 26, 1811. John Barham, BM.
Richard Bennett & Polly Bell, Feb. 25, 1811. John Sheppard, BM.
John Blackemore & Victory Rankin, Nov. 7, 1811. Wm. Hall, BM.
William Blasangam & Ann Collins, April 10, 1811. Wm. Hannah, BM.
Matthew C. Bowlen & Martha Short, April 24, 1811. Greenberry
    Howard, BM.
Durham Brock & Ann Marshall, March 1, 1811. John Layne, BM.
Samuel Bradley & Nancy G. Cardwell, March 18, 1811. Benjamine
    Clary, BM.
Thomas Bradley & Edith West, Nov. 6, 1811. John West, BM.
Henry Bradley & Nancy Merley, May 8, 1811. Wm. Hall, BM.
John Brooks & Jane Lambert, Aug. 8, 1811.
Daniel Browning & Vathle West, July 29, 1811. David Browning, BM.
Josiah Cane & Nancy Wilkerson, July 27, 1811. Joseph Barron, BM.
Robert Carel & Sally Cochran, Dec. 24, 1811. Thos. Carrel, BM.
William Cartwright & Elizabeth Goodall, Feb. 13, 1811. Ambrose
    Porter, BM.
John Cotton & Fanny Blackwell, June 24, 1811. Jonathan White, BM.
Nathan Davis & Eliza Rogers, March 30, 1811. David Bell, BM.
Samuel Dorris & Susanna Pitt, March 14, 1811. Wm. Dorris, BM.
Willis Dorsett & Nancy Panky, July 20, 1811. Adam Crump, BM.
James Doss & Nelly Graves, Nov. 23, 1811. John W. Byrns, BM.
Harry L. Douglass & Priscilla Shelby, Jan. 8, 1811. John H. Bower,
    BM.
James Douglass & Nancy Dodson, Nov. 28, 1811. Abram Trigg, BM.
John Doxey & Rebecca Dougherty, May 1, 1811. Stephen Doxey, BM.
Jarroth Dugger & Polly McAdam, Aug. 20, 1811. Flood Duggar, BM.
    Benjamine Taylor.
Samuel Durham & Sally Morris, Sep. 7, 1811. John Durham, BM.
Larkin Echols & Polly Spradlin, Jan. 15, 1811. Markey Key, BM.
Levi Ellis & Cynthia Bradford, March 16, 1811. Daniel Jones, BM.
William Empson & Betsey Morris, Feb. 4, 1811. Robert Parks, BM.
Clement Ferrell & Sulley Edwards, April 26, 1811. John Fillingham,
    BM.
Obadiah Finley & Mary L. Johnson, Feb. 22, 1811. Joel Echols, BM.
Isaac Forrest & Nancy May, July 6, 1811. Elisha Green, BM.
Lewis Graham & Patsey Wilson, April 12, 1811. Henry Hart, BM.
William Graves & Caty Rickmond, April 9, 1811. Wm. Barker, BM.
John Gregory & Sally Patton, Jan. 15, 1811. David Ormand, BM.
William Grisum & Caty Mouser, Dec. 27, 1811. Joseph Anthony, BM.
Henry Hawkins & Sally Hall, Jan. 10, 1811. David Hall, BM.
Charles Henderson & Anne Wilson, Aug. 19, 1811. John Henley, BM.
Achford Hodges & Anne Moody, Oct. 24, 1811. John Spradlin, BM.
William Huffman & Lucithe Edwards, Nov. 30, 1811. Richard Edwards,
    BM.
Thomas Hunt & Sally Griffey, July 16, 1811. Thos. Knight, BM.
James Itson & Cecilia Seffason (Seffaran, also found Saffarson),
    Feb. 27, 1811. Nathan Crenshaw, BM.
George Latimer & Catherine McKithen, Jan. 26, 1811. James Jackson,
    BM.
Thomas Marcum & Nancy Trible, Nov. 23, 1811. J. W. Byrns, BM.

Leoderith Mandrill & Nancy Ellis, Aug. 27, 1811. E. Phillips, BM.
Thomas Maxwell & Sarah Cavitt, Nov. 25, 1811. Moses Cavitt, BM.
Craddock H. May & Peggy Nemo, Dec. 13, 1811. Elisha Green, BM.
Isaac McKoun & Rebecca Owens, Jan. 18, 1811. Reddick Horn, BM.
Morris Miller & Caty Borene, Aug. 20, 1811. Francis Borene, BM.
Dinnon Moody & Patsy Durham, Nov. 20, 1811. Ambrose Hillburn, BM.
William Nickins & Polly Laurence, Jan. 7, 1811. Andrew McCormack,
  BM.
Stephen Norris & Drusilla Brake, July 10, 1811. Joel Brown, BM.
Peterson (or Paterson) Parrish & Nancy Johnson, Oct. 7, 1811, by
  S. Hunt, J.P. Edmond Bridges, BM.
William Patton & Fanny Sanderson, Dec. 30, 1811. B. Vinson, BM.
Robert Payne & Sally Beard, Dec. 16, 1811. Thos. Beard, BM.
Lemuel Perkins & Sally Rynes (or Ryner), Aug. 19, 1811. Daniel
  Barrett, BM.
Robert Pitt & Sally Hall, July 13, 1811. Stephen Pitt, BM.
William Reeder & Nancy Johnson, Nov. 11, 1811. Ashford Hodges, BM.
Thomas Rickman & Polly Henry, Nov. 2, 1811. Wm. Henry, BM.
Elijah R. Robertson & Nancy Parker, April 9, 1811. F. Brown, BM.
Albert Russell & Lockey Henderson, Jan. 26, 1811. Bennett Hender-
  son, BM.
Michael Shaver & Elizabeth Mock, Oct. 1, 1811. John Fuller, BM.
Anthony B. Shelby & Maryann Winchester, April 2, 1811. Abraham
  Shaifer, BM.
John Shepherd & Patsey Bennett, Sep. 6, 1811. Joseph Caine, BM.
John Sloss & Jane Motheral, Aug. 7, 1811. Joseph Motheral, BM.
James Smith & Jinny Young, Jan. 29, 1811. Michael Young, BM.
Samuel Snowden & Nancy Snowden, April 8, 1811. Henderson Parnel,
  BM.
John Stephens & Polly Bailess, July 2, 1811. Edmund Keen, BM.
Barton W. Stone & Celia Wilson Bowen, Oct. 30, 1811. John H. Bowen,
  BM.
Benjamine Taylor & Catherine Cattron, Aug. 28, 1811. Peter Cat-
  tron, BM.
John M. Taylor & Rachel West, Sep. 21, 1811. Herbert Avent, BM.
James Thompson & Nancy Dinning, Oct. 24, 1811. Andrew Dinning, BM.
William Travelstreet & Hannah Miers, Dec. 10, 1811. John Miers, BM.
Jacob Turner & Elizabeth Green, April 30, 1811. F. Miller, BM.
James Walker & Rhody Milburn, March 9, 1811. A. Walker, BM.
Charles White & Betsey Bloodworth, Oct. 3, 1811. Henry Bloodworth,
  BM.
Thomas Wilkerson & Sally Nemo, July 1, 1811. Francis Youree.
Montitian Wilson & Mary Martin, Dec. 19, 1811. Moses Wilson, BM.
Stephen Wilson & Polly McElurath, Dec. 3, 1811. Edwin Alexander,
  BM.
James Walton & Jane A. Parr, May 4, 1811. Thos. Gilbert, BM.
William Wright & Nancy McKinney, March 1, 1811. James McKinney,
  BM.
Marlin Alexander & Margaret Wygal, Dec. 30, 1812. Matthew Alexan-
  der, BM.
William Allen & Nancy Duvall, Jan. 23, 1812. Thomas Howel, BM.
William Alley & Judith Street, Dec. 24, 1812. Robert Cato, BM.
Andrew Anderson & Dorkass Clark, Oct. 15, 1812. Wm. Griggs, BM.
Samuel Anderson & Ann Clark, Aug. 25, 1812. Andrew Anderson, BM.

SUMNER COUNTY MARRIAGES

Benjamine Ashlock & Elizabeth Cooper, June 5, 1812. Thomas Knight, BM.
Philip Atkins & Salley Bradshaw, Oct. 24, 1812. James Lauderdale, BM.
John Baker & Mary Young, Dec. 4, 1812. S. K. Blythe, BM.
Jonathan Baringer & Kitty Goodall, Jan. 10, 1812. William Cartwright, BM.
Wright Barnes & Kitty Stone, Sep. 30, 1812. Orran Faulk, BM.
Adam Beard & Elizabeth Smith, May 12, 1812. Andrew Smith, BM.
William L. Bledsoe & Mary Sanford, Oct. 12, 1812. Jacob C. Cook, BM.
Richard Blythe & Mary Anderson, Nov. 4, 1812. S. K. Blythe, BM.
William Boren & Julian Dye, Dec. 2, 1812. Hugh W. Latimer, BM.
John Bowles & Polly Anderson, Feb. 17, 1812. Wm. Ogles, BM.
David Boyers & Charlotte Clark, Jan. 22, 1812.
John Bracken & Patsey Martin, Feb. 8, 1812. Edmund Browning, BM.
William Bradford & Nancy Boyles, March 26, 1812. Levi D. Ellis, BM.
Joshua Bradley & Jane Hall, May 26, 1812. John Bradley, BM.
Richard Bradley & Sally Martin, March 31, 1812. Jonathan Spooner, BM.
William Bradley & Sally Stalcup, June 19, 1812. John Taylor, BM.
John Brown & Octavia Conn, April 4, 1812. Sam'l Meredith, BM.
Robert Brown & Hanah Brown, June 12, 1812. Robert Patton, BM.
Robert Brown & Hannah Brown, June 11, 1812. Robert Patton, BM.
James Bruce & Peggy Lindsay, May 5, 1812. Isaac Lindsay, BM.
William Burney & Anne Guthrie, July 7, 1812. Isaac Armfield, BM.
Moses Cavitt & Elizabeth Tinnin, Oct. 19, 1812. William Tinnin, BM.
Richard Cavitt & Peggy Barrow, Aug. 4, 1812. Samuel Piper, BM.
Ezekiel Cherry & Jane Wilson, Nov. 5, 1812. Robert Collier, BM.
Andrew Clark & Polly Wilson, Nov. 3, 1812. Montetion W. Wilson, BM.
Enoch P. Connell & Nancy Walton, July 4, 1812. Will Trigg, Jr., BM.
John Crenshaw & Betsey Parker, May 18, 1812. Richard Gillespie, BM.
Hardy M. Cryer & Elizabeth L. Rice, Nov. 6, 1812. James Douglas, BM.
Larkin Dalton & Elizabeth Thornton, Nov. 11, 1812. W. H. Douglas, BM.
Starkey Daughtry & Lydia Forrester, Dec. 8, 1812. Abram Trigg, BM.
Jonathan Davis & Caty Hunt, Jan. 6, 1812. Thomas Hunt, BM.
James Derr & Sally Keiser, Sep. 21, 1812. Joseph Blair, BM.
Carson Dobbins & Betsey McMurry, March 4, 1812. James McMurry, BM.
William Dorris, Jr. & Polly Rippey, July 16, 1812. Robert Davis, Jr., BM.
William Dulass (Douglass) & Caty Garrison, Feb. 3, 1812. Daniel Montgomery, BM.
Henry Durham & Jane Richardson, Nov. 12, 1812. Goldsberry Thurman, BM.
Thomas Durin & Polly Winn, Aug. 24, 1812. Josiah E. Giles, BM.
James Elliott & Elender Inman, Sep. 10, 1812. John W. Byrn, BM.
John Ferneybough & Frances Gilbert, July 16, 1812. John Walters, BM.
John Fillingan & Prudence Valentine, April 29, 1812. Stephen Puckett, BM.
Reuben Forrest & Katy May, Oct. 2, 1812. Thomas Keefe, BM.
Richard R. Gillespie & Polly Duty, Feb. 10, 1812. Henry Bledsoe, BM.

Boswell Gregory & Patsey Bowman, March 30, 1812. Isaac Gregory, BM.
Abraham Grim & Betsey Wombledorff, Oct. 3, 1812. Charles Watkins, BM.
Benjamine Grissam & Betsey Richmond, Nov. 16, 1812. George Richmond, BM.
Watson Guestree & Elizabeth McGlothin, Aug. 29, 1812. Survellen Ellis, BM.
John Gwin & Polly Beard, Sep. 22, 1812. Thomas C. Beard, BM.
Moses Hall & Susan Blakemore, Sep. 15, 1812. Laurence Whitsitt, BM.
Reby Harel & Polly Wallis, Feb. 23, 1812. Israel Moore, BM.
Richard Harrison & Jane Tinnin, Dec. 7, 1812. Azariah Tinnin, BM.
Michael Heffman & Polly McDowell (or just Dowell), Aug. 22, 1812. John Tomkkins, BM.
Samuel Higganson & Peggy Rogan, Sep. 8, 1812. Nathan Crenshaw, BM.
William Hodge & Harriett Clark, Feb. 11, 1812. Robt. M. Boyers, BM.
Andrew Hoover & Mary Dyer, April 29, 1812.
Matthew Ing & Susannah Pickering, Dec. 18, 1812. Adam Crump, BM.
Frances Johnson & Kitty Foster, Sep. 22, 1812. Adam Starnes, BM.
Lewis Johnston & Salley Payne, Nov. 28, 1812. Joel Parrish, BM.
William Kennedy & Mary Stevens, Dec. 30, 1812. David Stuart, BM.
Strother Key & Margaret C. Graham, Jan. 16, 1812. Thomas Swann, BM.
John Lane & Elender Willis, Sep. 12, 1812. John Willis, BM.
George Litsinger & Elizabeth White, May 30, 1812. Robert White, BM.
Reuben Mansker & Polly Borders, Sep. 3, 1812. Peter Borders, BM.
Andrew Martin & Polley Montgomery, Aug. 26, 1812. Wm. Montgomery, BM.
Jasper Martin & Fanny Wilson, Oct. 29, 1812. James Wilson, BM.
William Martin & Sucky Knowell, April 23, 1812. Colson Lovell, BM.
James McCoy & Anna Chapman, Jan. 13, 1812. Red D. Barry, BM.
Joseph McDaniel & Maria Thomas, Aug. 17, 1812. Elisha Thomas, BM.
Joseph McGloughlin & Anne Boles, June 29, 1812. Isaac Boles, BM.
John McKinsey & Lucy Morrison, July 11, 1812. William McKinsey, BM.
Thomas Miers & Sally Wetherred, Dec. 15, 1812. Solomon Shoulders, BM.
Frederick Miller & Rhody Vinson, Jan. 27, 1812. Henry Vinson, BM.
Solomon Mitchell & Sarah Furgerson, Jan. 13, 1812. Bartholemew Ozburn, BM.
Robert Moore & Peggy Green, May 19, 1812. Orran Faulks, BM.
Jesse Morris & Anna Harper, April 30, 1812. Isaac Morris, BM.
Henry Newton & Jemima Woodall, April 4, 1812. James Bracken, BM.
Benjamine Parker & Susannah Robertson, Dec. 11, 1812. David Wilson, BM.
William Patterson & Rachel Clendening, March 10, 1812. James Hart, BM.
William Patton & Jane Lowry, Feb. 12, 1812. Daniel Stewart, BM.
George Pearce & Lucy Kirkham, Sep. 24, 1812. Jonathan Peaire, BM.
Eddin Phillips & Celia Melton, May 18, 1812. William Ogles, BM.
William Rame & Jane McDaniel, June 11, 1812. Wm. McAdams, BM.
Rhodam Rawlings & Sally E. Lucas, Aug. 31, 1812. John Shelby, BM.
Peter Reed & Elizabeth Hudson, May 30, 1812. Edmund Keen, BM.
Seth Russell & Polly Jackson, Feb. 27, 1812. James Alderson, BM.
Nathaniel Sanders & Harriet Sanders, Feb. 24, 1812. Abram Trigg, BM.

William Sanderson & Patsey Searcy, Jan. 13, 1812. John Christian, BM.

Randel Scott & Francis Adkison, Jan. 16, 1812. Andrew McCormick, BM.

William Snoddy & Elizabeth Alexander, July 7, 1812. David Orr, BM.

James Stalcup & Peggy Marlin, Sep. 2, 1812. Thomas Stalcup, BM.

John Stapleton & Eliza Joiner, Dec. 3, 1812. Enos King, BM.

William Thompson & Patsey Beasley, April 27, 1812. Hugh Latimer, BM.

Jordon Uzzell & Pully Dugger, Jan. 15, 1812. Leonard Dugger, BM.

Enos Vinson & Charity Baldridge, July 22, 1812. Wm. McCall, BM.

George Vinson & Sally Stalcup, March 4, 1812. Philip Turner, BM.

David Wallace & Peggy Williams, Aug. 10, 1812. William Goff, BM.

James Watts & Patsey Young, April 11, 1812. James Smith, BM.

Reuben Watts & Polly Morris, June 25, 1812. Robert Watts, BM.

Daniel West & Judith Hooper, June 30, 1812. Asa Hodges, BM.

Littleton Whoten & Anna Wilson, Nov. 28, 1812. Robert Whoten, BM.

Malchi Willis & Betsey Lane, Sep. 12, 1812. John W. Byrns, BM.

Edward Williams & Rachel Brackin, May 7, 1812. Thomas Stalcup, BM.

George Wilson & Sarah Sibles, Nov. 15, 1812. Thos. Blackwell, BM.

Robert Wilson & Jane Latimer, March 21, 1812. Thomas Shaw, BM.

Logan D. Wirt & Sally Wirt, Oct. 26, 1812. David West, BM.

Henry Workings & Lavinia Turner, Sep. 1, 1812. John Cloar, BM.

James Wright & Nancy Montgomery, Dec. 4, 1812. Gideon Wright, BM.

Beverly Young & Martha Wright, Feb. 6, 1812. Jamison Bandy, BM.

Silas Alexander & Nancy Anderson, April 29, 1813. Raven C. Follis, BM.

John Allsupt & Prudence Henderson, Oct. 6, 1813. David Allsupt, BM.

Jonathan Anderson & Elizabeth Condon, April 14, 1813. David White, BM.

Isaac Askew & Mabala Allen, Sep. 10, 1813. Webb Bloodworth, BM.

James Barnard & Jessia Short, Aug. 25, 1813. Zadoch Barnard, BM.

Hugh Barr & Katy Hodge, Nov. 23, 1813. Robt. Hodge, BM.

David Barrett & Patsey (Inge) Ingram, Dec. 11, 1813. George Barrett, BM. (Note: Patsy Inge sister of Joseph Inge).

Francis Barry & Sarah Frost, July 4, 1813. Jonathan Hady, BM.

Learner Blackman & Elizabeth Elliott, June 22, 1813. James Odom, BM.

Edmond Boaz & Betsey Proctor, Nov. 27, 1813. Samuel K. Blythe, BM.

Joseph Campbell & Milly Norris, Jan. 13, 1813, by S. Hunt, J.P. David Green, BM.

William Carroll & Cecilia M. Bradford, Sep. 1, 1813. Henry Bradford, BM.

Gideon Carter & Betsy Swaney, May 15, 1813. Joseph Carter, BM.

Joseph Carter & Betsey Mallard, June 30, 1813. Gideon Carter, BM.

Edward Choat & Sally Axcum (Axum), June 4, 1813. Christopher Woodall, BM.

Thornton Clayton & Fanny Beardon, March 6, 1813. John Bentley, BM.

Adam Cline & Sarah Black, Nov. 29, 1813. John Cline, BM.

Waid Davis & Patsey Dreweney (Drewney), May 23, 1813. Fieldin Hankins, BM.

Thomas M. Dement & Elizabeth Bowler, March 3, 1813. David Dement, BM.

John Dobb & Sarah Anderson, May 6, 1813. William Wygal, BM.

Jesse Douglass & Patsey Cunning, Sep. 8, 1813. Robert Payne, BM.
William Ring.
David Dowel & Elizabeth Shook, Aug. 13, 1813. Chas. B. Stubbins,
BM.
John Easley & Anny Worldrum, Nov. 25, 1813. Isiah Trasey, BM.
James Ellis & Susannah Cattron, Sep. 4, 1813. Everard Ellis, BM.
Beverly Fleming & Polly Aspy, Nov. 15, 1813. Joseph Moss, BM.
James Fleming & Polly Ross, Sep. 20, 1813. Isiah Lauderdale, BM.
William Garrison & Kesiah Smith, June 26, 1813. William Delapp,
BM.
Littleberry Green & Fanny Tyree, Jan. 12, 1813. Michael Green, BM.
Greenberry Greenhaw & Sally Bridges, June 19, 1813. Hugh Cowin,
BM.
John Gibson & Polly Trible, Aug. 5, 1813. Abram Trible, BM.
William Glover & Betsey Motherall, July 15, 1813. Samuel K.
Blythe, BM.
James Gourley & Violet Wilson, May 18, 1813. Jacob Houdeshall, BM.
Jesse Graham & Peggy Alexander, July 11, 1813. Zaddock Ingram, BM.
James M. Gray & Maria Saunders, Sep. 1, 1813.
Asa Hassell & Sally Edwards, Feb. 8, 1813. Nathan Edwards, BM.
William Henderson & Martha Henson, March 14, 1813. James Trap, BM.
Samuel Hendricks & Rebecca Dorris, Oct. 4, 1813. William Summers,
BM.
Edmund Hogin & Polly Walton, May 13, 1813. Hugh Tinnin, BM.
Thomas Hunt & Mary Davis, July 11, 1813. Jonathan Davis, BM.
William Hubbard & Sally Dalton, July 31, 1813. Joseph Motheral,
BM.
Vinson Lee & Lily Jenkins, Dec. 24, 1813. Thomas Jenkins, BM.
Joseph Lester & Rebecca Dorris, Dec. 4, 1813. William Capps, BM.
Stephen Lewis & Oma Laurence, Jan. 4, 1813. David Dement, BM.
King Luton & Caroline Walton, Oct. 8, 1813. John Perry, BM.
Thomas Keefe (Keese) & Peggy Evans, Feb. 2, 1813. Will Trigg,
BM.
Andrew Jackson & Betsey Dorris, March 18, 1813. Andrew Martin, BM.
Clem Jennings & Elizabeth Bennett, May 26, 1813. Richard B. Estes,
BM.
Thomas Johnston & Matheen Carson, Oct. 3, 1813. Benjamine Johns-
ton, BM.
Henry Martin & Hannah Carroll, Dec. 7, 1813. Benj. Seawell, BM.
James McGee & Matilda Wallace, Jan. 19, 1813. Joseph Wallace, BM.
William McKinnie & Cynthia W. Wilson, Dec. 14, 1813. James T.
Wilson, BM.
Jonathan Mercum & Betsey May, Aug. 7, 1813. Michiel Green, BM.
Daniel Miers & Mary Wilson, Oct. 18, 1813. Thomas Shoals, BM.
Miles Miers & Lucy Dukes, June 26, 1813. Solomon Shoulders, BM.
Thomas Miles & Esther Summers, April 30, 1813. Henry Hamilton, BM.
Hugh Morrison & Sarah Williamson, Feb. 27, 1813. John Morrison,
BM.
William Murphey & _____ (?), Nov. 6, 1813. Jacob Gregory, BM.
Robert Neely & Fanny Boswell, Aug. 11, 1813. J. D. Blackmore, BM.
William Owen & Martha Edwards, Feb. 5, 1813. William Crenshaw, BM.
David Parrish & Lucinder Hunt, July 3, 1813. Elijah Boddie, BM.
Isaac Pavatt & Thornin Eliss, May 3, 1813. Pavatt Cuffman, BM.
William Pitt & Jane Robertson, Jan. 9, 1813. Isaac Baker, BM.

SUMNER COUNTY MARRIAGES

Nicholas B. Pryor & Sally M. Thomas, Sep. 16, 1813. John Johnson, BM.
Barney Reyley & Peggy McKinsey, Oct. 12, 1813.
Elijah Russell & Sarah Drewry, April 5, 1813. Daniel Williams, BM.
James Sanders & Levisa Bowen, March 19, 1813. William Glover, BM.
Isaac Short & Polly Overby, July 22, 1813. Jacob Barnard, BM.
Joseph Sloss & Ann Hodge, Nov. 25, 1813. John Turner, BM.
Abraham Smith & Lydia Pearce, Jan. 13, 1813. George Reese, BM.
Stephen Stalcup & Margaret Pitt, Jan. 19, 1813. William Lawhorn, BM.
Barry R. Starks & Betsey Lindsey, July 16, 1813. James Wills, BM.
Jacob Straiter & Beady Dean, June 6, 1813. John Warren, BM. Nicholas Cocklereese.
William Snyder & Fanny Wadkins, May 20, 1813. Paul Tinsley, BM.
William Trail & Sally Hammon, Jan. 29, 1813. Willis Atchison, BM.
William L. Turner & Eliza B. Smith, Jan. 12, 1813. Benjamine Brown, BM.
Edmond Wagoner & Charity Wilson, Oct. 13, 1813. Joseph T. Wilson, BM.
John Wallace & Matilda Wilson, Sep. 1, 1813. Ezekiel Cherry, BM.
Daniel Williams & Mary Mayhue, May 18, 1813. Elmore Waggoner, BM.
Charles Wood & Elizabeth Reeves, July 26, 1813. Wm. H. Douglass, BM.
John Worldrum & Rhody Hide, May 20, 1813. William Henderson, BM.
Samuel Young & Betsey George, Aug. 24, 1813, by S. Hunt, J.P. John Douglass, BM.
William Young & Nancy Patterson, April 24, 1813. Samuel Young, BM.
William Stovall & Betsey Rickman, Nov. 3, 1814. George Stovall, BM.
Joseph White & Patsey Cunningham, Sep. 11, 1814. Kasper Mansker, BM.

NO RECORDS FOR YEAR 1815 (lost)

Philip Ashlock & Marian Melton, Jan. 15, 1816. David West, BM.
John Aspley & Milly Senter, July 12, 1816. William Aspley, BM.
Isaac Anderson & Polly Rogers, Oct. 25, 1816, by S. Hunt, J.P. William Cantrell, BM.
John B. Anderson & Nancy Stamps, Sep. 19, 1816. William Cantrell, BM.
Thomas Badget & Jane Badget, Sep. 16, 1816, by Jas. Douglass, J.P. James Johnson, BM.
Joshua Barker & Anne Smith, Sep. 17, 1816, by Hugh Kirkpatrick, M.G. James Kirkpatrick, BM.
Robert Bell & Margarett F. McGundy, June 4, 1816. Robert Desha, Jr., BM.
Nathan Benbrook & Sally McGuire, Nov. 9, 1816, by John Benbrook. Elijah Sneed, BM.
Lawrence Bevard & Betsey White, May 7, 1816. Thomas Scurry, BM.
Adam Biggs & Sally Miller, June 6, 1816. Thos. Scurry, BM.
Elijah Body & Mariah Elliott, Dec. 25, 1816, by Hardy M. Cryer. Ashley Stanfield, BM.
James Bowman & Elizabeth Bowman, May 31, 1816. John T. Bowman, BM.
Jesse Bradley & Lucinda Trible, Jan. 17, 1816, by James Gwin, M.G. Stephen Trible, BM.

27

John Bradley & Elizabeth Goostree, Jan. 17, 1816, by James Gwin, M.G. Stephen Trible, BM.
Luke Bradley & Agatha Woodall, Jan. 20, 1816, by Edward Gwin, J.P. Johnathan Woodall, BM.
Thomas Bradley & Betsey Ritter, Oct. 29, 1816. Thos. Scurry, BM.
Charles N. Brigance & Fanny Dyer, Jan. 2, 1816. John Brigance, BM.
Thomas Brookshire & Matilda Giles, March 25, 1816, by John Rutherford.
Oliver Bush & Nancy Cravens, Dec. 31, 1816, by Edw. Douglass. Jourdon Jackson, BM.
Charles L. Byrn & Mary C. Davidson, Nov. 23, 1816. William Cantrill, BM.
Nelson Cardwell & Nancy Hughs, Nov. 30, 1816, by C. Ballard. William Stovall, BM.
Benjamine Carless & Sally Rascoe, Dec. 10, 1816, by Hardy M. Cryer. William House, BM.
Mack Clark & Mary Ann Abbott, Dec. 1, 1816. Edw. Douglas, BM. Thos. Scurry, BM.
Spencer Clary & Winney Daniel, Nov. 30, 1816. Elisha Clary, BM.
Meredith Crenshaw & Elizabeth Pharr, Jan. 2, 1816, by John Rutherford. Enos Vinson, BM.
Thomas Crowder & Elizabeth Nemo, Sep. 18, 1816. Amos McCarther, BM.
John Curry & Margaret Cowen, Oct. 16, 1816. John McElurath, BM.
Thomas Daniel & Judy Thornhill, April 10, 1816, by Thos. Anderson, J.P. Michiel Green, BM.
Robert Denny & Elizabeth Davis, Sep. 16, 1816, by Wm. Montgomery, J.P. Thos. Scurry, BM.
George W. Dickason, Jr. & W. Turner, Aug. 2, 1816. Walter Dickason, BM.
Griffith Dickason & Matilda Williams, Nov. 29, 1816. J. W. Weatherred, BM.
William Dinning & Nancy Moody, July 15, 1816, by Edward Gwin, J.P. Burwell Hunter, BM.
Ephraim Dixon & Catherine Thompson, Aug. 31, 1816. William White, BM.
Anthony Donoho & Anna Coleman, July 1, 1816, by Daniel Latimer, J.P. James Stratton, BM.
James Donoho & Lotty Holmes, May 23, 1816. James McKain, BM.
John Dorris & Jane Dorris, Feb. 9, 1816. Isaac Dorris, BM.
Daniel Draper & Betsey Joyner, Oct. 19, 1816, by John McMurtry, J.P. Thomas Shaw, BM.
Wesley Dugger & Charlotte Dugger, July 10, 1816. Leonard Dugger, BM.
Elias Durlin & Lucy Burk, Aug. 7, 1816. Thos. Scurry, BM.
James T. Ellis & Susanna Wright, Aug. 29, 1816. Jacob Ellis, BM.
Elim A. Erwin & Elizabeth A. Duncan, Dec. 7, 1816.
Cornelius Evans & Anna Harrell, Aug. 7, 1816. Jno. Shelby, BM. Wm. H. Douglass.
Drewry Esley & Mary Tracey, Dec. 22, 1816, by Robert McClarey, J.P. Michael Tracey, BM.
Gideon Eson & Sally Herring, Feb. 6, 1816. Drury Herring, BM.
Nelson Ferguson & Roxey Tyler, Nov. 23, 1816. J. W. Byrn, BM.

SUMNER COUNTY MARRIAGES

John Garrison & Rhody Hampton, Dec. 14, 1816, by Wm. Montgomery,
   J.P. Jonathan Holly, BM.
Sherwood George & Anne Goldman, Feb. 15, 1816, by Jas. McKendree.
   Thos. Ferrell, BM. J. B. Anderson.
William Gilmore & Patsey Henderson, Oct. 3, 1816, by Robt. McClarey,
   J.P. Abram Bird, BM.
Joab Goodbread & Polly Henson, Sep. 16, 1816. Thos. Scurry, BM.
John Goodrum & Majory Carothers, Nov. 13, 1816, by S. K. Blythe,
   J.P. Geo. Elliott, BM. James White.
Henry Hamilton & Jane Frazor, April 24, 1816. Thomas Shaw, BM.
Wade Hampton & Mary Melton, Sep. 23, 1816. Benjamine Bush, BM.
Noah Harper & Rebecca Summers, June 29, 1816, by Daniel Latimre,
   J.P. Humphrey Miers, BM.
Robert Harper & Nancy Landers, Aug. 15, 1816. John Webb, BM.
John Harris & Polly Lembeth, Dec. 8, 1816. Elisha Long, BM.

John Harris
          Sir:
              I am engaged to be married to Miss Polly Lambath
          and have sent to you by Mr. Abram Martin, Jr. for
          license.
                  Test: Sam'l Martin
                                John Harris

          Sir:
              Mr. John Harris of Sumner County and my daughter
          Polly are engaged to be married. You will therefore
          send license for the solemnization of matrimony.
                  Test: Sam'l Martin
                                William Lambath

Mathew Harris & Milly Cockrum, Oct. 17, 1816, by Jas. McKendry.
   Thomas Shaw, BM.
William L. Harris & Anney Todd, Feb. 27, 1816, by Sam'l. Gibson.
   Wm. L. Bledsoe, BM.
David Herbert & Mildred Dickerson, Nov. 5, 1816, by Thos. Black-
   more. Benjamine Herbert,BM.
John Hermans & Sally Mitchell, Aug. 14, 1816. Nath. Prince, BM.
Asa Hodge & Lucy Williford, April 23, 1816, by Edwin Gwin. Jacob
   Seawell, BM.
Robert Hodge & Jane Sloss, Jan. 10, 1816. William Glover, BM.
Nathan Holloway & Sophia Crews, April 30, 1816, by John Pitts.
   Thos. Scurry, BM.
Jacob Houndershell & Jane Gourley, Aug. 27, 1816, by John Ruther-
   ford. John Rutherford, BM.
William House & Rachel Bowles, June 28, 1816. Samuel Rooney, BM.
William Hunley & Patsy Adams, Nov. 11, 1816, by John Wiseman.
James Isaacs & Mima McAdams, May 17, 1816. William McAdams, BM.
Henry W. Johnson & Sally Green, July 11, 1816, by Edw. Douglas;
   J.P. Lewis Green, BM.
John Joiner & Betsey Clemmons, May 28, 1816, by John McMurtry. Ely
   Stalcup, BM.
Moses Jones & Nancy Allen, Aug. 27, 1816. William Hannah, BM.
Joseph Kelly & Hevelina Penticost, Feb. 5, 1816. David West, BM.

James Knight & Sally Hanson, Dec. 20, 1816. Thomas Brookshire, BM.
Jonathan Knight & Polly White, April 22, 1816, by Thos. McGuire.
 John Cooper, BM.
Samuel Lamar & Nancy Randall, Nov. 7, 1816, by Robt. McClary.
 Forster Clayton, BM.
Warner Lambeth & Lucy Turpin, Oct. 17, 1816, by Daniel Latimer, J.P.
 Wm. Moss, BM.
John Lorance & Kitty Tinsley, Sep. 24, 1816. Jesse Daniel, BM.
Nathaniel Law & Rebecca Raines, Oct. 17, 1816, by Elijah Simpson,
 J.P. Edmond Haines, BM.
Rob. N. Lewis & Mahala Martin, Oct. 6, 1816; Edward Gaines, BM.
 Samuel Gwin.
David Lindsy & Nancy Purvis, Aug. 18, 1816, by L. Hunt, J.P.
Isaac Looney & Betsey Brigance, Feb. 29, 1816. Joseph Scoby, BM.
George Martin & Zela Dagner, May 24, 1816, by Dan'l Latimer, J.P.
 Robert Parks, BM.
Thomas Morton & Patsey Cage, Nov. 10, 1816. Edward Douglas, J.P.
 H. Cage, BM.
William Mansker & Avarilla Dugger, Aug. 21, 1816. Luke Dugger, BM.
Richard Moore & Polly McKendre, Feb. 8, 1816. James Gwin, M.G.
 Matthew Harris, BM.
William May & Christian McDaniel, Dec. 28, 1816, by Anderson, J.P.
 Webb Bloodworth, BM.
Amos McCarthy & Lewisa Crowder, July 11, 1816, by Jas. Douglass.
 Thos. Crowder, BM.
William McGuary & Elizabeth Williams, June 22, 1816, by John Mc
 Murtry, J.P. Anthony Williams, BM.
John McKennie & Fannie Wilson, Jan. 5, 1816. John Payne, BM.
James McKinsey & Betsy Josey, Feb. 24, 1816. James Cryer, BM.
John McMillan & Betsey Butt, Nov. 23, 1816, by Thos. Blakmore.
 Thomas Carothers, BM.
Joseph McReynolds & Tabitha McReynolds, Oct. 26, 1816, by Thos.
 Anderson. Isaac Lane, BM.
Arrey Meader & Elizabeth Clybourn, Dec. 29, 1816, by Elijah Simp-
 son, J.P. George Clyborn.
Thomas Milton & Nancy Ozbrooks, Jan. 20, 1816, by Thos. McGuire.
 William Martin, BM.
William Montgomery & Polly Martin, Sep. 16, 1816, by Hugh Kirk-
 patrick, M.G. James Robb, BM.
Ransom Moss & Charlotte Boyers, May 11, 1816, by Sam'l Blythe, J.P.
 Pleasant Tyree, BM.
Anthony B. Neely & Peggy D. Reed, Nov. 1, 1816. William Carr, BM.
Henry Nimmo & Polly Cockran, Oct. 17, 1816, by James McKendree.
 William Trigg, Jr., BM.
John Newlin & Prudence Blankenship, Dec. 19, 1816. Edmond Boze, BM.
James H. Owings & Sally Hudson, March 13, 1816, by Edward Gwin, J.P.
 William Hudson, BM.
David Parrish & Lutilda Hunt, June 5, 1816, by S. K. Blythe, J.P.
 Robert Desha, BM.
Joel Parrish & Betsy Rawlings, June 20, 1816. A. B. Shelby, BM.
James H. Patterson & Martha Clendening, July 4, 1816. Anthony B.
 Clendening, BM.
Matthew Phips & Elizabeth Wallace, Sep. 24, 1816. James Hutchin-
 son, BM.

SUMNER COUNTY MARRIAGES

Banjamine Pitt & Polly Busby, Jan. 4, 1816. S. Pitt, BM.
Sterling Pitt & Lavina Brigance, Jan. 18, 1816. Thos. Scurry, BM.
William Pend & Elizabeth Rice, Aug. 21, 1816, by John McMurtry, J.P.
    J. W. Byrn, BM.
William Powell & Mary Patton, April 5, 1816, by Daniel Latimre, J.P.
Daniel Price & Obedience Kent, Aug. 15, 1816. William Dickens, BM.
Nathaniel Prince & Betsy Harrison, Dec. 8, 1816. Joel Parrish, BM.
Silas Pruett & Sally Perry, March 25, 1816. Robert Desha, BM.
John Pyle & Sarah Allen, Feb. 24, 1816, by Wm. H. Anderson, J.P.
    David Crocket, BM. David Whipple.
William Randle & Nancy McReynolds, Oct. 21, 1816, by Robt. McClarey.
David Reddick & Milley Moore, Aug. 13, 1816. James Barry, BM.
George Roberts & Betsy Johnson, July 13, 1816, by B. Craighead.
    M. Winchester, BM.
Charles Robertson & Bethelhem (?) Day, March 23, 1816. Thos.
    Scurry, BM.
Micheil Robinson & Milly Patterson, Dec. 27, 1816. Jesse Rankin,
    BM.
Aaron Ruyle & Betsy Rogers, Feb. 10, 1816. William McAdams, BM.
Henry Ruyle, Jr. & Betsy Smith, May 13, 1816. Littleberry Smith,
    BM.
Jacob Sciva & Zelpha Bloodworth, June 8, 1816, by Wm. H. Anderson,
    J.P. John Pankey, BM.
John Senter & Rhody Durham, July 16, 1816. Logan West, BM.
Thomas Shaw & Euphy Hamilton, June 6, 1816, by Edward Gwin, J.P.
    Henry Hamilton, BM.
Abraham Sims & Nancy Keen, March 13, 1816, by Edward Gwin, J.P.
    Currel Keen, BM.
Munford Sneed & Susannah Lunsford, June 1, 1816. Peter Townsend,
    BM.
David Snoddy & Nancy Purvis, Aug. 18, 1816. Joseph McElurath, BM.
Obediah Spradlin & Lucinda Cockran, March 21, 1816, by Daniel Per-
    due, J.P. John Foster, BM.
Byard Stovall & Charlotte Dickison, July 5, 1816, by John Pitts.
    Robert Rickman, BM.
James Stovall & Polly Dephrest, March 5, 1816, by John Pitts.
    Nathan Holloway, BM.
John Summers & Margaret Jackson, Jan. 2, 1816, by Daniel Latimer,
    J.P. Levi Summers, BM.
Joel Swiney & Sally Tinsley, Dec. 4, 1816, by Washington C. Ballard,
    M.G. John Stone, BM.
William Teasly & Amy Pharr, April 22, 1816. Enos Vinson, BM.
John Thurmond & Nancy Gregory, Feb. 5, 1816. Morgan Penticost, BM.
Joseph Townsend & Polly Durin, Aug. 8, 1816. Griffin Bennett, BM.
Teriha Turner & Rachel Dickinson, Dec. 7, 1816. Will Trigg, BM.
Edmund Vinson & Merina Fleetwood, Dec. 4, 1816. Stokley Vinson, BM.
Stokley Vinson & Sally Fleetwood, March 9, 1816, by John Ruther-
    ford. Enos Vinson, BM.
Henry Virgin & Nancy Alley, March 20, 1816. William White, BM.
George Watson & Martha McAdams, Feb. 29, 1816. Edward Gwin, BM.
Thomas S. Watson & Sally Smith, Nov. 13, 1816. Abraham Trigg, BM.
David H. Whipple & Mary Smith, March 31, 1816, by Wm. H. Anderson,
    Jr., J.P. Wm. H. Anderson, BM.

Samuel Whitworth & Polly Hendin, Jan. 30, 1816. Jamison Bandy, BM.
   Will Trigg, Jr. Date performed, Feb. 4, 1816.
Jonathan Wilkenson & Anne Kirkpatrick, July 22, 1816, by John
   McMurtry, J.P. Joseph Kirkpatrick, BM.
John Wilks & Tabitha Green, Aug. 13, 1816. Jesse Haynie, BM.
Richard S. Wilks & Martha Winn, Aug. 31, 1816, by John Wiseman.
   William Hunley, BM.
Abisha Williams & Peggy Brigance, March 13, 1816.
Joseph Wilson & Amanda Alexander, Jan. 9, 1816. William Colbert,
   BM.
Thomas Wilson & Betsy Bull, April 2, 1816, by Thos. Anderson, J.P.
   Sam'l Anderson, BM.
John Williams & Peggy Morris, March 23, 1816, by S. L. Blythe.
   Robt. Parks, BM.
Hugh H. Withers & Dolly H. Avent, Jan. 27, 1816. Carter Moss, BM.
James F. Winn & Polly Hurt, Oct. 21, 1816, by John Jarratt. Thomas
   Meirs, BM. Wm. Moss.
Peter Winn & Polly Smith, Aug. 13, 1816. Jesse Hassell, BM.
Benjamine Woodruff & Polly Garner, March 8, 1816, by John Barr,
   J.P. Nathaniel Prince, BM. Abraham Trigg.
Thomas Wright & Polly Pitner, Sep. 30, 1816, by Robert McClary.
   Edward Maxey, BM.
Joshua Abston & Winny Joiner, March 26, 1817, by L. Hunt, J.P.
   Asa White, BM.
Aaron Adams & Catherine Harris, Feb. 11, 1817, by Elijah Simpson,
   J.P. Shadrick Rumley, BM.
James Adams & Elizabeth Tinsley, Dec. 23, 1817, by Washington C.
   Bullard. Richard Stone, BM.
Carter Adcock & Dolly Railey, Oct. 9, 1817. Isaac Pearis, BM.
Jeremiah Alderson & C. (Crisia) Nolin, Feb. 24, 1817. James Alder-
   son, BM.
James Anderson & Polly Briggs, Sep. 13, 1817. Adam Briggs, BM.
James Anderson & Sarah Buckhanan, April 2, 1817. Isaac Anderson,
   BM.
Robert Anderson & Permelia Winham, Feb. 27, 1817, by James Douglass,
   J.P. Thos. Scurry, BM.
William Anthony & Jane B. Marshall, June 11, 1817, by John Wiseman,
   M.G.
William Baker & Betsey Treadwell, June 21, 1817, by S. Hunt, J.P.
   James Douglas, BM.
Richard Bandy & Kesiah Pearis, Dec. 30, 1817. Jamison Bandy, BM.
John Barham & Fanny Markham, Jan. 7, 1817. Eli Giles, BM.
Turner Barnes & Betsey Anderson, March 26, 1817. John Bell, BM.
Zadeck Bernard & Hannah Kimbel, Oct. 29, 1817.
Allen Bond & Elizabeth Donoho, March 26, 1817. Jesse Dillon, BM.
Robert M. Boyers & Elizabeth Banks, Dec. 28, 1817. Joel Parrish,
   BM.
James Boyle & Nancy Campbell, Aug. 25, 1817. John Boyle, BM.
William Brantley & Mourning Morris, Oct. 29, 1817, by S. W. Blythe.
   William Harris, BM.
James Briley & Jane Bandy, March 21, 1817, by Dan'l Latimer, J.P.
   William Briley, BM.
Kendal Brinkley & Hannah Davis, Sep. 27, 1817, by David Webb, M.G.
   Robt. Cochran, BM.

Joseph Brown & Mary Calbert, Oct. 26, 1817. Isaiah Simmons, BM.
William Brown & Avarilla Malone, Oct. 4, 1817. John Brown, BM.
John Bruce & Betsey Williams, March 13, 1817, by Wm. Montgomery, J.P. Daniel Montgomery, BM.
Robert Bruce & Susannah Cobb, Oct. 3, 1817. William McQuay, BM.
Thomas Bruce & Polly Turpin, May 5, 1817, by John McMurtry, J.P. William Dorris, BM.
John H. Burford & Nancy McCollester, March 24, 1817. Jesse Clark, BM.
John Byrns & Polly Pruett, Dec. 24, 1817, by John Rutherford. James Pruett, BM. Amos Goyne.
Peter Bryson & Sally E. Saunders, July 23, 1817. John H. Bower, BM.
Larkin Carman & Elizabeth Barton, Nov. 5, 1817. Elijah Barton, BM.
Robert Carroll & Peggy Stuart, April 10, 1817. George Elliott, BM.
James Claxton & Polly Martin, March 3, 1817, by Sam'l Gibson, E.C.C. Thomas Scurry, BM.
Ezekiah Collum Barnes & Dotia Stone, Aug. 23, 1817, by James Douglas, J.P. John Moore, BM.
Turner Cook & Betsey Durham, Sep. 27, 1817. Allen Meirs, BM.
Lewis Corder & Rebecca Phillips, Sep. 11, 1817. Ebbon Phillips, BM.
William Crane & Nancy Rascoe, Aug. 7, 1817. Philip Turner, BM.
Shelton Dalton & Patsey Walton, Dec. 16, 1817. John Wiseman, J.P. Matthew Bathey, BM.
John Dorris & Jane Dorris, July 30, 1817. John McMurtry, J.P. Hugh Kirkpatrick, BM.
Alfred M. Douglass & Cherry Ferrell, April 26, 1817. James Stratton, BM.
Ezeas W. Earle & Rebecca W. Clark, Sep. 25, 1817. John W. Byrn, BM.
Benjamine Edwards & Patsey Miers, Nov. 16, 1817. John Bell, BM.
Joseph T. Elliston & Elizabeth Blackman, Dec. 10, 1817. A. B. Shelby, BM.
Leonard Escue & Polly Lee, June 4, 1817. S. W. Blythe, J.P. John Stewart, BM.
Sanford Fitts & Tabitha Hughes, Nov. 4, 1817. Washington Ballard, V.D.M. Thomas Scurry, BM.
Jacob Forrester & Polly McMurtry, July 17, 1817. Wm. Montgomery, J.P. John W. Byrn, BM.
Cullen Gardner & Sally Franklin, Jan. 8, 1817. Thos. Scurry, BM.
Reuben Gowen & Crisia Ford, Dec. 6, 1817. Sam'l Gwin, BM.
Simon Gray & Betsey McAllester, March 20, 1817, by James Douglas, J.P. Jacob Seawell, BM.
Ropher (Roper) Gregory & Martha Gregory, Feb. 20, 1817, by Wm. H. Anderson, J.P. John Stewart, BM.
Thomas Hails & Sally Justice, Oct. __, 1817. David Barrott, BM. Geo. S. Brigance.
John Harper & Nancy Linzey, March 14, 1817, by Elijah Simpson, J.P. John Barr, BM.
Thomas Harrison & Martha Morris, July 15, 1817. Thos. Scurry, BM. William Cantrill.
Cader Harroll & Polly Garrison, Nov. 2, 1817. Ambrose Porter, BM.
Joseph Hays & Tabitha Hobdy, Oct. 10, 1817. John Hobdy, BM.

Samuel Henry & Polly Carroll, Nov. 18, 1817. Wm. Reed, Jr., BM. Wm. Henry.

John Hobdy & Nancy Cummins, Oct. 4, 1817. Edward Gwin, J.P. Thos. Hobdy, BM.

John P. Hogan & Polly Hogan, Nov. 22, 1817. John W. Byrn, BM.

Daniel Holman & Polly Exum, April 26, 1817. Robert Desha, BM. George Elliott, James Barry.

Dred Holmon & Betsey Morris, Nov. 29, 1817. David Allen, BM. Caleb Boyman.

Thomas Holloway & Creasy Rogers, Dec. 22, 1817. John Garrison.

John B. Howard & Harriett Searcy, May 29, 1817. William Bracken.

Mathew Johnson & Lucy Head, Nov. 26, 1817. R. M. Boyers.

John Jones & Judy Little, April 12, 1817. Joshua Clarkson.

John Jones & Tiney Ruyle, July 26, 1817. Wm. Montgomery, J.P. Joshua Claxton.

Moses Jones & Priscilla Dement, Jan. 18, 1817. J. P. Cantrell.

Abram Joyner & Rebecca King, Jan. 2, 1817. James Hicks.

William Kerr & Polly Hanna, April 9, 1817. Washington G. Ballard, John Stewart.

Stanley Kumley & Betsey Smothers, July 17, 1817.

LaFayette Landis & Mary Smith, April 1, 1817. John Allen.

Isaac Lane & Elizabeth Camp, Sep. 17, 1817. Robert Morris Boyers.

Charles P. Laurence & Caty Crider, May 20, 1817. Wright Barnes.

David Logue & Polly Glasco, Sep. 10, 1817. William Cantrell.

Joshua Lovell & Vineny Moody, Oct. 17, 1817. Zachariah Lovell.

George A. Lucas & Polly Allen, Nov. 3, 1817. John Wiseman, M.G. Wm. Hadley.

Peter W. Lucas & Clementine Donoho, Oct. 29, 1817.

Wesley Malone & Patsey H. Hawkins, June 9, 1817. John Hunley.

Alfred Moore & Polly Hall, Jan. 25, 1817. D. Shelby, William Hall.

Nathan Morgan & Annie McCarty, Dec. 13, 1817. James Green, M.G. Thos. Scurry.

Nathaniel Nowlin & Mahalah Anderson, Sep. 27, 1817. Edmond Boaz.

Greenberry Orr & Elizabeth Burk, May 8, 1817. C. Ballard, Thos. L. Harris.

Jacob Overall & Jane Lee Tinsley, May 8, 1817. John W. Byrn.

Lewis Panky & Margaret Hainey, May 7, 1817. S. Blythe, J.P. Matthew Neal.

Nathaniel Parker & Betsey Collier, May 13, 1817. Daniel Parker, M.G. Richard Parker.

Lewis Paterson & Hanah Hunt, Oct. __, 1817. James Trousdale.

James Patterson & Olive Bates, Nov. 27, 1817. Joshua Claxton.

Simpson Payne & Elizabeth Green, Oct. 13, 1817. Hugh Crawford.

William Powell & Mary Patton, see 1816. John H. Bowen.

James Preestley & Caroline Pavatt, Nov. 15, 1817. Hugh Kirkpatrick, M.G. Zebuton Cantrell.

Mark Rainey & Betsey Smith, Nov. 8, 1817. Allen McDaniel.

_____ Ramsey & Margaret Brackin, Feb. 5, 1817. Nath. Prince.

Amos Randel & Rebecca Finn, Nov. 6, 1817. Robert McClarey, George Mercum.

King Rice & Polly Pond, Jan. 18, 1817. Frances Moore.

Allen Robertson & Anny Day, Jan. 12, 1817. Jesse Day.

Elijah Robinson & Betsey Mitchell, July 7, 1817. D. Webb, M.G. Thomas White.

William Robertson & Polly Bohann, Sep. 14, 1817.
William L. Robinson & Selina Winchester, June 17, 1817. William Hadley.
Robert F. Rogers & Nancy Clary, March 5, 1817. Henry Willard.
Richard Rose & Lalinda Street, June 17, 1817. Thos. Scurry.
Stenley Rumby & Betsey Smothers, July 17, 1817. Jonathan Clampit.
Christian Ruminger & Jane Farr, Nov. 27, 1817. Meredith G. Crenshaw.
Haley Russell & Rachel Kingsall, Oct. 15, 1817. John McMurtry, J.P. Jacob Forrester.
Henry Ruyle & Polly Berry, Aug. 20, 1817. W. H. Anderson, J.P. John W. Byrn.
Patrick Ryons & Lucy Barnett, July 17, 1817.
Reuben Satterfield & Betsy Carson, March 28, 1817. John Reeves.
Edward Scruggs & Frances S. Blackmore, Oct. 24, 1817. Jonathan Clay.
William Shall & Jane Fulton, Dec. 23, 1817. John White.
David Shelton & Rebecca L. Dickason, Dec. 3, 1817. John Wiseman, M.G. Robert Bradley.
John Smith & Elenor Pearce, Jan. 27, 1817. Peter W. Lucas.
Adam Snoddy & Prudence Alexander, April 9, 1817. W. Alexander.
Graham Snoddy & Frances M. Liggor, May 26, 1817. James Stratton.
William Snoddy & Sally Withrey, Sep. 27, 1817. Joseph McElurath.
William Stalcup & Clarey Foster, Sep. 15, 1817. Saml. Stalcup.
Alsey Stinson & Rhody Smothers, July 24, 1817. John Barr, J.P. John M. Rice.
Daniel Stone & Betsey Ford, May 26, 1817. John Bowen.
Richard Stone & Frances Adams, April 10, 1817. William Hunley.
Thomas Stovall & Betsey Sanders, Aug. 1, 1817. L. W. Weatherred.
Hugh Stuart & Sarah Shaw, Dec. 11, 1817. Robert Shaw.
James Suddarth & Elizabeth Turner, Sep. 25, 1817. Thos. Miers.
Cornelias Summers & Nancy Briley, Aug. 8, 1817. Samuel Smith.
Levi Summers & Louise Hatchett, March 18, 1817. Alexander Summers.
Peter Summers & Sally Armfield, June 28, 1817. Joshua Clark.
Hubert Tarpley & Elizabeth Catron, July 15, 1817. John McMurtry, J.P. James Ellis.
Champion Terry & Nancy Pitt, Dec. 9, 1817. Jonathan Looney.
Edmund Traylor & Elizabeth Joyner, March 8, 1817. J. W. Byrn.
Daniel Tramell & Nancy Wooten, March 11, 1817. Thos. Henderson.
Philip Turner & Mary Vinson, ___ 18, 1817. Frederick Miller.
William Volner & Polly Weeks, July 3, 1817. Elijah Simpson, J.P. Ely Smothers.
William Ward & Polly Yandle, Feb. 6, 1817. Samuel Yandle.
John Weeks & Deliah Roykin, Oct. 18, 1817. Thos. Simpson.
Charles White & Sally King, July 12, 1817. Elijah Boddie.
Benjamine Wilkinson & Betsy Givins, Dec. 24, 1817. Josiah Cain.
James Wilson & Anne Wilson, March 4, 1817. Jas. T. Wilson.
William Winbane & Margaret Anderson, Oct. 23, 1817. Amos Payne.
Reubin Woolbanks & Nancy Barrett, Feb. 12, 1817. Jas. Gwin, M.G. Thomas Scurry.
Henry Young & Sally T. Humphrey, Sep. 11, 1817. John Lauderdale.
Armstead Alderson & Elizabeth Orr, Sep. 14, 1818. John Gilbert, J.P.
Lytle Allen & Eliza Smith, Dec. 16, 1818. John Bell.

Lewis Banton & Mary Abston, Nov. 24, 1818. Asal White.
James Barrett & Nancy Lanford, Sep. 19, 1818. William L. Bledsoe.
Asail Bateman & Milly Johnson (Johnston), April 30, 1818. Richard
  Moore.
Solomon Beardon & Nancy Morris, Sep. 30, 1818. John Riggs.
Joseph M. Bell & Elizabeth C. Essex, Aug. 27, 1818. James McBride.
Micajah Bell & Peggy Lee, April 9, 1818. James Johnson.
Abraham Bradley & Zelpha Dorris, June 27, 1818. John Hilbert J.P.
  David Bradley.
David Bradley & Lucy Kirkum, Jan. 12, 1818. Joshua Bradley.
Robert Bradley & Nancy Bradley, Jan. 5, 1818. Samuel Mading.
John Brigance & Rebekah Stuart, Nov. 16, 1818. Isaac Looney.
Jesse Brown & Ellen Pritchet, Dec. 24, 1818. John McMurtry, J.P.
  John Ralph.
Jacob A. Browning & Polly Beckman, Dec. 19, 1818. Edward Browning.
William Cantrell & Joice E. Bugg, April 9, 1818. Wm. Trousdale.
Thomas Carey & Martha Brewster, April 16, 1818. W. C. Ballard,
  M.G. James Adams.
John Chadbourne & Tabitha Brassell, July 13, 1818. John Bell.
Michael Clyne & Margaret Ogle, Nov. 25, 1818. Wm. Alderson.
John Coleman & Nancy Lewis, Aug. 13, 1818. Ansil D. Bugg.
Solomon Debeard & Polly Franklin, March 9, 1818. John McMurtry,
  J.P. George Reed.
William Dinning & Lucky Alderson, April 17, 1818. Wm. Alderson.
Robert B. Dobbins & Jane Bratney, March 30, 1818. Thos. C. Beard.
Robert Dorris & Jinny Rippy, July 18, 1818. Addison Foster, J.P.
  William Dorris.
Elmore Douglass & Eliza Fulton, Oct. 22, 1818. T. B. Craighead,
  A. Donnell.
Alexander D. Duval & Margaret Gwin, March 9, 1818. Wm. C.
  Stribling, M.G. George Blain.
Robert Fleming & Polly Barr, Nov. 13, 1818. Thos. Scurry.
John W. Ford & Elizabeth Rolin, July 23, 1818. Wm. C. Dew.
Joshua Ford & Barbara Kittle, March 4, 1818. S. W. Blythe.
Donald Frazer & Julia Jane Anthony, July 29, 1818. Wm. Hume, D.D.
' J. Moore, Jas. Robb.
Cama Freeman & Charity Baber, Feb. 5, 1818. David Redditt.
William George & Sally Griffin, Jan. 3, 1818. Andrew Cavitt.
Willie Gibson & Cyntha Morrow, Sep. 16, 1818. Samuel Rooney.
Milton Giles & Juliana Westfall, March 4, 1818. John Rutherford,
  A. Gilmore.
Matthias Gillehand & Caty Hendricks, Jan. 17, 1818. John W. Byrn.
George Gillespie & Mary Clark, Jan. 1, 1818. Anthony B. Shelby.
Zachariah G. Goodall & Eliza B. Winston, May 18, 1818. Samuel
  Sullivan.
Hambleton Gregory & Sally Duren, Sep. 15, 1818. W. C. Ballard,
  M.G. Sanford Fitts.
Richard Hale & Mary Young, March 12, 1818. Charles L. Humphrey.
Cader Harroll & Polly Garrison, Nov. 22, 1818. John McMurtry, J.P.
Henry Hellmontoller & Betsy Velentine, Nov. 23, 1818. Jas. Douglas,
  Eli Stalcup.
James Henderson & Jannet Pack, May 23, 1818. Samuel Pack.
John Hendricks & Tabitha Dorris, July 25, 1818. John McMurtry,
  J.P. Saml. Gwin.

SUMNER COUNTY MARRIAGES

John Hanson & Caty Wainscott, July 20, 1818. Wm. Cantrill.
John A. Hickison & Lucretia Patton, Aug. 13, 1818. Samuel D.
    Hickison.
Etheldred P. Horn & Priscilla King, Jan. 7, 1818.
William House & Sally Gardner, Dec. 15, 1818. S. Hunt, J.P.
Warner Howard & Esther Morris, Oct. 17, 1818. John H. Nanney,
    Reuben Searcy.
Sterling Howell & Elizabeth Wilson, April 16, 1818. John Ruther-
    ford, M. W. Wilson.
James B. Hughes & Sally Jane, July 23, 1818. John Tompkins.
John Hunt & Sally Follis, July 25, 1818. Carson Dobbins.
John Hutchinson & Nancy Moore, Jan. 6, 1818. Henry M. Johnson.
Moses Jacobs & Celia Clarey, Oct. 21, 1818. Isaac Lindsay, M.G.
    Henry Williams.
William L. Jiams & Sally Grooms, Feb. 3, 1818. Jacob Kingslow.
William Jones & Jane Brown, Jan. 23, 1818. William Murrel.
David King & Jemima Stanford, April 4, 1818. James Douglas, Samuel
    King.
Joseph Kirkpatrick & Judah Jefferson, March 7, 1818. John McMur-
    try, J.P. Lewis Marlen.
Champness Kiser (Keesee) & Elizabeth Mills, Oct. 27, 1818. Wm.
    Henry.
George Kittrell & Betsey Rutherford, Feb. 14, 1818. Joseph McEl-
    urath.
Ellet Lacy & Sarah Hughes, April 2, 1818. John Hughes.
Laurence Lauler & Polly Neely, Feb. 12, 1818. James Douglas.
Isaac Lee & Mary Berdin, Sep. 2, 1818. John Gilbert, William Ver-
    din.
Sylvanis Lockwood & Polly Jackson, March 25, 1818. Jas. Douglas,
    J.P. Wm. Finley.
Jourdan Loyd & Betsey Loyd, Nov. 6, 1818. John Barr, J.P. Thos.
    Murry.
Campbell Lucas & Polly Ellis, Nov. 27, 1818. James Gwin, M.G.
    L. Ellis.
Henry Martin & Hannah Carroll, Dec. 7, 1818. James Carr.
James Martin & Elizabeth Guthrie, Feb. 25, 1818. George Martin.
Moses Mayhew & Nancy Abshur, Nov. 28, 1818. Addison Foster, J.P.
    Thomas Harrison.
Duncan McDougal & Peggy Leshley, Oct. 3, 1818. Wm. Montgomery,
    J.P. M. Green.
William McElurath & Nancy Bennett, Aug. 11, 1818. J. Rutherford,
    John McElurath.
Alexander McFarland & Lucky Lindsey, Dec. 8, 1818. Isaac Lindsey,
    M.G. Amos Joyce.
John McLean & Nancy Campbell, Dec. 24, 1818. Colin Campbell.
James McMurtry & Polly Dobbins, June 3, 1818. James Mitchell.
Joseph McReynolds, Jr. & Margaret Anderson, June 4, 1818. Thos.
    Anderson, J.P. William Wallace.
Jobe Meader & Nancy Donoho, May 19, 1818. E. Simpson, Elijah Simp-
    son.
John Meek & Jane Wilson, Dec. 10, 1818. James Bratton.
Joseph Morris & Nancy Inman, April 13, 1818. John Gilbert, J.P.
    Joel Parrish.
Uriah Nanny & Polly McCarty, Sep. 26, 1818. James Green, M.G.

Andrew Neal & Nancy Neal, Sep. 25, 1818. James Neal.
William Nickins & Elizabeth Love, Sep. 3, 1818. William White.
Nathaniel Nowlin & Mahalah Anderson, Sep. 27, 1818. S. Hunt, J.P.
Bartholemus Osburn & Betsey Bandy, Oct. 8, 1818. Horatio Bandy.
Joel Parrish & Mary Motherall, June 4, 1818. Joseph Scoby.
Lewis Parrish & Polly Lane, June 27, 1818. Isaac Lindsey.
Lewis Parrish & Polly Lindsey, June 11, 1818. William Crane.
Isaac Pearce & Polly Jones, Jan. 24, 1818. John Smith.
Asa Perry & _____ Valentine, Nov. 7, 1818. James Douglass, J.P.
Charles Perry & Polly Lasiter, Nov. 4, 1818. Edward Phillips.
Jonathan Payton & Angelina Peyton, July 2, 1818. John Bell.
John W. Phillips & Sally Marcum, May 23, 1818.
Simon Prescott & Polly Garrison, Dec. 4, 1818. James Green.
Parkin Pridgen & Milley Miers, Sep. 1, 1818. Joel Pridgen.
Adkins Powell & Nancy Potts, July 18, 1818. Thos. Potts.
James C. Rice & Polly Allen, Dec. 7, 1818. S. Hunt, Solomon
    Shoulders.
David H. Rickman & Peggy Henry, Sep. 8, 1818. Samuel Henry.
Robert Rickman & Catharine Reed, Feb. 2, 1818. Robert White.
Joseph Rieff & Lydia Burton, July 20, 1818. John Brown.
James Rhodes & Sally Snoddy, Jan. 17, 1818. Joseph McElurath.
John Ruyle & Lucy Dyer, June 6, 1818. John McMurtry, J.P. Moses
    Ruyle.
Moses Ruyle, Jr. & Spicy Smith, June 23, 1818. John McMurtry, J.P.
    John Bone.
John Ross & Polly Bandy, Dec. 5, 1818. Reuben Ross.
William Rousey & Amey Tucker, Dec. 7, 1818. James Carr, Benjamine
    Seawell.
Laurence Rowe & Martha Charlton, Jan. 8, 1818. Sam McCorcle.
William Shaw & Elizabeth Carr, Feb. 10, 1818. John Barr.
Samuel Sillers & Agnes Hannah, April 21, 1818. Hardy M. Cryer.
David Sims & Elizabeth Mitchell, July 16, 1818. Joseph M. Bullers.
William H. Smith & Nice Duty, May 12, 1818. William Smith.
Thomas Smothers & Courtney Powell, Nov. 7, 1818. John McMurtry,
    J.P. William Glover.
John Stills & Mary Goldman, April 15, 1818. Eli Stalcup.
Thomas Summers & Polly Briley, Sep. 12, 1818. Nat Price, Samuel C.
    Tyree.
Thomas Thurman & Jane Morrison, May 14, 1818. John Rutherford,
    Moses Wilson.
Jonathan Trousdale & Elizabeth Young, Feb. 8, 1818. Elijah Simp-
    son, J.P. Joshua Draper.
Thomas Valentine & Lucky Vinson, Feb. 4, 1818. Solomon Barnes.
Edmund W. Vaughn & Eliza Graham, March 16, 1818. J. Rutherford,
    John Marlin.
Mathew Vaughn & Rachel Phillips, Aug. 22, 1818. Wm. Melton.
Mathew Vaun & Catharine Potts, Oct. 2, 1818. Saml. Gwin.
Walter Wade & Susan Tinner, Jan. 27, 1818. S. H. Blythe, William
    A. Tinner.
John P. Wagnore & Mary Sanders, Nov. 5, 1818.
John P. Walker & Elizabeth H. Saunders, July 1, 1818. Will Trigg,
    Jr.
Joseph B. Wallace & Malissa Wilson, March 17, 1818. S. H. Blythe,
    J.P. Samuel Wilson.

William Walton & Matilda Baker, Feb. 12, 1818.
Jourdan Webb & Socky Davis, Aug. 24, 1818. William Glover.
Lewis Wimberley & Mary Bush, Jan. 26, 1818. William Bush.
Tandy Wood & Elizabeth Ashley, May 11, 1818. Edward Gwin.
Woodson Wynn & Jane Wilks, July 18, 1818. Richard Wilks.
William Yandell & Milley Heffington, Jan. 23, 1818. Edward Gwin,
    J.P. Abram Trible.
James Adams & Polly Harrison, Feb. 20, 1819. S. H. Blythe, J.P.
Lothwick B. Alford & Lindy R. Hall, Jan. 12, 1819. S. Hunt, J.P.
    Daniel McAuley.
James Andrews & Elizabeth McDaniel, Jan. 29, 1819. Wm. L. Alexan-
    der, J.P. John Allen.
John Angel & Polly Shaver, Dec. 13, 1819. Enos Harper.
Walthett Angel & Polly Robertson, Feb. 15, 1819. Thos. Murrey.
Archibald C. Armstrong & Sally Reddick, Jan. 23, 1819. Jas.
    Harrison, Nathaniel Prince.
Willie Balthrop & Mary Dodson, Jan. 12, 1819. William Glover.
John Barnett & Betsey Hunter, Dec. 26, 1819. Dempsey Hunter.
Thomas Barton & Judah Knight, Feb. 16, 1819. S. H. Blythe, J.P.
    Ezekiel Carothers.
John B. Bond & Kitty Stone, Dec. 20, 1819. John Stamp.
Williamson Bonner & Marino Redditt, Jan. 18, 1819. Lewis Schulter.
Archibald Bowling Duval & Adaline M. Duval, June 28, 1819. James
    Gwin, M.G. Samuel Gwin.
William Bracken & Levesta Bell, Feb. 22, 1819. Addison Foster,
    J.P. Jeremiah Spencer.
A. B. Breedlove & Mary Wood, Aug. 11, 1819. John Hunley.
Thomas Bunton & Betsey Turner, April 27, 1819. Robert Desha.
William Bush & Louiza Powell, Sep. 4, 1819. Hugh Kirkpatrick, M.G.
    Joseph Kirkpatrick.
Jese Butterworth & Sally Clay, Aug. 7, 1819. John Parvat.
John Butterworth & Lucy Tally, March 17, 1819. Isaac Lindsey, M.G.
    Zach Talley, Jr.
David Carr & Sally Guthrie, Nov. 4, 1819. Hugh Kirkpatrick, M.G.
    Robert Guthrie.
Samuel Chappell & Musa Henderson, June 21, 1819. Samuel Gibson,
    E.C. Nathaniel Prince.
Jennings Charlton & Anna Robertson, Aug. 16, 1819. Francis Day.
John I. Choate & Chris-(?) Hassell, Dec. 1, 1819. A. H. Douglass.
Andrew Clairy & Polly Blackard, Nov. 25, 1819. John McMurtry, J.P.
    John McMurtry.
George Cobb & Sarah Burnley, April 17, 1819. James Carr.
Richard Cope & Keziah Best, Sep. 7, 1819. James Gwin, J.P. Thomas
    White.
George Cowen & Margaret Carothers, April 13, 1819. Elmore Harris.
Jacob Crabtree & Patsey Binley, Dec. 28, 1819. Wm. Hadley.
Josiah Crawford & Lydia Sears, Aug. 26, 1819. J. Rutherford,
    Elisha Long.
Benjamine Crews & Susan Crenshaw, Oct. 30, 1819. Richard Higgan-
    son.
William Davenport & Nancy Boyer, March 4, 1819. John Mitchell.
Benjamine Desha & Telitha Stams, May 31, 1819. Ashel W. Reese.
John Dickson & Polly Gillespie, Nov. 23, 1819. William Dickason.
Bowles Dinning & Martha Bowles, Dec. 18, 1819. Andrew Dining.

John Donoho & Sally Crews, Nov. 27, 1819. Walter Donoho.
Stephen Etheridge & Betsey Itson, Sep. 7, 1819. Edward Briant.
Milton Easley & Rachel Alsup, March 6, 1819. John Henson, Josiah
    Henson.
John Ferguson & Anny Bates, Nov. 27, 1819. John Bates.
Benjamine French & Patsey Boiles, Sep. 9, 1819. John Barr.
Jesse Gambling & Mary Cotton, May 26, 1819. Arthur Cotton.
Isaac B. Gibson & Polly Crosswaite, July 26, 1819. Samuel Gibson.
William W. Gift & Elizabeth Dodson, Oct. 1, 1819. Edmund Turner.
James Gillespie & Mary Grider, July 24, 1819. John Barr, David
    Starnes.
James Glasgow & Ann Maupin, Aug. 26, 1819. Wm. L. Alexander, Austin
    Maupin.
Moses S. Goff & Margaret Biggs, Sep. 10, 1819. Adam Biggs.
John Goodall & Sally McDaniel, June 23, 1819. John Hunley.
James M. Grayor & Charlotte Hassell, Sep. 1, 1819. Geo. Elliott.
Robert W. Guthrie & Nancy Foster, Oct. 6, 1819. Hugh Kirkpatrick,
    M.G. Andrew H. Guthrie, BM.
David R. Gwin & Nancy Towell, Aug. 26, 1819. Isaac Lindsey, M.G.
    Daniel Latimer.
James Gwin & Sally Bailey, June 14, 1819. Benjamine Wilkerson.
Samuel Hall & Elizabeth Strother, Oct. 1, 1819. George Sarver.
James Hamilton & Amy Rice, Sep. 23, 1819. Thomas Hamilton.
Adam Hamton & Agnes Douglas, Jan. 26, 1819. King Carr.
Jonathan Hardin & Peggy Moore, April 14, 1819. Edw. Douglas, Lewis
    Green.
James Harrison & Emily Smith, March 18, 1819. Mathew Johnson.
Abel Hasten & Nancy Jackson, May 31, 1819. Sylvanus Lockwood.
John Hendrick & Ruth Strader, June 3, 1819. John Dining.
John Hinton & Polly Hendrick, Aug. 23, 1819. John Hendirck.
Richard Hobdy & Betsey Cotton, March 3, 1819. Hardy M. Cryer,
    Arthur Cotton.
Meredith Hodges & Catharine _____, Jan. 9, 1819. Addison Foster,
    Isham Hodges.
Charles Hersley & Lucinda Stovall, June 16, 1819. Talbot Horsley.
Burrell Hunter & Betsey Brigance, Nov. 20, 1819. Geo. S. Brigance.
Reuben Hunter & Mahali Brigance, Aug. 19, 1819. James B. Thorn-
    hill.
David Hutcherson & Anna Boyd, March 9, 1819. Hugh Kirkpatrick,
    Geo. Reir.
William Hutcheson & Nancy M. Hargrove, July 24, 1819. James
    Hutcheson.
Joseph Irby & Sally Horsley, May 19, 1819. William Hunter.
Lemuel Jackson & Jane Dishman, March 20, 1819. John Dishman.
Ralph Jones & Eliza Hogg, Nov. 19, 1819. Nath'l Sanders, Michael
    Emry.
Logan D. Key & Polly Stovall, July 5, 1819. John Pitts.
Solomon Key & Nancy Stoval, Dec. 1, 1819. Joel Stoval.
Lewis King & Dicy Allen, Nov. 29, 1819. John L. Swaney, John Bent-
    ley.
Jessie Kirk & Frances Gray, Dec. 13, 1819. J. W. Hall, Amos Joyner.
Jacob Latimer & Sally Liggett, Jan. 30, 1819. Wm. Montgomery,
    James Kirkpatrick.
Robert Leonard & Dorias Barnard, May 1, 1819. John Rice, Jacob

Barnard.
Andrew Lewis & Sidney Boyers, Dec. 25, 1819. John M. Boyers.
Giles Liggett & Elizabeth Shaw, March 1, 1819. Wm. Montgomery,
John Connolly.
Joseph Logan & Abegail Dorris, Dec. 31, 1819. John Logan.
Jonathan D. Looney & Harriett Hassell, Nov. 8, 1819. Adlae Don-
nell.
Reuben Lowry & Easter Davis, June 9, 1819. John McMurtry, John
Mitchell.
Landy Lyles & Peggy _____, Oct. 13, 1819. Thos. Scurry &
Nat'l Prince.
James Lytle & Rebeckah Cook, July 13, 1819. John H. Bowen.
Charles Morgan.
Benjamine Mabry & Elizabeth Robertson, Dec. 28, 1819. Francis Day.
William Mandrell & Peggy McMillan, Feb. 12, 1819. Addison Foster,
Solomon Mandrell.
George Martin & Margaret Montgomery, March 6, 1819. George Martin.
James Martin & Betsy Thompson, Jan. 23, 1819. Zebulon Cantrell,
Elmore Douglas.
James L. Martin & Frances Rickman, Aug. 19, 1819. Robert M. Boyers.
William McConahay & Amariah Moor, Sep. 8, 1819. Edward Gwin, Cur-
rie Keen.
Mathias McDaniel & Rachel Stilts, March 9, 1819. John W. Byrn.
Robert McKethen & Sally Latimer, Aug. 19, 1819. Hugh Kirkpatrick,
Edwin Latimer.
John Moody & Rebecca Settle, Oct. 25, 1819. John Dining.
Ziga Moore & Tenesy Stewart, Nov. 9, 1819. John Wallace.
Joseph Murrey & Sarah Davis, Feb. 24, 1819. James Gwin, M.G.
John McGlothlin.
Nathan Newby & Catey Potts, Aug. 23, 1819. Alfred H. Douglas, Wm.
Glover, John Hastin.
James Odom & Polly Hamson, Feb. 20, 1819. Micahel Green.
James Oneil & Betsy Wright, March 12, 1819. John Foster.
Green B. Orr & Mary Brown, June 22, 1819. Thos. L. Harris.
Robert A. Osburn & Dovy Hart, May 17, 1818. Wm. L. Alexander, Wm.
Hart.
Smith Pack & Peggy Ferrell, Nov. 1, 1819. Alisha Williams.
S. N. Parker & Judy Prophet, Oct. 29, 1819. James Stratton,
Solomon Shoulders.
Henderson Parnell & Malinda Sincleer, Jan. 2, 1819. John McClelan.
Joseph Payne & Betsy Ward, July 9, 1819. Wm. L. Alexander, John
Brown.
Asa Perry & Sarah Valentine, Nov. 7, 1819. William White.
John Perry & Sally Glasgo, Aug. 11, 1819. John McMurtry, John
Stewart.
Jesse Ragon & Elizabeth Gregory, May 13, 1810. N. Sanders, Josiah
Simmons.
James Robinson & Nancy Thompson, March 20, 1819. James Gwin, M.G.
Joseph Ainsworth.
William Ritter & Peggy Granger, Dec. 19, 1819. David Bradley.
Robert Ritchey & Evaline Kennedy, June 16, 1819. Cullin Gardner,
Danl. Kennedy.
Britton Rogers & Polly Pitt, April 17, 1819. James Jackson.
John F. Schubert & Sally Tonville, Oct. 12, 1819. N. Sanders,

SUMNER COUNTY MARRIAGES

Robert Shaw & Nancy Wells, Oct. 16, 1819. Wm. Cantrell.
Levy C. Shy & Rachel Boyle, Sep. 2, 1819. John Bracken.
John W. Simpson & Jane Montgomery, Sep. 18, 1819. John Mitchell, John Overton.
Len. S. Sims & Elizabeth Carroll. Sep. 9, 1819. Isaac Lindsey, M.G. John Briding.
Robt. W. Sloan & Rthua Jones, Dec. 5, 1819. Hezekiah Reid.
Abram Smelton & Sally Nevill, Feb. 4, 1819. John McGlothlin.
George Smith & Sally Fleetwood, June 26, 1819. Wm. Turner.
Harrison Smith & Jane Mankin, Oct. 16, 1819. Geo. Elliott.
William K. Smith & Cassandra Johnson, July 20, 1819. Robert Parks.
John Stewart & Betsey Brown, July 21, 1819. Wm. L. Alexander.
Thomas Stewart & Sally Summers, July 28, 1819. Wm. Cantrell.
William Stratton & Elizabeth Daughtry, Dec. 1, 1819. John Mc-Elurath.
James Taylor & Sally Charlton, Dec. 1, 1819. Robert Desha.
William Thompson & Nancy Ligon, Oct. 2, 1819. John Wiseman, Thomas Ligon.
John Townsend & Elizabeth Adams, Nov. 27, 1819. John Wiseman, Joseph Townsend.
Frederick Travelstreet & Polly Bunton, Dec. 7, 1819. Wm. Shell, Joel Parrish.
Richard Townsend & Malinda S. Payne, Oct. 26, 1819. William Hunley.
Temple Hunley & Mackey R. Harris, Dec. 28, 1819. John McKendre.
Boyd M. Turner & Mary Booker, Dec. 30, 1819. John L. Swaney, John Clear.
Nathan Underwood & Judy Martin, June 17, 1819. John Underwood.
Henry B. Vaughan & Delia Graham, Dec. 22, 1819. Ashley Standfield.
John S. Vaughn & Sally D. Boyer, Oct. 19, 1819. John Wiseman, Ashley Stanfield.
George Walton & Polly Terry, March 16, 1819. S. Simpson, Martin Hire.
Hardy Watson & Elizabeth Taylor, June 2, 1819. James Carr, Geo. F. Keesee.
Joseph White & Betsey Hainey, Nov. 23, 1819. George Elliott.
Nathan White & Penelope Lyon, May 18, 1819. Wm. L. Alexander, Wm. Hadley.
William Wilks & Polly Brown, Nov. 15, 1819. Woodson Wynn.
John V. Williams & Mrs. Matilda Dickerson, Sep. 27, 1819. Daml. Gibson, E.C.C. Alexander Neilly.
Joseph Williams & Lucy Dugger, June 22, 1819. Floyd Dugger, Reuben Talley.
Joseph H. Wise & Elizabeth Armstrong, March 23, 1819. Jacob Turner.
William H. Wright & Elizabeth M. Sanderson, July 1, 1819. John Wright.
John L. Wynn & Elizabeth A. Gillespie, Aug. 25, 1819. Wm. Hadley.
John Yates & Jane Yates, July 20, 1819. Ashley Stanfield.
William Young & Mariah Starr, Oct. 18, 1819. John L. Swaney.
Gilford Bass & Polly Proctor. Aug. 18, 1820. John Beardin, Jr.
Mathew Bayne & Phebe Carman, Jan. 19, 1820. Thomas Pritchett.
Isaac Bell & Sally Stubblefield, May 31, 1820. Jas. Carr, John Brown.

SUMNER COUNTY MARRIAGES

Moses Biram & Elizabeth Crawford, Aug. 10, 1820. Joshua Smith.

Fieldon N. Blackmore & Rebeckah Johnston, Feb. 2, 1820. Stephen R. Roberts.

Dalton Booker & Rebecca Wooten, Sep. 25, 1820. John Wiseman, Olive Dickason, John R. Dalton.

Robert Boyd & Margaret Watkins, April 5, 1820. Wm. Montgomery.

Moses Brock & Nancy Ashlock, Aug. 22, 1820. James Durham.

John Braham & Marian Parker, May 10, 1820. John Wiseman, Pascal Head, Wm. Hall.

Jacob Brown & Dovy Foster, Sep. 18, 1820. Meredith Hodges, Joseph Spradling.

William A. Bull & Mary Anderson, Sep. 20, 1820. Thos. Anderson, Ramsey L. Mason.

Lemuel Byram & Francis Bradford, Jan. 23, 1820. Ashley Stanfield.

Noah Byrom & Mina _____, Jan. 11, 1820. Jamison Bandy.

John Caffry & Eliza Bradford, Jan. 10, 1820. Dixon Stroud.

Samuel Calhoun & Martha King, Jan. 27, 1820. John Shelton.

David Alloway & Nancy Ferguson, Dec. 15, 1820. E. Cross, V.D.M. John Fuller.

James B. Cantrell & Hannah Brown, May 13, 1820. James Gwin, M.G. Jacob Brown.

William Carter & Polly Duncan, Feb. 21, 1820. W. H. Hart.

Samuel Elim & Elizabeth Jones, July 27, 1820. Dan'l. McAuley, Daniel H. Slater, Ethelbert N. Sanders.

John C. Clark & Benta Hughes, Feb. 4, 1820. Numbleton Gregory.

William P. Carr & Peggy Reed, March 29, 1820. J. W. Byrnn.

Henry Davis & Susanna Dowell, April 17, 1820. Francis M. Weathered.

Gabriel Dillard & Sarah Jones, May 31, 1820. Hugh Kirkpatrick, Ezekiel Crain.

John Donoho & Betsey Dossit, Jan. 8, 1820. James Cartwright.

Isaac C. Douglass & Eliza W. Baker, June 1, 1820. Wm. Trousdale.

Willie J. Douglas & Eliza Watkins, June 13, 1820. Edw. Douglas, Cullen Edwards.

Jeremiah Doxey & Hannah Wise, Aug. 28, 1820. John L. Doxey.

Thomas Duke & Sally Boyd, Aug. 5, 1820. Isaac Lindsey, E.M.E.C. Eusebues Stone.

Hiram Duncan & Sally Key, April 15, 1820. Ricely Defrees.

Buckner S. Durham & Susan Rippy, Dec. 14, 1820. Addison Foster, John Durham.

James Durham & Lydia Gillespie, July 14, 1820. George McGuire.

Ely Dyer & Sally Derman, Oct. 7, 1820. Isaac Lindsey, Mathew Rice.

Samuel Edson & Nancy Dorris, Feb. 8, 1820. Samuel Dorris.

Jacob Ellison & Elizabeth Crenshaw, Feb. 20, 1820. Thos. Anderson, Thos. Scurry.

John Ferguson & Any Bates, Nov. 27, 1820. John L. Swaney.

Mathew Figures & Eliza A. Thomas, July 27, 1820. William Hadley.

James Foster & Catey Yandell, Jan. 3, 1820. Joseph Spardling.

George Frazor & Polly Bates, Nov. 27, 1820. Wm. Montgomery.

Thomas Frazor & Ibby Kirkpatrick, Sep. 4, 1820. Hugh Kirkpatrick, M.G. James Frazor.

Taylor G. Gillum & Mary Meador, July 10, 1820. Wm. Austin.

Asa Green & Rebecca Forrester, June 15, 1820. Wm. H. Anderson, John Connelly.

SUMNER COUNTY MARRIAGES

Andrew H. Guthrie & Peggy Kirkpatrick, April 6, 1820. David Foster,
  M.G. Robert Guthrie.
John Hall & Rebecca Lambeth, May 27, 1820. Wm. Lambeth.
Hugh Harshey & Frances Burk, Jan. 3, 1820. Joel Parrish.
Thomas Harris & Lotty Watson, July 26, 1820. Daniel Muse.
Hugh Harshaw & Jane Curry, July 6, 1820. John Curry.
William Hays & Eupha Hamilton, Aug. 16, 1820. John Cotton.
Tavanah Head & Polly E. Smith, Sep. 5, 1820.
Benjamine J. Henley & Susanna Napier, Nov. 30, 1820. Wm. Woodall,
  Esq. John Napier.
Hugh W. Hill & Eunice Donnell, June 9, 1820. Adlae Donnell.
William Hodges & Sarah West, Sep. 26, 1820. Meredith Hodges.
James Holaway & Milly White, May 15, 1820. Wm. Smith, Elisha
  Roberson.
Jesse Holt & Lucretia Crossland, Nov. 2, 1820. Daniel McAuley,
  Robert Patton.
James Hudson & Betsey Savely, Dec. 7, 1820.
Thomas Huston & Sarah Motheral, Oct. 27, 1820. Hugh Kirkpatrick,
  M.G. Joel Parrish.
Benjamine Jackson & Wineford Carpenter, Oct. 3, 1820. Addison
  Foster, John N. Byrn.
Thomas Jarrett & Elizabeth Byson, Oct. 30, 1820. Armstead Rogers.
James P. Jenkins & Judah Cobbs, July 19, 1820. Rice Cobbs.
Robert Joiner & Lucretia Latimer, Oct. 4, 1820. Hugh Kirkpatrick,
  M.G. Robert Taylor.
William Justice & Christiana Meaders, Feb. 14, 1820. Jesse Meadors.
John Keilley & Margaret Dorris, March 18, 1820. Valentine Bernard.
William Key & Betsey Tuttle, July 17, 1820. Moses Gaines.
Charles Keys & Elizabeth Bruce, June 7, 1820. John Barr, James
  Mills.
John Kisen & Fanny Blair, April 8, 1820. Henry Williams.
John Kittle & Elizabeth Holt, Dec. 26, 1820. John Lea Swaney, John
  Carman.
John Laurence & Betsey McKinsey, Oct. 12, 1820. Mathew Neal.
Lemuel Laurence & Nancy Rogers, Feb. 3, 1820. Jesse Donnell.
Robert Laurence (Uun) & Lucinda Patton, Dec. 20, 1820. Thos. Ander-
  son, Thomas Smith.
William Lowhorn & Eliza Trice, March 15, 1820. Robert Crighton,
  Abram Martin.
Little Berry Mason & Nancy Durham, Aug. 28, 1820. John Gilbert,
  John W. Byrn.
John McClelan & Gilley Parnel, Aug. 20, 1820. David Lovell.
Andrew McGlothlin & Jemima Gilbert, March 9, 1820. William Woodall.
William McGlothlin & Nancy Skeen, Jan. 13, 1820. Joseph McGlothlin.
John McMurtry & Sarah Blackard, Sep. 30, 1820. Thomas Blackard.
Sterling Nicholl & Jane Scruggs, Jan. 28, 1820. Pleasant Tyree.
Henry P. Noel & Elender Ellis, July 22, 1820. Samuel Ellis.
William Norris & Elizabeth Collier, April 6, 1820. Wm. H. Douglas.
Bird Nowlen & Polly Horn, May 29, 1820. John Gilbert, Wm. Milton.
John Osburn & Kisiah Stone, Aug. 10, 1820. Solomon Shoulders.
Archibald Overby & Sally Barnard, Oct. 14, 1820. Isaac Short.
William W. Ozbrooks & Betsey Hodges, Jan. 29, 1820. Joseph Spard-
  ling.
Mathew Perdue & Nancy Webb, Jan. 3, 1820. Joseph Spradling.

SUMNER COUNTY MARRIAGES

Josiah Perry & Sally Jarritt, Jan. 25, 1820. Allen Gardner.
Norflect Perry & Betsey Garrett, April 19, 1820. Josiah Walton.
Joseph B. Pitt & Sally Bandy, Nov. 21, 1820. Wm. Pitt.
John Pritchett & Betsey Rimmers, Dec. 11, 1820. John McMurtry,
    Thomas Durham, Thomas Ralph.
Lewis Ralph & Polly Smith, Jan. 4, 1820. Moses Mills.
Benjamine Ray & Lucintha Allen, Jan. 27, 1820. James C. Rice.
Stephen S. Ray & Margaret Graham, Nov. 1, 1820. Charles Henderson.
Marmaduke Redditt & Sally Rullage, June 13, 1820. Thomas Scurry.
John Rice & Mary Gilbert, March 4, 1820. John Grove.
William Savely & Elizabeth Jones, Oct. 17, 1820. William Davenport.
Solomon Shoulders & Sally Pierce, Jan. 8, 1820. James Cartwright.
Joseph Simons & Amelia Taylor, May 17, 1820. N. Sanders, Benj.
    Hawkins.
John Sneed & Jane Winn, July 8, 1820. Wm. Hall.
David Sterns & Elizabeth McNeill, Feb. 7, 1820. John McNeill.
Joel Stovall & Rebeckah Rickman, Aug. 22, 1820. Rich Johnson,
    Mathew B. Cathey.
Benjamine Strator & Catey Morris, Jan. 17, 1820. Geo. D. Blake-
    more.
Henry Strictlen & Elizabeth Ritter, Sep. 21, 1820. David Lovell.
James Strother & Sally Stewart, Aug. 25, 1820. Charles N. Brigance.
Dixon Stroud & Lucretia Hunt, Aug. 22, 1820. Saml. Hunt, Alfred
    M. Douglas.
James B. Stuart & Francis Buckley, Dec. 15, 1820. J. L. Swaney.
Levi Summers & Polly Price, Jan. 8, 1820. James Strother.
Richard Taite & Margarett _____, July 19, 1820. J. Lockalear,
    R. S. Mayson.
James B. Thornhill & Reuella Stewart, April 20, 1820. Samuel Wil-
    son.
Nelson Turner & Betsey Bunton, Dec. 5, 1820. Richard Johnson,
    Stephen H. Turner.
Jesse Tuttle & Patsey Mandre, Aug. 14, 1820. Daniel Webb, M.G.,
    Wm. Key.
David Vance & Jane Gillespie, Aug. 8, 1820. Isaac Laeth.
Jonathan Wallace & Dicy Tilley, Sep. 19, 1820. Thos. Anderson,
    Joseph McReynolds.
Samuel Webb & Elizabeth Johnson, Aug. 14, 1820. Owen Griffith,
    John Templeton.
Baker Welch & Sally Alexander Hawkins, March 7, 1820. Benj. Haw-
    kins.
Berry Wilkerson & Susannah Malone, Dec. 7, 1820. S. M. McMury.
Samuel Wilson & Betsey Anderson, Sep. 7, 1820. Thos. Anderson,
    Alex. Bull.
Grissim Williams & Delia Honeycut, July 3, 1820. Wm. Hadley.
William Williams & Sara Moore, March 22, 1820. Cage Hall.
Henry Wright & Susannah Crane, March 15, 1820. Lewis Crane.
Richard Wynn & Nancy Wilks, Sep. 19, 1820. Richard Wilks.
Levi Allen & Elizabeth Allen, Nov. 3, 1821. S. Hunt, Webb Blood-
    worth.
Robert Armstrong & Caty Hogg, Dec. 28, 1821. S. K. Blythe, John
    Hogg.
Elisha Askew & Patsey Eubanks, Jan. 20, 1821. John McMurtry, M.G.
    Richard Garrison.

John G. Atchinson & Nancy Mabry, Dec. 11, 1821.
Benjamine Baber & Malinder R_____, Dec. 18, 1821. S. Hunt.
Stephen Boren & Susan Wimbelly, April 19, 1821. John Gilbert,
    Francis Baren.
Thomas Barham & Elizabeth Perry, July 23, 1821. V. Landers. John
    Barham.
Josiah Barrett & Louisa Teysdale, Dec. 17, 1821. Nicholas Latimer.
Jesse Beaver & Sarah B. Wems, June 18, 1821. Jas. Carr.
James Barton & Betsey Childress, Aug. 30, 1821. Larkin Carman.
Alfred Bell & Jane Hainey, July 5, 1821. S. K. Blythe, Mabene
    Anderson.
Henry Belote & Harriett Boon, April __, 1821. W. Smith, John
    Swaney.
George D. Blackmore & Patsey Hannah, Dec. 31, 1821. Ashley Stan-
    field.
Reuben Blackmore & Betsey Bently, March 28, 1821. John Belote.
Job. Blakard & Biddy Trusty, Dec. 31, 1821. Andrew Clarey.
Hugh Boyle & Eliza Spooner, March 10, 1821. Abram Martin.
Ledewick Broddie & Matilda Anthony, Nov. 26, 1821. Hardy Cryer.
Jeremiah Brown & Nancy Hodges, March 13, 1821. Anderson Darnel,
    M.G. Holly Hodges.
Enock W. Brookshire & Emisia Bradford, May 12, 1821. S. Hunt, R.
    M. Boyers.
Littleton Bruce & Jane Duff, April 2, 1821. Isaac Lindsey, Adam
    Turner.
Arthur D. Bugg & Tabitha J. Smith, Oct. 11, 1821. Ethelbert
    Sanders.
Wm. Bush & Elizabeth Groves, Oct. 6, 1821. Arch Marlin.
Martin Byrns & Rebecca Yarborough, Nov. 30, 1821. Wm. Mayberry.
Andrew Chandler & Ann Hutchison, Sep. 15, 1821. John Boyd.
John F. Clark & Matilda Wormington, Oct. 13, 1821. John J. King.
Martin Cowgill & Sally Brooks, Sep. 24, 1821. Thomas Brooks.
Drury Cruze & Elizabeth Crenshaw, Nov. 26, 1821. Richard Johnson,
    Josiah Lauderdale.
John Dalton & Malinda Patterson, June 11, 1821. Alexander Sadler.
Jesse Daniel & Ann Cotton, Jan. 23, 1821. Jesse Gambling.
Ricely Defrees & Elizabeth Holloway, Dec. 21, 1821. Hiram Duncan.
Joseph Defriece & Maryann Day, May 3, 1821. Robert Fleming.
Reuben Denton & Nancy Busby, Dec. 24, 1821. Wm. Busby.
William Dorris & Nancy Right, Dec. 21, 1821. John Gilbert, John
    Mitchell.
Augustine Downs & Polly Tilley, Dec. 24, 1821. Thos. Anderson, C.
    H. May.
John Downs & Clarissa Rutland, Feb. 9, 1821. M. Anderson.
Drew Edwards & Catherine Dorris, Nov. 23, 1821. Thos. Edwards.
Thos. Crutchfield & Lotey Valentine, July 17, 1821.
William Edwards & Mary Cantrell, Oct. 21, 1821. Hugh Kirkpatrick,
    M.G. A. W. Reese.
Joseph Edison & Peggy Dorris, Feb. 9, 1821. Samuel Edison.
Alfred Erwin & Polly Ball, Dec. 15, 1821. James Carr, Abner Erwin.
Jesse Evans & Sarah Deshazor, Aug. 17, 1821. Cornelius Evans.
Robert Fleming & Mary Gourley, Feb. 16, 1821. Wm. Jackson.
William Franklin & Evaline Douglass, Oct. 6, 1821. Edward Douglass,
    Wm. Edwards.

William Frainham & Nancy Norwell, Oct. 29, 1821. Jesse Morris.
George Frazor & Polly Kisor, Nov. 27, 1821. James Jackson.
Daniel Gaines & Francis Ford, June 14, 1821. David Allen.
Robert Gilbreath & Nancy Alvis, July 17, 1821. Andrew Gilbreath.
Willie Gilbert & Patsey Williams, Jan. 15, 1821. John Logan.
John Gillespie & Polly Ball, March 23, 1821. Jas. Carr.
Isaac Glasgow & Mariah Perry, Nov. 17, 1821. Wm. Montgomery.
Wm. Gooster & Catherine Taylor, Oct. 6, 1821. Jesse Hall.
Samuel Graves & Susan Durning, June 2, 1821. Isaac Lindsey, John
    Roberts.
Mel S. Gregory & Julia White, Dec. 19, 1821. A. Moore.
William Hale & Patsey Tinsley, Dec. 28, 1821. William Stone.
James Guild & Mary E. Williams, March 27, 1821. I. Clark, M.G.
    Nath. Sanders.
Thomas Hamlet & Sally Proctor, July 21, 1821. Wright Barnes.
Higdon Harper & Verdela Turner, July 17, 1821. J. C. Cook, Byrd
    Stovall.
John Harris & Anna D. Brown, Nov. 9, 1821. Robert Brown.
John Hart & Matilda Blackemore, April 2, 1821. Humphrey Bate,
    Richard Johnson.
Samuel Haw & Betsey Blackard, Oct. 23, 1821. Wm. Montgomery,
    Ezekiel Crane.
John Henry & Beky M. Mitchell, Dec. 20, 1821. Moses Henry.
John J. Henry & Nancy Kirk, Jan. 30, 1821. Peter H. Martin.
Lemuel S. Hunter & Frances Cotton, Jan. 14, 1821. A. W. Reese.
James Hutchinson & Peggy Frazor, March 3, 1821. Isaac Evans.
Francis Hyronimous & Permelia Bunch, July 26, 1821. Henry C.
    Williams.
Joseph Lng & Violet Armfield, Nov. 6, 1821. David Barrett.
John Jackson & Polly Alderson, June 25, 1821. Addison Foster,
    James Alderson.
Joseph Justice & B. Foster, Feb. 26, 1821. M. Hodges, Joseph Mc-
    Minn.
John Kerby & Sally Woodall, Feb. 6, 1821. Wm. McConneley.
Christopher Kitring & Polly Kirkpatrick, Nov. 17, 1821. Peter
    Kitring.
Samuel Kirkpatrick & Eveline McMurtry, Dec. 12, 1821. Hugh Kirk-
    patrick.
James Lauderdale & Mary Gillespie, May 18, 1821. John Wiseman,
    John Malone.
William Lowrey (Laurey) & Nancy Davis, Jan. 27, 1821. John Mc-
    Murtry, Thos. Durran.
William Lee & Polly McAdams, July 9, 1821. Cabel Woolf.
Thomas Lewis & Nancy Cummings, Aug. 1, 1821. John Durham.
James Markham & Sally Correll, Feb. 9, 1821. Francis Weatherred.
Abraham Martin & Mary Parker, Dec. 25, 1821. Richard Johnson,
    Milton Parker.
Edward Mann & Harriett Buckner, Jan. 29, 1821. Jesse Ellis.
John McCaffry & Eliza Bradford, Jan. 1, 1821. S. Hunt.
Wm. B. McCullock & Leddy Phipps, Nov. 30, 1821. Miles McCorkle.
Henry McDole & Betsy Goff, July 12, 1821. Wm. Woodall, David Lov-
    ell.
Frederick Martin & Nancy Black, May 19, 1821. Henry Pearson.

William McMillen & Rachel Kennedy, June 18, 1821. Valentine Bernard.
Bennett Meador & Judith Meador, Dec. 3, 1821. James Carr, Taylor Gilliam.
James L. Mills & Mary T. Duncan, Nov. 27, 1821. James Car-(?), P. C. Mills.
Pinkey C. Mills & Hannah Gaines, July 26, 1821. James Carr.
Peter Minsey & Elizabeth Gregory, June 19, 1821. Thos. Coddle.
James Mitchell & Sally Donoho, Nov. 17, 1821. Richard Johnson, Stephen Norton.
Austin Moore & Sarah White, April 23, 1821. John White.
Isaac W. Moore & Mourning Baker, Oct. 1, 1821. Wm. Montgomery, James House.
Peter Moore & Mary Jones, July 23, 1821. John Mitchell.
Elijah Morris & Nelly Twopence, Jan. 11, 1821. Dan'l McAuley.
Jacob Morris & Betsey Dossett, Oct. 12, 1821. Isaac Morris.
John Morris & Polly Harrison, Jan. 24, 1821. John Harrison.
Moses Morris & Jenny Barnard, March 18, 1821. Elisha Barnard.
Britton J. Neal & Betsey McNealy, Dec. 21, 1821. John Wright.
William Parker & Frances Bowen, Sep. 25, 1821. Richard Johnson.
James Parrish & Martha Little, Aug. 29, 1821. Benj. Parrish.
Scarborough Penticost & Fanny Crews, Sep. 29, 1821. Andrew Blythe.
Willis Perry & Nancy Mandrell, March 16, 1821. W. Johnson.
Amos Phelps & Betsy Gant, June 21, 1821. Lewis Albright.
Thomas Phelps & Nancy Browning, April 26, 1821. John Browning.
Benjamine Price & Patsey Strother, Dec. 31, 1821. W. G. Marlin.
Jesse Rains & Keziah Izzard, June 12, 1821. Lewis Izzard.
Thomas Ralph & Charity Powell, May 23, 1821. J. G. Ellis.
William Ralph & Charity Fairless, July 13, 1821.
William Reddett & Fanny Padgett, Feb. 20, 1821, by John Swaney.
James Reddick & Nancy Gaines, Sep. 21, 1821.
James Rickman & Elizabeth Henry, Nov. 22, 1821. Benj. Smith.
James Rickmond & Elizabeth Henry, Nov. 22, 1821. Wm. Stone.
John Rider & Nancy Morris, April 15, 1821. Claiborn Morris.
Samuel Rogers & Mariah Kelly, Feb. 19, 1821.
Jacob Runnells & Polly Black, Feb. 3, 1821. John Troutt.
Alexander S. Sadler & Patsey Parsons, June 6, 1821. John Dalton.
Charles G. Sanders & Eliza Douglass, May 8, 1821. Nathan Sanders.
John Sanders & Jane McConnell, Oct. 31, 1821. Olive Dickison.
William Savely & Elizabeth Jones, Oct. 17, 1821. Wm. Fuqua.
Harvey L. Scobey & Patsey Parnell, May 14, 1821.
John Settles & Polly Covington, Aug. 1, 1821. Dempsey Hunter.
Joseph Sloan & Nancy Barr, Feb. 13, 1821. Robert Lauderdale.
Childress Smith & Riley Harper, Jan. 9, 1821. E. Hunter.
Andrew Soper & Polly Wilkison, Nov. 3, 1821. Townsend Wilkison.
Jesse Spann & Niona Mifflin, March 5, 1821. Stewart Mifflin.
John Stalcup & Nancy Hastings, July 25, 1821.
Alexander Stewart & Polly Carr, Feb. 1, 1821. Ozri Alexander.
Milus Stewart & Nancy Mitchell, Oct. 18, 1821. W. H. Henry.
Eusibus Stone & Elizabeth Boyles, April 18, 1821. John B. Bond.
Thomas Talbott & Elizabeth Parr, Sep. 4, 1821. J. H. Talbott.
James Taylor & Rebecca Phillips, Jan. 16, 1821. Wm. L. Bledsoe.
John Taylor & Mary Helms, Dec. 26, 1821. Abraham Bradley.
Lawrence Tinnin & Mary Tinnin, Oct. 15, 1821. Andrew Blythe.

SUMNER COUNTY MARRIAGES

Wayne Thomas & Peggy Perkins, April 20, 1821. John Joyner.
George Trout & Nancy Bell, June 23, 1821. John Trout.
Phillip Vance & Patsey McKnight, Dec. 17, 1821. Mathey Erwin.
John Wakefield & Sally Cummings, Dec. 12, 1821. Thos. Cummings.
Douglass Walton & Eliza Exum., Dec. 26, 1821. Daniel Carney.
James Wallace & Nancy Daniel, Aug. 23, 1821. Samuel Wallace.
Frederick Watkins & Nancy Cage, Sep. 24, 1821. Orville Cage.
John K. Watson & Sophia Starks, Aug. 11, 1821. Bartholomus Watkins.
John West & Polly Allen, Jan. 23, 1821. William Allen.
Robert West & Mary Currey, Nov. 8, 1821. William White.
John L. White & Elizabeth Harrice, Feb. 2, 1821. Carson Dobbins.
Samuel S. Wilks & Mary Stanfield, Sep. 17, 1821. Woodson Winn.
William Whittington & Rachel Adams, Dec. 17, 1821. Edmond Hanes.
Thos. Woods & Mary Bruce, Oct. 8, 1821. Thos. Bruce.
Aza H. Wormington & Anna Holly, Nov. 10, 1821. John J. King.
James Wright & Patsey Endsley, March 27, 1821. Lemuel May.
Ebenezer Arnold & Evelina Dodson, Feb. 9, 1822. A. W. Reese.
Volentine Austin & Maria _____, July 6, 1822. Isaac G. Coles.
James Ball & Anna Carr, Jan. 12, 1822. James Carr.
Epson Bandy & Harriett Pearce, June 2, 1822. Allen Smith.
Jamason Bandy & Elizabeth Wright, May 10, 1822.
James Barnard & Betsey Hunter, Sep. 6, 1822. John Hinton.
James Barton & Betsey Childress, Jan. 29, 1822. Stephen Brundige.
Daniel Benthall & Frankey Patton, Jan. 28, 1822. William McCall.
Joshua Biggers & Polly Deans, March 6, 1822. James Dickerson.
Michael Black & Isabella Fikes, Jan. 7, 1822. Jacob Graves.
Hugh Bogle & Rachel Bogle, Dec. 23, 1822. James Bogle.
David Bradley & Jinny Allen, March 29, 1822. Wm. H. Douglas.
Alfred A. Brevard & Mary B. Alexander, July 15, 1822. Geo. Thompson.
John A. Brinkley & Polly Golden, June 8, 1822. Samuel A. Bailey.
Moses Brock & Susan Richardson, April 18, 1822. John Browning.
Manaweather Brown & Clarissa West, Dec. 18, 1822.
David Bundy & Frances Martin, Nov. 20, 1822.
Elijah Busby & Lucy Busby, Jan. 29, 1822. Solomon Shoulders.
Frederick Carpenter & Lucinda Chambers, Jan. 21, 1822. James Alderson.
William Carter & Nancy Rickman, July 29, 1822. John Dalton.
John Chapman & Peggy Baldridge, Nov. 26, 1822. Enos Vinson.
Isaac Charlton & Elizabeth Black, March 24, 1822. Shadrick Finn.
Samuel Cochran & Milly Brown, Dec. 3, 1822.
Wiley Cook & Betsey Barns, May 5, 1822. John Underwood.
John Crunk & Betsey Connor, Jan. 19, 1822. Ezekiell Young.
Thomas Crutchfield & Lotey Valentine, July 17, 1822. Benj. Parrish.
Alexander Cunningham & Frances Smith, Sep. 1, 1822. James Baker.
Josiah Dalton & Elizabeth Pruett, March 10, 1822. Jonathan Davis.
Philip Day & Betsey Burns, Dec. 10, 1822.
John Dennis & Jane Dalton, Aug. 31, 1822.
William Dillon & Elizabeth Tracy, Dec. 19, 1822.
Lewis G. Donalson & Nancy Rogers, Nov. __, 1822.
Abasuerus Dyer & Elizabeth Morgan, March 23, 1822. John Piles.
Hugh H. Eagan & Sally Bandy, April 4, 1822. Elisha Green.
William Edwards & Judy Brazel, Jan. 21, 1822. Solomon Shoulders.
William Jackson & Sally Branham, Feb. 23, 1822. John Branham.

Benjamine Johns & Patsey Day, Aug. 5, 1822. Malcom Smith.
Thomas A. Johnson & Nancy M. Johnson, Jan. 8, 1822. David Johnson.
Warren Kelly & Margaret Rogers, Nov. 23, 1822.
Elias Kennedy & Isabella Dobbins, Feb. 9, 1822. Alexander B.
   Dobbins.
Jeffery King & Rebeccah Shelton, Jan. 9, 1822.
James Lawhorn & Thankful Brigance, Jan. 22, 1822. William Lawhorn.
William Lawson & Jane C. Graham, Nov. 22, 1822. Stephen Wray.
Waman Leftwitch & Rebecca Rowland, April 4, 1822. John Ford (Jno.
   W. Ford).
Joseph B. Lindsey & Elizabeth Anderson, May 18, 1822. Sam'l H.
   Hodge.
David Lovell & Betsey Parnell, Feb. 22, 1822. William Glover.
Reason L. Mayhew & Sealah Wilson, Oct. 7, 1822.
George Martin & Abagile Lichingo, Feb. 25, 1822. Stephen Turner.
James Mays & Mary Dennon, July 14, 1822. John Hinton.
Andrew McGlothlin & Jemima Gilbert, March 9, 1822. A. W. Reese.
Stephen McKelbury & Lucinda Rogers, Feb. 4, 1822. Hugh McAdem.
James Mickelbury & Polly Roper, Jan. 26, 1822. Solomon Shoulders.
Samuel Middleton & Nancy Lambert, Feb. 5, 1822. William Lambert.
William Miller & Hannah Carr, Dec. 30, 1822.
Daniel Montgomery & Sally Garrison, Jan. 1, 1822. Richard King.
Samuel Morris & Betsey Harrison, Feb. 27, 1822. William Morris.
Morgan R. Penticost & Betsey Aspley, May 20, 1822. M. H. Henry.
Rolls Perry & Matilda Shaver, March 11, 1822. John Angela (Anglea).
Noah Phillips & Lucinda Troffilsted, June 28, 1822. William Robin-
   son.
John Pirtle & Betsey Winbourn, Aug. 1, 1822. John Moore.
Benjamine Ragland & Nancy Dotson, Sep. 9, 1822. James Alderson.
Daniel Rigsby & Sally Dill, March 12, 1822. Jacob Gregory.
John Rippey & Betsey Robinson, March 23, 1822. Josiah Rippey.
John Ross & Sarah Seat, Jan. 11, 1822. James R. Boyles.
Daniel Saffarns & Betsey Beeler, April 1, 1822. Wm. Porter.
William Sanders & Judith Bradley, Jan. 26, 1822. James Sanders.
Samuel Savely & Dicy Joiner, Nov. 20, 1822. John Brown.
James Shackleford & Polly Hollowell, Jan. 17, 1822. John Grooms.
Martin Shelton & Elizabeth Sample, Dec. 14, 1822.
Jeremiah Stark & Nancy Searcy, March 23, 1822. Chas. Watkins.
George Steel & Margaret Martin, Nov. 28, 1822.
Abraham Stephens & Salley Stuart, April 6, 1822. John Stuart.
John Stewart & Caty _____, May 20, 1822.
James Stratton & Joyce Thompson, Feb. 21, 1822. Stephen Forrester.
Nicholas Thompson & Naomah Jacobs, April 9, 1822. Tyre Yancy.
William Volentine & Peggy Love, Aug. 22, 1822. Wm. White.
Ephraim Waggoner & Selah Willson, Oct. 7, 1822. Reason L. Mayhew.
Robert Watson & Margaret Price, Sep. 12, 1822.
Samuel Watson & Nancy Vance, March 18, 1822. James Story.
W. G. Williamson & Susan Beacham, April 1, 1822. Benjamine Patton.
Robert Winham & Mary Moore, June 12, 1822. Wm. Porter.
Hiram Woolbanks & Sarah Dowell, Feb. 16, 1822. John Dowell.
Moses Wood & Polly Crane, March 8, 1822.
William R. Wood & Mariah Evans, Dec. 10, 1822.
William Wright & Polly Barrott, Jan. 29, 1822. John H. Turner.
William Yandel & Polly Sneed, Dec. 2, 1822. William Ward.

SUMNER COUNTY MARRIAGES

George Xericon & Mary Armfield, July 23, 1822. John Armfield.
Jeremiah Alsup & Lucy Brown, Nov. 20, 1823. Daniel Webb.
Lemuel Aspley & Nancy Hannah, Dec. 24, 1823. Richard Johnson.
Josiah W. Baldridge & Sarah Hodges, Feb. 27, 1823.
John Bandy & Elizabeth Martin, Dec. 31, 1823.
Edwin Bane & City Rackley, Dec. 10, 1823.
Robert Barr & Cynthia Jones, Dec. 27, 1823.
Willis Benthal & Darcus Poteet, Oct. 23, 1823.
David Bernard & Pheby Ferguson, Feb. 22, 1823. Patrick Rains,
    Thos. Edwards.
John Biggs & Nancy Barrow, June 14, 1823. Edw. Edwards.
Thomas Blackard & Elizabeth Lay, Sep. 9, 1823. Wm. Montgomery.
Lee C. Blakemore & Charlotte Johnson, March 18, 1823. Lucilius
    Winchester.
Thomas Bonner & Mary Ferguson, June 21, 1823.
George Bowling & Nancy Kirby, Jan. 23, 1823. Meredith Hodges.
James A. Bowman & Sarah Stanfield, Feb. 4, 1823.
Jacob Brown & Anna Tatum, Jan. 16, 1823. Asa Hodges.
Nimrod Brown & Susanna T. Brown, Sep. 22, 1823. Reuben D. Brown.
Reuben S. Brown & Kisiah Sarver, March 15, 1823.
John Browning & Abigail Rippey, Sep. 10, 1823.
John Butt & Nancy Todd, Nov. 29, 1823.
James Campbell & Hannah Phelps, Dec. 19, 1823. William Allbright.
John S. Carr & Martha Hanna, Oct. 7, 1823.
William W. Chambers & Eveline Donoho, Dec. 6, 1823. George Thomp-
    son.
Archibald Chapman & Polly McGuire, March 15, 1823. Hanson Hunt.
George Chapman & Elizabeth Thompson, Aug. 11, 1823. Hugh Boyle.
William Chapman & Margaret Bull, Jan. 15, 1823. Thos. Anderson.
Austin Corley & Milly Turner, April 12, 1823. Benjamine Johnson.
Isaac G. Coles & Mary Ann Walters, May 14, 1823. John Walters.
Solomon Day & Elizabeth Gillespie, Jan. 6, 1823. Green Daniel.
John B. Dickason & Sarah White, Dec. 20, 1823.
Livingston Dickason & Frances Turner, June 11, 1823.
Cosby Dickerson & Leathy Grey, Oct. 6, 1823. Sumpter Turner.
Isaac Dillon & Polly Vaughn, May 8, 1823. Edmund Alvis.
Jeremiah Dixon & Pincey Beaver, Sep. 3, 1823.
Henry Dobbins & Sophia Allen, Oct. 27, 1823. Alexander B. Dobbins.
John Dorris & Elizabeth Hinson, Nov. 25, 1823. Ezekiel C. Hodges.
Tilley Downs & Jane Robertson, Dec. 23, 1823. Baley May.
John Duncan & Lucinda Center, Aug. 2, 1823.
Edmund Hides & M. J. Davis, Dec. 9, 1823.
Benjamine Ezell & Rhodia Hampton, April 9, 1823. William Lilley.
Thomas Foxall & Mary Cryer, March 6, 1823.
Smith Garrett & Caroline Matilda Ragsdale, Dec. 20, 1823. John
    Garrett.
Elisha Gibson & Martha Rice, July 9, 1823. Henry Rice.
John Gilbert & Mary Gower, Aug. 16, 1823. Charles Morgan.
Edward Giles & Susan Mathews, Feb. 28, 1823.
John W. Gregory & Elizabeth Adams, Jan. 18, 1823. Robt. W. Sanford.
Obadiah Gregory & Lucretia Spain, April 1, 1823. John Spain.
Thomas W. Hanna & Sally W. Turner, March 8, 1823. James B. Hanna.
John F. Harris & Elizabeth Agees, May 19, 1823. Francis M.
    Weathered.

William Hicks & Sally Derning, Feb. 19, 1823. Lewis Derning.
Exekial C. Hodges & Rebecca Dorris, Oct. 17, 1823.
Isaiah Hodges & Martha Hodges, Sep. 6, 1823. Jeremiah Brown.
Isham Honeycutt & Catharine Ogburn, Oct. 18, 1823. Benj. Bush.
John Horton & Polly Leat, Dec. 28, 1823.
Samuel Houghton & Elizabeth Dorris, Nov. 18, 1823.
Seaton H. Hunter & Desha Payne, Jan. 1, 1823.
Alexander Hutchinson & Pemmy Rutherford, June 14, 1823.
John Johnson & Elizabeth Jackson, Nov. 4, 1823. William Franklin.
Thomas Jones & Susanna Crenshaw, Jan. 20, 1823. John H. Dickinson.
James Lambert & Delinda Dickason, June 30, 1823.
Price Lambert & Eliza Dickason, July 4, 1823. James Charlton.
William Lane & Eliza Allen, June 6, 1823. John Bell.
Bennett Lane & Catharine Dickinson, Aug. 27, 1823.
William Laurence & Harriett McKinney, Jan. 4, 1823.
Amaziah Lyles & Mary Ann Murden, Jan. 3, 1823. Samuel V. Gilles-
pie.
Stephen Marlow & Aly Reynolds, Feb. 22, 1823.
Mead May & Polly Clenny, Jan. 9, 1823.
Joseph Meader & Lucinda Latimer, Aug. 2, 1823.
George Mills & Elizabeth Guthrie, April 9, 1823. Eli Guthrie.
Marcus Moore & Susan Crabb, April 8, 1823. Alfred Ing.
John Morris & Jememiah Bailey, Aug. 15, 1823. Noah Philips.
James Neal & Nancy Neel, April 1, 1823. Henry Beard.
James Nichols & Polly Allen, Dec. 25, 1823.
Eli Odam & Catey K. Phagan, July 17, 1823.
Robert Patton & Elizabeth Perry, Oct. 17, 1823. Hugh Kirkpatrick.
Warren W. Peden & Sarah G. Mills, Aug. 15, 1823. Henry Kerby.
Isaac Perry & Elizabeth Gardner, May 12, 1823. James Baker.
Thomas Perdew & Mary Deal, Dec. 1, 1823.
William Peyton & Milly Thomas, March 22, 1823.
James R. Riper & Elizabeth Morgan, Sep. 16, 1823. Edward Edwards.
Joshua Pyle & Nancy Allen, March 27, 1823. John Pyle.
James Ralph & Dosha Barton, Dec. 30, 1823. Caswell Smith.
Mathew Rice & Sally Ponds, Feb. 10, 1823. Levi Smith.
Robert Rose & Elizabeth Howerton, Nov. 11, 1823, John Ross.
George R. Roister & Mary Stewart, Feb. 22, 1823. M. Neale.
Jared Sample & Nancy Sample, Nov. 18, 1823. Martin Shelton.
Robert Sanderson & Mary M. Franklin, July 3, 1823.
Ethelbert M. Sanders & Theodotia Trigg, Sep. 9, 1823. John R. Bain.
William Seay & Ann Stanfield, July 13, 1823. Richard Johnson.
John Shields & Elizabeth Derryberry, Nov. 13, 1823. John Dowell.
Caswell Smith & Rebecca Sharlock, Oct. 27, 1823. John McMurtry.
John Spain & Milly Gregory, Jan. 23, 1823. Hugh K. Patterson.
William Spicy & Louisa Lee, Feb. 4, 1823. Elmore Douglas.
James Stephens & Nancy Head, March 26, 1823. Charles Watkins.
Asa Stewart & Nancy Crabb, Dec. 27, 1823. Charles Watkins.
Strother P. Suttle & Polly Cunningham, June 7, 1823.
John Taylor & Nancy Sherry, Jan. 23, 1823. John Alderson.
Richard Taylor & Mary Fronville, Dec. 11, 1823.
John K. Taylor & Jane M. Caldwell, Nov. 7, 1823. Robert Taylor.
Reuben Thornhill & Nancy Deshazo, June 20, 1823. David Brooke.
William Toombs & Elizabeth Henderson, Dec. 27, 1823. Thomas Jour-
dan.

Wily Tilly & Sally Robinson, Jan. 15, 1823.
Walter Trimble & Mary G. Mitchell, Feb. 26, 1823, by A. D. Camp-
    bell, M.G. (Pastor of Nashville Presbyterian Church). John J.
    White, BM.
William Wallace & Polly May, Nov. 13, 1823. Thos. Anderson, J.P.
Harris Walton & Mary Crenshaw, April 16, 1823, by Richard Johnson.
    Garrison Stubblefield, BM.
Harbard Wallace & Elizabeth White, Sep. 6, 1823.
Isaac Warren & Rebecca McKendree, March 26, 1823. James Gwin, M.G.
Philip Watkins & Eliza Lay, Oct. 13, 1823.
John Williams & Polly Gilmore, Aug. 18, 1823. Jonathan Davis, J.P.
Samuel Wilson & Nancy Moore, March 26, 1823, by James Douglas.
Joseph B. Winns & Mary Barry, Nov. 13, 1823. E. A. White, BM.
Samuel T. White & Nancy Thomas, Oct. 20, 1823. John Parson, BM.
John Wood & Annah Weathered, March 18, 1823. Thomas Miers, BM.
John Anderson & Nancy Grooms, Dec. 24, 1824, by Richard Johnson.
    William F. Sadler, BM.
James Anglea & Susanna Briley, July 3, 1824. Thomas Jourdan, BM.
Jourdan Baker & Elizabeth Early, July 17, 1824. Merry S. Bottom,
    BM.
Alfred. M. Beard & Louisiana Vinson, July 29, 1824, by Thomas Ander-
    son, J.P. Alfred M. Beard, BM.
Jacob Bernard & Charlotte Bandy, Sep. 28, 1824. Elisha Bernard,
    BM.
Jefferson Blakemore & Lena Willis, Dec. 3, 1824. Joseph Rice, BM.
Lemuel Bloodworth & Polly Camhorn (Lamhorn (?)), Feb. 5, 1824.
    William Bloodworth, BM.
Richard Boren & Miley Bush, Sep. 20, 1824, by Wm. Hobdey, J.P.
    Stephen Boren, BM.
James Boyles & Malinda Williams, May 4, 1824. Ferrin Bandy, BM.
James B. Bracken & Eliza Bracken, April 20, 1824. Meredith
    Hodges, J.P. Sam'l Tyree, BM.
Luke Bradley & Sally Brigance, Dec. 8, 1824. Sam. C. Cochran, J.P.
Benjamin Brassell & Rebecca Hall, Aug. 11, 1824, by James Douglas.
    William Winham, BM.
James H. Britton & Sarah M. Lauderdale, Feb. 2, 1824, by John
    Wiseman, M.G.
Richard G. Bugg & Prudence Chapill, Dec. 13, 1824, by J. H. Swaney,
    J.P. Thomas Gregory, BM.
George Burns & Marjory Day, Aug. 14, 1824. Thomas Coddle, BM.
George Bush & Catharine Stoode (Strode), Sep. 14, 1824. Allen
    Gardner, BM.
William Bush & Sally Gardner, July 2, 1824. William Cooly, BM.
Henry Butler & Fanny Week, Feb. 16, 1824, by Daniel Webb, M.G.
    Daniel Allsup, BM.
Shelton Carney & Susan Charlton, Feb. 24, 1824, by James Walton,
    J.P.
James Carter & Polly Morris, Nov. 8, 1824, by John Parker, L.D.
    John Morris, BM.
Abner Caton & Elizabeth Johnson, Jan. 24, 1824, by L. Landers, J.P.
    James Dickey, BM.
Thomas Chapman & Rachel Garrison, Oct. 25, 1824, by John McMurtry,
    J.P. James G. Elliss, BM.
Abner Charlton & Polly Anglea, Dec. 21, 1824. Jarratt Taylor, BM.

Thomas B. Clendenning & Elizabeth Frazor, July 5, 1824, by Joseph Kirkpatrick.

Austin Coats & Lucinda Dismuke, Nov. 14, 1824. Thomas W. Royster, BM.

Thomas Collier & Susan Donnell, Dec. 29, 1824, by John Parker, L.D. William Parker, BM.

James Cope & Annis Murdin, Oct. 29, 1824. Henry Sarver, BM.

Hugh Crawford & Patty Worker, Feb. 8, 1824, by Charles Watkins. Moor Cotton, BM.

John Crow & Nancy Martin, Aug. 15, 1824, by Charley Simmons.

Lewis W. Crump & Susan Clenny, Jan. 17, 1824, by Thomas Anderson, J.P.

John R. Dalton & Elizabeth Wooton, March 5, 1824, by John Wiseman, M.G.

John Richard Dinning & Fanny Kirby, March 22, 1824, by Robt. Norvell, M.G. David Kirby, BM.

Fielding Dickason & Polly Todd, July 15, 1824, by J. L. Swaney, J.P. Wm. L. Harris, BM.

Latimer Donnell & Susan _____, March 8, 1824, by Richard Johnson.

Persis Donnell & Sally Hassell, Jan. 22, 1824, by John R. Bain. Robert A. King, BM.

John Duty (Doty) & Elizabeth C. Harvel (Harrel), March 16, 1824. Wm. Turner, BM.

Francis Duffy & Pamelia Parker, Nov. 10, 1824, by John Wiseman, M.G. Charles Morgan, BM.

Joseph B. Dunn & Poley Mahn (?), Feb. 29, 1824, by Jonathan Davis, J.P. Daniel Allsup, BM.

Hiram Duty & Emaline Banks, Feb. 21, 1824, by James Walton.

Alexander Elliston & Cynthia Hart, March 2, 1824, by John Wiseman, M.G.

John Emery & Susannah Emery, Aug. 3, 1824. Ralph Jones, BM.

John Eskew & Anny Stone, March 27, 1824. James Charlton, BM.

Thomas W. Essex & Nancy Malone, July 6, 1824. S. H. Lauderdale, BM.

Isaac Evans & Mary Rutherford, Aug. 6, 1824, by Caleb Crane. James Hutchison, BM.

Lanty Fairless & Elizabeth Ralph, April 3, 1824, by John McMurtry, J.P. Lewis Ralph, BM.

Hardy Fleetwood & Harriett Pagitt, May 16, 1824, by J. L. Swaney, J.P.

James Fleming & Elizabeth Rasco, Aug. 12, 1824, by J. B. Wynns, M.G.

John Graves (Groves) & Salley Skeen, May 19, 1824, by Alexander D. Duval, J.P. William Tyree, BM.

David Garrett & Louisa G. Rhodes, March 31, 1824, Chas. Watkins, J.P.

Edward Green & Mary Simons, Dec. 28, 1824, by M. M. Cryer, E.C. James Knight, BM.

Daniel Gregory & Polly Wood, July 24, 1824, by Robert Norvell, M.G. Jacob Gregory, BM.

Jonathan Gregory & Diner Wood, July 24, 1824, by Robt. Norvell, M.G. Jacob Gregory, BM.

SUMNER COUNTY MARRIAGES

Thomas E. Gregory & _____(?), Dec. 4, 1824. John O. Higgerson, BM.

John Grooms & Harriett Hanes, April 6, 1824. James Harrison, BM.

Anderson Harlon & Frances Reddit, Dec. 21, 1824, by W. J. Swaney, J.P. Patrick Buckley, BM.

Robert Harris & Anne Alderson, Aug. 4, 1824, by Robt. Norvell, M.G.

Manuel Head & Prunetta Dugger, June 14, 1824, by John McMurtry, J.P. Thomas Head, BM.

Middleton Head & Francis Stone, April 7, 1824, by Richard Johnson.

Solomon Henson & Fanny Hall, Dec. 22, 1824, by M. Hodges, J.P. Joshua Bradley, BM.

Hawkins Hill & Nancy Douglass, Aug. 28, 1824. Wade Hampton, BM.

Hizikie Holand & Sally Poole, Oct. 24, 1824. G. Haley Ernest, BM.

Mitchell Holloway & Catherine Volentine, Dec. 20, 1824. Richard Parker, BM.

Samuel W. Harper & Jane L. Tinsley, Oct. 9, 1824. Richard Townsend, BM.

John House & Susan Cope, July 17, 1824. Samuel Roney, BM.

Leroy Jackson & Sarah Donoho, Aug. 19, 1824, by Jonathan Dougal. Wm. Donoho, BM.

Martha (?) Jernigan & Ann Groves, May 16, 1824, by Harvey Sawyers. Nathaniel Rice, BM.

Thomas Johnson & Sally Ann Moore, Dec. 28, 1824, by H. H. Cryer, E.C. Alfred Moore, BM.

Jefferson Joiner & Nancy Haines, Aug. 16, 1824, by James W. Patton, J.P. Asa B. Douglass, BM.

William Joiner & Sally Flack, Aug. 17, 1824, by Richard Harrison, J.P. John P. Hogen, BM.

Donelson Joyner & Nancy Towpence, July 17, 1824, by Thos. Anderson. Frank Dancy, BM.

Thomas Key & Patsy Asply, May 7, 1824. Hiram Duncan, BM.

David Kirby & Mary Ann Beason, March 1, 1824, by Wm. Hobdy, J.P.

Stewart Kirkpatrick & Elizabeth Kirkpatrick, Jan. 26, 1824. Thomas Frazor, BM.

William Kirkpatrick & Elizabeth Kirkpatrick, July 24, 1824, by Robt. Guthrie, M.G. Stewart Kirkpatrick, BM.

William Lane & Jane Brown, Feb. 14, 1824, by Richard Johnson. Richard Allen, BM.

Walter C. Langley & Hannah Doxey, Jan. 27, 1824. Isaac Lindsey, BM.

Jonathan Latimer & Harriett Kelly, Feb. 7, 1824, by John McMurtry, J.P. William Bush, BM.

Eli Lawson & Patsy Rodgers, Dec. 13, 1824, by Josiah Walton, J.P. Webb Bloodworth, BM.

William Leffler & Vina Mertin, Nov. 9, 1824. George Windle, BM.

William Lovell & June Alderson, Feb. 22, 1824, by Alex D. Duval, J.P.

Archibald E. Mansker & Mary Burns, May 27, 1824. Robert Patton, BM.

Joseph K. Martin & Polly Wood, Oct. 25, 1824. James L. Martin, BM.

Absolam May & Phebe Farris, Aug. 12, 1824, Craddock May, BM.

Morris May & Patsey Overstreet, April 28, 1824, by Thos. Anderson, J.P.

William McAdams & Polly Lee, Sep. 22, 1824, by S. Davis, J.P.

Charles McIlmore & Elizabeth G. Miles, Aug. 17, 1824. Harvel McIlmore, BM.
John McMurtry & Sarah Blackard, Sep. 30, 1824.
Jacob Miller & Elizabeth Frailey, Nov. 4, 1824, by Samuel Davis, J.P. Jacob Miller, BM.
Jacob Morris & Elizabeth Taylor, May 7, 1824. Jesse L. Keen, BM.
Ashford Napier & Nancy Echols, July 28, 1824. Currel Keen, BM.
Henry Neale & Clarissa Browning, Nov. 29, 1824, by Robert Guthrie, M.G. Henry Beard, BM.
Thomas Nelson & Catharine Farmer, Nov. 18, 1824. John Majors, BM.
James Norvell & Patsey Burrow, Jan. 8, 1824. Alexander Cavitt, BM.
William Orean & Nancy Durham, March 8, 1824, by Wm. Smith, J.P. James Durham, BM.
Isaac N. Parker & Mary Lafferty, June 10, 1824, by John Crenshaw, J.P. William Winham, BM.
Henry Parrish & Patsy Proctor, March 16, 1824, by John L. Swaney, J.P.
Simpson Payne & Elizabeth Turner, Sep. 21, 1824, by Edwards _____. Charles Morgan, BM.
Lafayette Posey & Louisa Mitchell, Jan. 26, 1824. John L. Bugg, BM.
Payton Rasco & Nancy C. Rice, Sep. 14, 1824, by James Gwin, M.G. Mebane Anderson, BM.
Thomas N. Rasco & Sally Combs, Dec. 29, 1824, by J. B. Wynns, M.G. Harvey C. Douglass, BM.
Beverley Read & Aceny Dalton, May 25, 1824. David Vance, BM.
William Richardson & Cinthy Jones, July 30, 1824. John McMurtry, J.P. William B. Jones, BM.
Jeremiah Rice & Mossy Bandy, July 19, 1824, by William Peter _____. John Spiller, BM.
George Rider & Alsa Bush, July 3, 1824, by Robt. Norvell, M.G. John Rider, BM.
Anthony B. Reid & Henrietta Sanford, Dec. 24, 1824. D. Lauderdale, BM.
Isaac A. Robinson & Elizabeth Green, May 7, 1824, by Thos. Anderson, J.P.
Abel Rule & Polly Lynch, Aug. 26, 1824, by John McMurtry, J.P. Thomas Pritchett, BM.
John F. Shapell & Sarah Essex, Nov. 15, 1824. John Bell, BM.
Enoch Shields & Minta Kirby, Jan. 17, 1824, by Robt. Norvell, M.G.
Eli Shy & Ally Smith, Jan. 17, 1824, by Robert Norvell, M.G.
Benjamine Smith & Sally Cloar, April 13, 1824, by J. O. Cook, J.P.
John Soper & Mary New, Dec. 21, 1824. A. M. Reese, BM. John Franklin, William Franklin.
John Spiller & Nancy Bandy, June 30, 1824. John Spiller, BM.
Hutchinson Standly & Catherine Bradley, Oct. 25, 1824. William Bradford, BM.
John Stanford & Polly Cartwright, Dec. 8, 1824, by Demcey Ashford, J.P. Samuel King, BM.
Ashley Stanfield & Margaret M. Russell, Nov. 18, 1824, by John R. Bain. William Trousdale, BM.
Michael Tracy & Patsey Gregory, Sep. 3, 1824, by Jonathan Davis, J.P. Stephen Gilliam, BM.

David Trusty & Sally Williams, April 22, 1824. Andrew H. Guthrie, BM.

Sumpter Turner & Rachel Dalton, Jan. 7, 1824, by Richard Johnson.

Robert Tuttle & Patsey Perry, July 22, 1824. William Key, BM.

Wesley Watts & Mary C. Breene, Dec. 11, 1824, by John Wiseman. Horace Lawson, BM.

Chipley Williams & Polly Garrett, March 18, 1824. William Delass, BM.

Thomas Williams & Willy Lovel, Sep. 30, 1824, by Samuel David, J.P. Jonathan Williams, BM.

William Williams & Sarah Covington, Jan. 5, 1824, by Wm. Fuqua, M.G. Enoch Powell, BM.

William Willoughby & Kesiah Smith, Nov. 8, 1824. Wm. Alderson, BM.

Zacheus R. Wilson & Keziah Stone, Nov. 6, 1824, by Stephen R. Roberts, J.P. James T. Wilson, BM.

John Woodall & Ruby Kerby, Nov. 9, 1824. Reuben Searcy, BM.

Joel L. Abston & Louisa Cage, Dec. 30, 1825, by Chas. Watkins, J.P. George Douglass, BM.

Dudley Adams & Sary Anne Townsend, Sep. 1, 1825, by Richard Johnson. H. Smith, BM.

Alfred Allen & Franky Benthall, Dec. 31, 1825, by Elijah Boddie, J.P. David Allen, BM.

John C. Allen & Nancy Holmes, March 24, 1825, by Wm. Smith, J.P. James Holmes, BM.

Luke P. Allen & Margaret Parker, Aug. 15, 1825, by J. Parker. John Parker, BM.

Fielding Alley & Susanna Bradley, Jan. 23, 1825, by Samuel Cothran, J.P.

Henry Anthony & Amelia Shy, Jan. 21, 1825. Levi Shy, BM.

Jacob Anthony & Evaline A. Graham, April 11, 1825. Wm. McCullock, BM.

Thomas Armstrong & Sinai Roney, Oct. 27, 1825. E. Edwards, Stephen H. Turner, BM.

Levi A. Baker & Kitty Walton, Dec. 10, 1825, by Hugh Kirkpatrick, M.G. William Walton, BM.

David Bales & Rebecca Tracy, July 13, 1825, by Samuel Dorris. Elijah Butler, BM.

Wright Barnes & Nancy Doughtry, Nov. 5, 1825, by Elijah Boddie, J.P. Solomon Shoulders, BM.

Joseph W. Beard & Lurena Neal, Nov. 14, 1825, by Francis Johnston, M.G. David Beard, BM.

William Bentley & Nancy Youree, Jan. 3, 1825, by Jno. Swaney, J.P. Reuben Blackemore, BM.

James Bever & Mariah Bunch, Feb. 27, 1825. Joel Meador, BM.

James Biggs & Jane Carney, Nov. 10, 1825. Edmond Barrow, BM.

Siras Boyd & Rosey Savely, April 19, 1825. Thomas Duke, BM.

William Bracken, Jr. & Rachel Morris, May 4, 1825. John Morris, BM.

Isaac Bradly & Catherine Gough, Aug. 20, 1825. Robt. Bradley, BM.

William Bradley & Sally Goff, Jan. 24, 1825. David Bradley, BM.

Elisha Brily & Rebecca Harper, Oct. 1, 1825, by S. H. Turner, J.P. Thomas Summers, BM.

James Brown & Elizabeth Kirkpatrick, Aug. 23, 1825. Jeremiah Durgess, BM.

Patrick H. Buckly & Frances Dickinson, June 30, 1825. James Taylor, BM.

Anderson Busby & Parizade Coelman, Feb. 8, 1825. John Mitchell, BM.

Josiah Bush & Caty Rider, March 2, 1825. William Bush, BM.

James Cain & Karen Savely, Aug. 13, 1825. Caleb Willis, BM.

William Caldwell & Cinderilla Stanfield, Feb. 13, 1825. Wm. Murry, BM.

David Cannon & Sary Piles, Dec. 20, 1825.

Joshua Carney & Mary Charlton, Dec. 21, 1825. Olive Dickerson, BM.

James Carr & Elizabeth Williams, July 15, 1825, by John McMurtry, J.P. Wm. Kennedy, BM.

Jarrett Carter & Sally Tuttle, April 4, 1825, by W. Smith, J.P. Gideon Carter, BM.

Thomas W. Cartwright & Elizabeth Cook, July 14, 1825. John Stanford, BM.

Thomas Cherry & Amy Justice, Aug. 29, 1825, by Samuel Cochran, J.P. Mark Justice, BM.

Richard Clark & Betsey Jones, March 2, 1825, by Jonathan Davis, J.P. Richard Philips, BM.

William Cole & Fanny Law, Oct. 15, 1825, by Samuel Davis, J.P. Joseph Cole, BM.

Benjamine Cook & Nancy Barnes, May 7, 1825. Solomon Shoulders, BM.

Moor Cotton & Lovy Edwards, Jan. 10, 1825, by Josiah Walton, J.P. Bright Harris, BM.

John Crews & Rushia Bloodworth, March 5, 1825, by C. Crane. Wm. Griffin, BM.

Cage Crowder & Mary Rogers, Dec. 8, 1825, by Thos. Anderson, J.P. Thos. James, BM.

Thomas Culbertson & Sarah Guthry, Dec. 22, 1825, by James Guthrie, M.G. George Wills, BM.

Richard Daulton & Poley Taylor, July 13, 1825. Andrew Taylor, BM.

Hiram David & Polly Ford, Sep. 11, 1825, by Wm. Smith, J.P. Thomas Coddle, BM.

Bird Debow & Ann Crawford, Nov. 10, 1825, by Charles Watkins, J.P. John L. Blackwell, BM.

Charles Degraffenried & Mary Herndon, Oct. 13, 1825. John Roberson, BM.

James Dempsey & Susan Clark, March 3, 1825, by Richard Harrison, J.P. Edy Jacobs, BM.

Thomas Downs & Sally Soper, Dec. 28, 1825, by Thos. Anderson, J.P. Samuel Works, BM.

Auston Duffer & Sally Hunt, Oct. 8, 1825, by J. David, J.P.

Alexander C. Ewing & Cloe R. Sanders, May 17, 1825, by Thos. Joyner. Wm. Hadley, BM.

William R. Ewing & Sally Byson, Sep. 14, 1825, by Thomas Joyner. Alexander Ewing, BM.

Birtis W. Ferrell & Sally T. Hunt, Nov. 3, 1825. Burl Bender, BM.

William Fin & Sealy Mayhew, Aug. 23, 1825, by Samuel Davis, J.P. Benjamine Wilson, BM.

John Galbreath & Mary Hatchell, Feb. 23, 1825. Elisha Hatchell, BM.

John Gardner, Jr. & Malvina Baker, Sep. 26, 1825, by Elijah Boddie, J.P. James House, BM.

SUMNER COUNTY MARRIAGES

Edward S. Giles & Nancy Jackson, Aug. 25, 1825. Robert Desha, BM.
Jacob Gillespie & Nellie Graham, Jan. 12, 1825, by John Crenshaw,
J.P. Ashley Stanfield, BM.
William Gillespie & Jane P. Barr, Sep. 27, 1825. George Byrn, BM.
John Granger & Polly Suttle, Dec. 13, 1825. John Stalcup, BM.
James Gregory & Elizabeth Gregory, Aug. 29, 1825. James Gibson,
BM.
William Griffin & Patsey Bloodworth, Jan. 7, 1825. John Crews, BM.
Jeremiah W. Hale & Jemima Ann Scruggs, Dec. 1, 1825, by Thos.
Anderson, J.P. John H. Dew, BM.
Henry N. Beard & Elizabeth B. Stalcup, Nov. 7, 1825. William Neal,
BM.
Noah Hampton & Nancy Shaw, April 9, 1825. John Garrison, BM.
Thomas Hanes & Elizabeth Law, May 5, 1825, by Samuel Davis, J.P.
Henry Law, BM.
Thomas A. Hardy & Elizabeth Busby, July 23, 1825, by Josiah Walton,
J.P. Elijah Busby, BM.
Benjamine S. Harper & Nancy Tinsley, Nov. 30, 1825. Dickson Tuck-
er, BM.
Lowe Harrison & Jane Cole, March 2, 1825, by Richard Harrison, J.P.
Richard Harrison, BM.
James Hartin (or Martin) & Eunice Brown, Aug. 1, 1825. Samuel
Brown, BM.
Robert Holmes & Polly Lavinor, July 18, 1825, by Joshua Walton,
J.P. John Crews, BM.
David Ingram & Polly Johnson, Feb. 7, 1825, by Richard Harrison,
J.P. Wm. Ward, BM.
George H. Jefferson & Elizabeth P. Moor, March 7, 1825, by Thos.
Joyner. Joseph Moor, BM.
John Jennett & Mary Barr, April 25, 1825. Hezekiah Jennett, BM.
Thomas Johnson & Elizabeth Barham, Dec. 21, 1825, by Stephen
R. Roberts, J.P. John Parson, BM.
Thomas Johnson & Nancy Tavenor, Aug. 30, 1825. Wm. Cummins, BM.
Frederick Justice & Terry Crowder, July 2, 1825. Andrew Martin,
BM.
Jonathan Latimer & Nancy West, Feb. 26, 1825, by William Peter.
Wm. Moore, BM.
James Lee & Francis Philips, Nov. 23, 1825. James Durham, BM.
William Maddox & Marget Simmons, July 2, 1825, by Samuel Davis,
J.P. George Simmons, BM.
Richard Marshall & Sary Carr, Dec. 27, 1825. Wesley Oglesby, BM.
Mathew Martin & Elizabeth Caps, Dec. 26, 1825, by Hugh Kirkpatrick,
M.G. Andrew Jackson, BM.
William Martin & Sarah Ann Sanders, Oct. 27, 1825. John P. Wagnor,
BM.
Pleasant Mays & Viney Dorris, Jan. 10, 1825. Wm. Parker, BM.
Henry McLaffey & Elizabeth Laurence, Dec. 1, 1825, by Thos. Ander-
son, J.P. Stephen Forester, BM.
John McMurry & Barbary Evans, Feb. 23, 1825, by Hugh Kirkpatrick,
M.G. Samuel K. Blythe, BM.
James McReynolds & Sarah Mayhew, March 2, 1825, by Sam'l Davis,
J.P. Josiah Benson, BM.
Armstead Meredith & Elizabeth Wever (Weaver), July 12, 1825. Wm.
Alderson, BM.

Jesse Meador & Polly Austin, March 20, 1825. Moses Henry, BM.
Adam Meek & Priscilla Hale, March 21, 1825, by James Wallace, J.P.
Israel Moore, BM.
Edward Moor & Lucinda Hunter, Sep. 19, 1825, by Thos. Joyner.
Jas. B. King, BM.
Joel Morris & Mary Tally, Feb. 23, 1825, by Thomas Joyner. Reuben
Tally, BM.
Walter B. Morris & Cinthia E. Elliott, May 4, 1825, by John R.
Bain. John F. Fulton, BM.
John Ogles & Annes Wilson, Dec. 1, 1825, by Samuel Davis, J.P.
Benj. Wilson, BM.
Austin Oneal & Ally Smith, Jan. 13, 1825, by Samuel Davis, J.P.
V. Smith, BM.
Joseph Payne & Sophiah Glasgow, Sep. 15, 1825. Lewis Green, BM.
Joel Philips & Sally Wilson, July 7, 1825. James Campbell, BM.
John H. Pickard & Jane H. Crews, July 30, 1825, by Josiah Walton,
J.P. Wm. Griffin, BM.
William Pile & Margaret Allen, June 16, 1825. Jeshu Pile, BM.
John Poe & Polly Tinsley, Sep. 26, 1825, by Josiah Walton, J.P.
Jesse Daniel, BM.
Joshua Predaux & Betsey Ann Latimer, May 6, 1825, by Demcey Ash-
ford, J.P. James Stratton, BM.
James Ray & Eliza Graham, Sep. 2, 1825, by John Wiseman, M.G.
Stephen Ray, BM.
John H. Ray & Martha T. Cage, May 10, 1825, by John Wiseman, M.G.
John Overton Cage, BM.
Henry Rigsby & Judy Brooks, Oct. 28, 1825, by James Wallace, J.P.
Martin Cowgill, BM.
John Rippey & Betsey Bell, March 3, 1825, by M. Hodges, J.P.
William Roper & Margaret Spencer, March 5, 1825.
James Sanders & Leutitia Cavy, March 21, 1825, by James Patton,
J.P. John Mitchell, BM.
Henry Sarver & Mary O. Rice, April 22, 1825, by James Gwin, J.P.
Samuel Gwin, BM.
Benjamine Seawell & Margaret Rickman, Feb. 3, 1825. Hardy Seawell,
BM.
William W. Seay & Ann Stanfield, July 13, 1825. Robert Chappell,
BM.
Orville Shelby & Elizabeth Caroline Winchester, Jan. 29, 1825.
Joseph C. Guild, BM.
Thomas Short & Betsey Anderson, Dec. 11, 1825, by Jonathan Davis,
J.P.
George W. Shreve & Jane White, March 30, 1825, by William Peter.
James Fleming, BM.
Eli. Smothers & Margaret Piles, Jan. 13, 1825, by John T. Carr,
J.P. Jacob Smothers, BM.
Robert Steel & Harriett Baily, Dec. 31, 1825, by Richard Johnson.
Saml. Barr, BM.
Edward Stevenson & Eliza A. Mann, Oct. 3, 1825, by L. P. Allen.
Robt. Weatherred, BM.
William B. Stovall & Mary Ann Cruise, Dec. 10, 1825. Mathew Ca-
they, BM.
Robert Stubblefield & Martha Jackson, Jan. 31, 1825, by John Cren-
shaw, J.P. William Gillespie, BM.

SUMNER COUNTY MARRIAGES

John B. Sturgeon & Elizabeth Watts, April 5, 1825, by James Charlton. James Fonvial, BM.
Edward Summers & Patsey Dalton, Dec. 8, 1825, by Jonathan David, J.P. Daniel Dalton, BM.
Robert Summers & Sally Briley, Sep. 13, 1825, by Edward Edwards. James Briley, BM.
John Swan & Nancy Pryor, Nov. 28, 1825. Lewson Barlow, BM.
Thomas Sweringer & Nancy Goodard, Dec. 13, 1825. John Stalcup, BM.
John Taylor & Amela Simons, Oct. 1, 1825, by James Charlton. William Glover, BM.
Berkly Thomas & Sally Tally, Jan. 31, 1825, by Thomas Joyner. Reubin Tally, BM.
Henry Townsend & Frances A. L. Wynn, Aug. 3, 1825, by Richard Johnson. George H. Smith, BM.
Dixon Tucker & Sally H. Rickman, Dec. 21, 1825. Samuel D. Higgarson, BM.
John G. Turner & Mary T. Parker, Dec. 10, 1825, by Wm. Smith, J.P. George H. Smith, BM.
William Turner & Elizabeth P. Smith, July 27, 1825, by Thomas Joyner. Jesse Garret, BM.
John Vanable & Ann Tilley, Nov. 14, 1825. William Downs, BM.
Pleasant Walker & Mary Boykin, Aug. 4, 1825, by Richard Harrison, J.P. James McKinly, BM.
Gray Walton & Susan McConnel, Jan. 3, 1825, by James Walton. Olive Dickerson, BM.
Isaac Walton & Elizabeth Mansker, July 26, 1825, by John McMurtry, J.P. Josiah Walton, BM.
Joel Walker & Martha Measles, July 16, 1825. David Higgason, BM.
Robert Weatherred & Martha W. Mann, July 26, 1825. Humphrey Bates, BM.
Thomas Wilkerson & Sarah Soper, Jan. 27, 1825, by John Parker, J.P. John Parker, BM.
John Wilks & Mary A. Townsend, Jan. 17, 1825, by John Wiseman, M.G. Richard Wilks, BM.
Anthony Williams & Sally Harpole, Oct. 22, 1825, by John McMurtry, J.P. Chesley Williams, BM.
James Williams & Anny Brown, May 1, 1825. Hardy Caldwell, BM.
John H. Williams & Polly Dunigan, Dec. 21, 1825, by S. Blythe, J.P. John Bell, BM.
Jesse Willis & Elizabeth Sherlock, July 9, 1826, by Richard Harrison, J.P. John Sharlock, BM.
Matthew T. Will & Mary H. Guthrey, Sep. 10, 1825, by Hugh Kirkpatrick, M.G. Peter Hellartin, BM.
Montition Wilson & Lucy Ann Johnson, Nov. 3, 1825, by Richard Johnson. Jas. R. Wilson, BM.
Willis Winn & Jane Townsend, May 19, 1825. John Townsend, BM.
John Woodall & Judy Kirby, Dec. 1, 1825, by Reubin Searcy, J.P.
Joseph Woodcock & Ready Cleborn, April 1, 1825. Thomas Woodcock, BM.
Alfred R. Wynn & Almira Winchester, March 14, 1825, by John R. Bain. John L. Bugg, BM.
John G. Wynn & Lucretia Hunt, June 27, 1825. James House, BM.
Wm. Yarborough & Margaret King, April 7, 1825. Alexander Mayberry, BM.

William Albright & Asneth Stalcup, Aug. 23, 1826, by Frances Johnson, M.G. John Stalcup, BM.

William Alderson & Tabitha Dinning, Feb. 17, 1826, by Robert Norvell. John Dinning, BM.

William Austin & Frances Mitchell, Nov. 4, 1826, by W. Smith, J.P. Henry Vaughn, BM.

Nathan Barnes & Elizabeth Holliman, Jan. 2, 1826. Ashley Stanfield, BM.

Caleb Barr & Priscilla Miers, July 4, 1826, by Wm. Walton, J.P. Solomon Shoulders, BM.

Edward Blakemore & Sophia J. Murry, Oct. 21, 1826. James Hail, BM.

John Blakemore & Dolly L-(?) Butterworth, Nov. 12, 1826, by Isaac Lindsey, E.M.C. Granville L. Pearce, BM.

John Booker & Lucretia Townsend, Aug. 23, 1826. Wm. A. Lauderdale, BM.

Robert Boyd & Margarete Watkins, April 5, 1826. David Hutchinson, BM.

William Bracken, Jr. & Rachel Harris, May 4, 1826, by W. Smith, J.P.

Robert Bradley & Lurany Osbourn, Jan. 7, 1826. John Graves, BM.

Edmund Brooks & Mary Wright, Oct. 17, 1826, Thomas James, BM.

Pleasant Brooks & Sarah Christmas, Jan. 2, 1826, by Silas Potts, J.P. John Brooks, BM.

John Brown & Sara Foster, Dec. 4, 1826, by Meredith Hodges, J.P. William Dorris, BM.

Richard Brown & Lucinda Landrum, Nov. 15, 1826. Mathew Johnson, BM.

Samuel Brown & Barshaba Evans, Oct. 26, 1826. David Johnson, BM.

Jonathan Browning & Elizabeth Stalcup, Nov. 7, 1826. Clifton G. Browning, BM.

Reuben Bruce & Jemima Brown, Dec. 9, 1826, by Stephen R. Roberts, J.P. Simon Bruce, BM.

Levi Bryant & Nelly Hall, Aug. 15, 1826. Joseph Spradlin, BM.

Dickison Burris & Jane Fraley, Aug. 10, 1826. Daniel Miers, BM.

Elijah Butler & Elizabeth Doss, March 11, 1826, by Samuel David, J.P. Joshua Doss, BM.

Lemuel Byram & Francis Bradford, Jan. 23, 1826. Thomas Joyner, BM.

David Campbell & Mary Ann Iacky, Oct. 4, 1826. Colin Campbell, BM.

John H. D. Carey & Frances Sanders, July 4, 1826. Richard H. P. Carey, BM.

Wilson L. Carr & Jane L. Baskerville, May 8, 1826. James B. Hanner, BM.

Felix Chenault & Nancy Ann Trigg, Nov. 11, 1826. David M. Sanders, BM.

Jacob S. Claspill & Rebecca Hays, Nov. 13, 1826. Jo. C. Guild, BM.

John H. Coats & Harriett S. A. Duncan, Feb. 27, 1826. Richard P. Hall, BM.

Thomas Coleman & Eliza D. Cage, Oct. 19, 1826. G. N. Douglas, BM.

Isaac Collier & Jane Bowman, Dec. 27, 1826, by James Charlton, J.P. Daniel Escue, BM.

William B. Connell & Ollivia Walton, April 19, 1826, by Hugh Kirkpatrick, M.G. George Million, BM.

Lewis Conner & Nancy Preston, Jan. 4, 1826. Robert Crocket, BM.

Martin Cowgill & Sally Perry, Nov. 19, 1826. Zach W. Baker, BM.

Hezekiah Crafton & Sally Massey, Aug. 15, 1826, by Silas Polk.

Edward Crews & Sally Bently, Dec. 20, 1826. James Anglea, BM.

SUMNER COUNTY MARRIAGES

Peter Davis & Polly Crafton, Aug. 13, 1826, by Silas Potts, J.P.
Thomas Davis, BM.
Joseph Dearman & Mary Mansker, April 15, 1826, by Ed. Edward. Wil-
liam Shaw, BM.
William L. Denney & Susan Wise, July 8, 1826. James Biggs, BM.
Joseph A. Dew & Elizabeth M. Green, Feb. 2, 1826, by Thomas Joyner.
John H. Dew, BM.
James B. Dews & Sally Blair, Feb. 9, 1826. Francis E. Garrett, BM.
Thomas C. Dobbins & Ann Beard, Oct. 18, 1826, by Robert Guthrie.
John Dobbins, BM.
Noah Donoho & Polly Williams, Aug. 8, 1826. Robert Guthrie, M.G.
Jacob Parks, BM.
Levi A. Dorris & Mary Campbell, Nov. 16, 1826. Jehosephat Campbell,
BM.
George Douglas & Polly White, Dec. 28, 1826, by C. Cram. M. C.
Abston, BM.
Norval Douglas & Priscilla Cage, Jan. 31, 1826. John F. Fulton, BM.
George I. Erwin & Milley H. Duncan, Dec. 26, 1826, by P. C. Wills,
J.P. James Mills, BM.
Mathew Erwin & Irena Stephens, Jan. 10, 1826, by John Wiseman, M.G.
Jas. Robb, BM. Elim A. A. Erwin.
Samuel Esken & Nancy W. T. Watts, May 20, 1826. James C. Shaver,
BM.
Thomas Essex & Mildred Bledsoe, Oct. 3, 1826. John F. Shabel, BM.
Alexander Garrison & Nancy Phenix, Feb. 7, 1826, by Silas Polk,
J.P. Henry Harmon, BM.
John Gibson & Polly Tomlinson, June 2, 1826. Craddock H. May, BM.
Milton Giles & Sally M. Hamilton, Dec. 15, 1826, by Thos. Anderson,
J.P. Franklin Hamilton, BM.
William H. Giles & Sidney Stone, Sep. 25, 1826, by Stephen R.
Roberts, J.P. Wm. F. Anderson, BM.
Charles Golston & Catharine Rule, Jan. 7, 1826. William Peyton, BM.
Joseph C. Guild & Catharin Blakemore, Dec. 19, 1826. Balie Peyton,
BM.
Joseph Guthery & Mary McNeely, Sep. 18, 1826. Andrew Martin, BM.
Thomas Guthrey & Nancy Hunt, Feb. 9, 1826, by C. Green. B. Babb,
BM.
Thomas W. Gwin & Mary Winburn, Oct. 12, 1826. Samuel Gwin, BM.
Richard T. Hall & Cinthia Dalton, Feb. 6, 1826. Richard P. Hall,
BM.
Thomas Hamilton & Polly Blair, July 17, 1826. John Summers, BM.
Henry Pearson.
Wm. Hannah & Nancy Jones, Oct. 2, 1826, by Luke P. Allen. James
Hannah, BM.
Jesse Harper & Sally Gregory, Aug. 24, 1826. John Gregory, BM.
Joel Harper & Permelia Vinly, Feb. 25, 1826. Elisha Carr, BM.
Pascal Head & Providence Philips, April 20, 1826, by John Wiseman.
Volney Stamps, BM.
William Henderson & Mary Dodd, Nov. 4, 1826, by Stephen R. Roberts,
J.P. Moses Lomax, BM.
William Henson & Susan Baynes, April 11, 1826, by J. Davis, J.P.
Jonathan Davis, BM. William Culwell.
John Holms & Nancy Williams, June 16, 1826. William Cooley, BM.

SUMNER COUNTY MARRIAGES

Bradley (Bradlet) Honeycutt & Celia Williams, July 15, 1826. Joel
 Yates, BM.
Hiram Hounshell (Houdshell) & Polly Gibson, May 31, 1826, by Samuel
 Davis, J.P. James Edison, BM.
Ambrose Houser & Pheobe Rimmer, Jan. 10, 1826, by John McMurtry,
 J.P. Benjamine Rimmer, BM.
James Hudson & Felisa Wallace, Sep. 13, 1826, by William Walton,
 J.P. Samuel Wallace, BM.
James Hunt & Fanny H. Hawkins, Sep. 17, 1826. Seaton Duffer, BM.
Reuben Johnston & Rosy Ann Fishback, Oct. 3, 1826, by Silas Polk,
 J.P. Peter Martin & J. Moore, BM.
Hugh Joiner & Minerva Smith, Nov. 21, 1826. William Smith, BM.
John Joiner & Peggy Dunagin, Jan. 14, 1826. Isaac Douglas, BM.
Robert Joiner & Polly Hargrove, Aug. 7, 1826. Absalom Joiner, BM.
Samuel Jopes & Mary Ann Cain, March 11, 1826. William Lee, BM.
Joseph Key & Sally Durham, March 28, 1826, by Jonathan David, J.P.
 John Blair, BM.
Macklin Key & Susan Rippy, April 15, 1826, by Francis Johnston, M.G.
 William Key, BM.
Peterson Key & Polly Rippy, May 27, 1826. Hiram Duncan, BM.
William King & Jane Phelps, Nov. 13, 1826, by Demcy Ashford, J.P.
 Demcy Ashford, BM.
Alfred Kirkpatrick & Elizabeth Patton, June 1, 1826. William
 Patton, BM.
Archibald F. Kirkpatrick & Betsey Brown, March 16, 1826, by W.
 Smith, J.P. Jeremiah Dugger, BM.
Jese Lassiter & Raney Brown, July 17, 1826, by Isaac Lindsay. Sol-
 omon H. Volentine, BM.
William Lawhorn & Ann Busby, Nov. 4, 1826, by Josiah Walton, J.P.
 L. B. Edward, BM.
Marmaduke Lay & Martha Watkins, Dec. 5, 1826. Philip Watkins, BM.
John Leddy & Mary Ann Armstrong, Oct. 23, 1826, by Charles Watkins,
 J.P. B. Watkins, BM.
Lewis Malone & Martha Beard, April 29, 1826, by Francis Johnson,
 J.P. Henry Beard, BM.
Solomon Maddock & Hannah Morris, Feb. 14, 1826, by Sam'l Davis, J.P.
 Jesse Tuttle, BM.
Armstead Marcum & Polly Corder, May 25, 1826. William N. Bain, BM.
John Martin & Nancy Blar (Balir), Aug. 14, 1826. William Shaw, BM.
Balie May & Magdalene Wallace, Feb. 23, 1826, by Tho. Anderson, J.P.
 Wm. H. Anderson, BM.
Joseph G. Meador & Malinda Brackin, July 3, 1826, by Robert Norvell.
 Moses Henry, BM.
Valentine Meadows & Susan Brown, March 15, 1826. Jeremiah Sarver,
 BM.
Michael Miller & Elizabeth Biddle, June 17, 1826. Wiley Vinson, BM.
Robert S. Mills & Susannah Goodrum, Aug. 14, 1826. George Stovall,
 BM.
John Minnick & Patey King, March 9, 1826, by Jonathan David, J.P.
Isham L. Moore & Catharine Gwin, Aug. 2, 1826. Hardy M. Cryer, BM.
William M. Nuner & Bediah Rogers, March 29, 1826. Armstead Rogers,
 BM.
Alfred Peatey & Loving Meggs, Oct. 25, 1826. Stephen Weatherford,
 BM. Jesse Thomas.

SUMNER COUNTY MARRIAGES

James Phillips & Elizabeth Stewart, March 3, 1826. S. M. Turner,
J.P. James Stewart, BM.
Aron Piles & Jailey Parker, Nov. 9, 1826, by John T. Carr, J.P.
Geo. Erwin, BM.
Elijah Pond & Nancy Scruggs, Aug. 23, 1826, by J. P. Hogan, J.P.
William Smith, BM. Henry Rice.
William Prince & Eliza Howell, Dec. 19, 1826. Wm. Edwards, BM.
William Ramsey & Diana Austin, April 30, 1826. John R. Dickason,
BM.
James Rigsby & Packy M. Brooks, May 5, 1826. Thomas Brooks, BM.
Eli Rippey & Maria Murrell, Nov. 4, 1826, by Meredith Hodges, J.P.
John M. Foster, BM.
Stephen R. Roberts & Elizabeth Jackson, April 13, 1826, by John
R. Bain, Lucilius Winchester, BM.
Edmund Rucker & Louisa Winchester, Oct. 25, 1826. J. W. Baldridge,
BM.
John Rule & Ann Gilpin, April 5, 1826. William Peyton, BM.
Alfred Ruyle & Sally Blackston, Jan. 23, 1826, by J. P. Hogan, J.P.
Moses Ruyle, BM.
Casten Sarver & Polly Fraly, Dec. 14, 1826, by Samuel Davis, J.P.
Robert Scott & Spicey Tinsley, Feb. 23, 1826. David Wilson, BM.
James Shaver & Eliza Giles, Dec. 12, 1826. Stephen H. Roberts, J.P.
Winston S. McDaniel, BM.
Alfred Shoulders & Polly Ann Bledsoe, Nov. 8, 1826. John M. Hen-
ley, BM.
Benjamine T. (F) Simpson & Eliza O. Tarver, Aug. 3, 1826, by Alex
D. Duval, J.P. Alex D. Duval, BM.
George H. Smith & Eliza B. Turner, May 19, 1826. R. A. Romkins
(Tomkins), BM.
Joseph Smothers & Polly Wigington, Aug. 1, 1826. David Ingram, BM.
William Smothers & Nelley Smothers, Oct. 22, 1826. Eli Smothers,
BM.
Thomas Spears & Elizabeth Dalton, Dec. 17, 1826. Charles Simmons,
BM.
Jesse Spiller & Jane Bandy, Sep. 26, 1826. Perrin Bandy, BM.
Elijah Stalcup & Elizabeth Allbright, April 22, 1826. William All-
bright, BM.
John Stalcup & Martha Stalcup, Sep. 1, 1826. Alexander Stalcup,
BM.
Eli Staly & Angelina Stamps, Feb. 13, 1826.
John M. Staley & Derinda H. Gibson, Aug. 1, 1826. Geo. W. Blake-
more, BM.
Jonathan Standley & Sally Jinnings (Jennings), Nov. 27, 1826.
David Standley, BM.
Greenville P. Stone & Tabitha Caviness, June 17, 1826. Wesley
Blakemore, BM.
James N. Swaney & Elizabeth Wigginton, Sep. 3, 1826. Samuel Boy-
kin, BM.
Hardy S. Sypert & Ann C. Donelson, Jan. 5, 1826. John H. Dew, BM.
Archibald Thomas & Edith H. White, July 28, 1826. Peter M. White,
BM.
Daniel L. Thomas & Martha Jones, Jan. 23, 1826, by C. Crain. Wil-
liam Jones, BM.
Henry Towell & Martha Joyner, May 3, 1826. Benjamine Taylor, BM.

Darham Tracy & Eadey Allsup, Feb. 19, 1826. John Bradley, BM.
John Taylor & Sally Allen, Nov. 20, 1826. William Stone, BM.
John Walton & Charity Perry, Jan. 19, 1826.
Baryholomur Watkins & Margaret Rawlings, Aug. 8, 1826. Wm. Edward, BM.
Stephen F. Weatherford & Bricey Moodey, Aug. 5, 1826.
Elijah Williams & Elizabeth Martin, May 8, 1826. Andrew S. Dickey, BM.
Green B. Williams & Martha Phipps, June 6, 1826, by Elijah Boddie, J.P. George Elliott, BM.
William Williams & Elizabeth Henderson, Sep. 27, 1826. Robert Holmes, BM.
William Williams & Elizabeth C. Bennett, Jan. 2, 1826. Josiah W. Baldrudge, BM.
Addison Wilson & Ann Moore, Aug. 2, 1826, by James Wallace, J.P. Samuel Wilson, BM.
John Wilson & Margaret Strode, April 22, 1826. Granville R. Morris, BM.
Pleasant Wilson & Sarah Stone, Dec. 26, 1826. Richard A. Tomkins, BM.
Francis Wood & Lucy Milton, July 3, 1826. Jacob Reynolds, BM.
Gideon Wood & Betsey Gibson, Aug. 4, 1826. Jacob Gregory, BM.
Thomas Woodcock & Polly Cliborn, Aug. 17, 1826.
Berry Wynne & Catherine Weathered, Sep. 6, 1826. Walter B. Morris, BM.
George Abbott & Frances Watson, July 25, 1827, by P. C. Mills, J.P.
John Alderson & Polly Hodges, Sep. 26, 1827. Greed Hodges, BM.
Hugh Alexander & Adaline Orr, Dec. 18, 1827. Samuel Brown, BM.
Fling Anderson & Mary May, July 30, 1827. William Parker, BM.
Sampson Anderson & Elizabeth Hinton, July 23, 1827. Albert G. Holmes, BM.
George Anthony & Nancy Borrin, July 25, 1827, by Wm. Hobdy, J.P. Francis Borrin, BM.
Dickinson Austin & Sally Hall, Dec. 24, 1827, by Reuben Searcy, J.P. Thomas Potts, Jr., BM.
Edward Bandy & Evaline Harper, Sep. 11, 1827. James Cain, BM.
Patton Bell & Jane Gilbert, April 28, 1827, by Wm. Hobdy, J.P. Jacob Brown, BM.
Daniel Benbrook & Margaret Boyer, Dec. 18, 1827. A. F. Young, BM.
Richard Boyles & Any Center, May 27, 1827. Michael Tracey, BM.
Cyrus W. Brevard & Pollyanna Mills, Jan. 22, 1827. Horace Lawson, BM.
Richard C. Brizendine & Frances Ashford, July 26, 1827. Young P. Brizendine, BM.
John Brooks & Nancy Brizindine, Dec. 1, 1827, by Robert Norvell. J. B. Brizendine, BM.
Abel Broughton & Eleanor Soaper, Dec. 20, 1827, by William Barr, J.P. James Gwin, BM.
John Brown & Fanny Simons, Jan. 4, 1827. Edw. Stratton, BM.
James G. Browning & Polly Ann Neale, Nov. 20, 1827. Jno. Dobbins, BM.
Lewis Burke & Elizabeth Letzinger, June 8, 1827. Green L. White, BM.
Dickson Burris & Jane Fraley, Aug. 10, 1827, by Jonathan Davis, J.P.

John Busby & Polly Barrett, Jan. 1, 1827. Arioch Thomas, BM.
Larkin Carmon & Elizabeth Cochran, Aug. 16, 1827. James Cochran,
    BM.
Robert Caruthers & Sally Saunders, Jan. 15, 1827. Baily Payton, BM.
James C. Carr & Harriett Belote, Sep. 25, 1827, by John Parker, L.D.
    Lucilius Winchester, BM.
John Casney & Nancy Summers, March 27, 1827. Ed. Edwards.
Green H. Cato & Rhody Alley, July 1, 1827, by Samuel Gwin, J.P.
Benjamine Chapman & Rebecca Bull, Aug. 6, 1827. Joseph McReynolds,
    BM.
Michael Cline & Nancy Rippy, Feb. 27, 1827. John Rippy, BM.
Bownden H. Coleman & Patsey Hall, March 13, 1827. James Coleman,
    BM.
Dempsey Cook & Polly Watkins, Nov. 12, 1827. Phillip Watkins, BM.
Martin Congill & Sally Perry, Nov. 19, 1827, by Wm. Walton, J.P.
Richard Cornelius & Betsey Reynolds, April 28, 1827. John Crump-
    ler, BM.
Washington Covention (Coventon) & Eliza Hughes, Sep. 19, 1827.
William Covington & Sarah Hunter, March 13, 1827. Demcy Ashford,
    J.P.
Eppa Cunningham & Caroline Lassiter, Nov. 10, 1827. Robert Patton.
Wyatt Dalton & Matilda Rowling, Feb. 13, 1827. Francis Duffy, BM.
Isaac Day & Elizabeth Scott, Dec. 17, 1827. Francis Day, BM.
Martin Douglas & Margaret Warren, Nov. 25, 1827. John Douglas, BM.
Ballard Downs & Polly Joiner, July 18, 1827, by C. Crain. Wm.
    Towpence, BM.
Nicholas L. Drumheln & Eliza Hollis, April 7, 1827. James Hollis,
    BM.
Abner Dunn & Polly _____, Nov. 16, 1827. Benj. Wilson, BM.
    Josiah Henson.
Seaborn Edwards & Sally Hodges, June 9, 1827. Ransom Hodges, BM.
John H. Foster & Maranda Martin, Sep. 17, 1827. A. W. Wormington,
    BM.
James Frudle & Susan Boyles, Nov. 27, 1827. John Bell, BM.
Benjamine Fowler & Marguritt Williams, June 11, 1827, by Robert
    Patton. Richard Harrison, BM.
Marcus L. B. Gibson & Matilda Osbourn, Dec. 14, 1827, by Meredith
    Hodges, J.P. Jeremiah Sarver, BM.
Robert K. Gillespie & Adaline Cage, April 12, 1827. Wm. Cantrell,
    BM.
Stephen R. Gilliam & Nancy Duffer, April 22, 1827. Setan Duffer
    (Seton), BM.
Robert Grainger & Martha McDole, May 21, 1827. William Lovell, BM.
Thomas Gregory & Mary Markham, March 25, 1827, by Stephen R.
    Roberts, J.P.
James Gwin & Polly Harper, April 26, 1827. Able Broughton, BM.
William Hale & Hannah Clark, March 18, 1827, by John F. Carr, J.P.
    James Carr, BM.
Gilbert Harding & Adah Stark, July 12, 1827, by Isaac Lindsey, M.G.
    Thomas Stark, BM.
Hugh N. Harris & Celia Bowman, Jan. 10, 1827, by James Charlton,
    J.P. Robert Chapp, BM.
John Harper & Jane Gardner, April 4, 1827, by John F. Carr, J.P.
    Simon Millar, BM.

SUMNER COUNTY MARRIAGES

John M. Henley & Mary Ann Turner, Oct. 18, 1827, by Wm. Walton,
  J.P. John H. Lewis, BM.
William D. Higgason & Milly Turner, Jan. 1, 1827. Samuel Higgason,
  BM.
Urish How & Mary Blair, Dec. 22, 1827, by C. Crain. William Jones,
  BM.
Thomas Howell & Ann Phipps, March 10, 1827. William Prince, BM.
W. C. Huffman & Lucy Ann Goodall, Aug. 30, 1827, by John Wiseman,
  M.G. S. H. Lauderdale, BM.
Clavin Hunter & Susanna Mayes, Nov. 30, 1827, by Demcey Ashford,
  J.P. John Hunter, BM.
Isaac Hunter & Elizabeth Cook, Nov. 3, 1827. Pollard W. McCarty,
  BM. Thos. Cook.
Willis Hunter & Mary Yarborough, Dec. 10, 1827, by D. Ashford, J.P.
  John Hunter, BM.
Mathew Ing & Sarah Summers, Jan. 29, 1827, by Ed. Edwards. William
  Jackson, BM.
Benjamin Israel & Edy Jacobs, June 26, 1827. David Ingram, BM.
Francis Jackson & Martha Crenshaw, Nov. 8, 1827. Jacob Reese, BM.
John Jackson & Delia Lovell, Oct. 24, 1827. John Stalcup, BM.
William Jackson & Charlotte Griffin, Feb. 17, 1827, by Josiah Wal-
  ton, J.P. Joseph Ing, BM.
Charles Johnson & Catharine White, Nov. 21, 1827, by John R. Bain.
  Charles Jackson, BM.
John Johnson & Malinda Roney, Feb. 10, 1827. Wm. K. Smith, BM.
Faountain P. Jones & Lucretia M. Wynne, Dec. 3, 1827, by J. B.
  Wynns. David W. Parrish, BM.
Willie E. Jones & Elizabeth H. Butterworth, Jan. 23, 1827, by Isaac
  Lindsey, E.M. Moses C. Preston, BM.
Charles Keys & Elizabeth Draper, Sep. 19, 1827, by John T. Carr,
  J.P. Marshall B. Duncan, BM.
Anderson Kirkpatrick & Eliza Moss, June 27, 1827, by Thos. Ander-
  son. James Vinson, BM.
William Lambert & Rebecca Nanny, Aug. 17, 1827. James Nanny, BM.
John Larrell & Susannah Jackson, Aug. 14, 1827.
William Lassiter & Susan Joiner, Oct. 17, 1827, by Robert Patton.
  James Crossley, BM.
John Marlin & Margaret Griffin, Dec. 19, 1827, by Josiah Walton,
  J.P. John Jackson, BM.
Frederick Martin & Rebekah Smith, Jan. 25, 1827, by Silas Polk, J.P.
Daniel McAllister & Loucissa Moore, March 21, 1827, by James
  Wallace, J.P. Samuel Wilson, BM.
Pollard W. McCarty & Esther Stephens, Nov. 3, 1827, by William
  Hobdy, J.P. Isaac Hunter, BM. Thomas Cook.
James McGowen & Mary Cartwright, May 23, 1827. William McCall, BM.
Jacob McLain & Hannah Boykin, July 22, 1827, by B. P. C. Mills,
  J.P.
John McMane & Nancy Charlton, March 27, 1827. Charles Jackson, BM.
Leonard McReynolds & Elizabeth Lambert, April 20, 1827. David
  Lamberth, BM.
Robert Michel & Miley Woodall, Jan. 18, 1827. John Henry, BM.
James Miller & Matilda Tyomas, Jan. 30, 1827. John Carr, BM.
Spencer Moody & Susan Hendrix, Oct. 10, 1827. Cyrus Lovell, BM.
  John Moody.

Abraham W. Mornington & Patsey Turpin, Feb. 26, 1827. David Ingram, BM.

John Murphy & Polly Hall, April 14, 1827. Jacob Strather, BM.

John Norvell & Susan Jackson, Aug. 14, 1827. J. W. Gilliam, BM.

Elisha Oglesby & Ann Allen, Jan. 3, 1827. Robert Pursley, BM.

Benjamine Pearce & America C. Stovall, Dec. 28, 1827.

Gideon Pitt & Roxanna Furgason, April 28, 1827. Solomon Shoulders, BM.

Fountain E. Pitt & Martha Britt, Aug. 14, 1827. Henry Sarver, BM.

David M. Porter & Eliza Buckner, April 30, 1827. William M. Swain, BM.

Joseph Potts & Malinda Roney, Jan. 9, 1827. Willis Wilkins, BM.

Benjamine Rainey & Catharin Towell, Oct. 30, 1827. Samuel Towell, BM.

Joseph Randle & Rebecca Colquit, Aug. 16, 1827. Wade David, BM.

Joseph Rice & Malissa Ambrose, Jan. 22, 1827. B. L. Rutherford, BM.

William Rice & Centhia Cotton, Oct. 31, 1827. Jesse Gambling, BM.

John Richmond & Sally Mandrill, Oct. 29, 1827. Solomon Mandrill, BM.

Josiah Rippy & Margaret Bell, July 21, 1827. William Rippy, BM.

Green B. Sanders & Mildred B. Tinsley, March 21, 1827. James Harrison, BM.

Caston Sarver & Polly Fraley, Feb. 15, 1827. John Snow, BM.

Willie W. Scruggs & Harriette Scruggs, Nov. 10, 1827. David Saunders, BM.

Samuel Senter & Nancy Crenshaw, May 7, 1827, by Richard Johnson. Benjamine Crews, BM.

Harvy Shannon & Mary Gibb, Jan. 15, 1827, by Lewis Parker. Samuel Towell, BM.

Solomon Simmons & Josiah Henson (?), Oct. 25, 1827. Sam'l David, Jr., BM.

Charles E. Smith & Frances B. Whitted, Aug. 7, 1827, by C. L. Jefferies, BM.

James Smith & Margaret Troutt, Jan. 11, 1827. Joseph Carter, BM.

William W. Smith & Elizabeth M. McMurry, Oct. 9, 1827, by John R. Barn. William H. Bowman, BM.

Andrew Smothers & Polly Summers, Aug. 13, 1827. John Summers, BM.

Edward Spurrier & Janthe Cuffman, Oct. 31, 1827. Robert Montgomery, BM.

John Stanly & Sally Lomux, Dec. 27, 1827. Moses Lomux, BM.

Noah Summers & Polly Bryly, Aug. 13, 1827. Robert Guthrie, M.G. Thomaas Summers, BM.

Augustus N. Tally & Polly McClain, Jan. 27, 1827, by S. L. Blythe, J.P. Ezekiel Gwin, BM.

John A. Todd & Rachel Shepley, Nov. 5, 1827. Wade Davis, BM.

William Trousdale & Mary Ann Bugg, Jan. 30, 1827. H. H. Douglass, BM.

Henry Trout & Polly Robinson, March 20, 1827. George Troutt, BM.

Jacob Troutt & Suesy Clay, Feb. 13, 1827, by Jonathan Davis, J.P.

Matthew Turner & Tabitha Richardson, April 14, 1827. Richard Allen, BM.

Terrisha Turner & Priscilla Parish, Aug. 20, 1827. Robert Bell, BM.

William Twopence & Julia Early (alias Julia Holcum), Jan. 6, 1827.
David Twopence, BM.
Jordan Taylor & Patsy Busby, Jan. 4, 1827. Stephen Taylor, BM.
William Watson & Catherine Vane, Dec. 18, 1827, by B. P. C. Mills,
J.P.
James Weathers & Patsy Yarborough, Jan. 30, 1827. Jacob Taylor,
BM.
William Wilson & Margaret Null, Nov. 13, 1827. Addison Wilson, BM.
John W. Williams & Polly Moss, Oct. 31, 1827, by Luke P. Allen.
Thomas Williams, BM.
Lewis Williams & Eliza Buckly, May 21, 1827. Wesley Blakemore, BM.
William J. Winn & Tabitha Wilks, Aug. 2, 1827. Richard Wilks, BM.
Benjamine H. Young & Milly Took, June 9, 1827. John A. McKendree,
BM.
Benjamine Adams & Polly Lacy, Nov. 10, 1828. Reuben Searcy, J.P.
William Adkinson & Malinda Parker, Nov. 27, 1828. M. Short, BM.
David Allen & Susannah Emory, Dec. 22, 1828, by Elijah Boddie, J.P.
Daniel Arnold & Dicey Draper, Sep. 24, 1828, by V. Swaney. George
W. Lance, BM.
Joseph Aust & Rebecca Williams, May 8, 1828, by Archd. D. Duval.
Frederick Aust, BM.
Samuel M. Banks & Ann R. McCarty, Nov. 29, 1828, by S. R. Roberts,
J.P.
Zachariah Barns & Elizabeth Jops (or Tops), June 14, 1828. Nicho-
las Drumbhelln.
Henry Beason & Sally Ross, Sep. 8, 1828. David Beason, BM.
Elbert Benbrook & Polly Chapman, April 22, 1828, by Robert Norvell.
James Alderson, BM.
David Beson & Polly Short, Oct. 16, 1828. Wm. Clendenning, BM.
James Biggs & Martha Cohorn, March 22, 1828. William Franklin, BM.
Thomas E. Blake & Amanda Bridgewater, Dec. 1, 1828. Wm. Turner,
BM.
William Black & Nancy Clay, July 24, 1828. Jacob Nunaly, BM.
David Bledsoe & Elizabeth Charlton, June 19, 1828.
James B. Bradley & Catharine McAden, Feb. 5, 1828. Henry Strange,
BM.
Joseph Brannon & Elizabeth Lomax, July 9, 1828, by S. R. Robus,
J.P. Thos. Jourdan, BM.
John C. Brevard & Mary H. Bilbo, Oct. 17, 1828, by Thos. Joyner.
C. Hart, BM.
Young P. Brizendine & Amy Woodall, Sep. 24, 1828. Wm. Woodall, BM.
William Brown & Fanny Hodges, March 29, 1828. Holly Hodges, BM.
Greenberry Bush & Rebecca Dorris, Sep. 8, 1828. Lewis Dorris, BM.
Tenny Bush & Hollen Nest, Oct. 17, 1828, by Wm. Montgomery.
Phillip Butt & Jincy Sadler, Nov. 3, 1828. Samuel Butt, BM.
David Caldwell & Elizabeth P. Stanfield, Feb. 2, 1828. Josiah
Stanfield, BM.
Robert Chappell & Elizabeth Brown, Feb. 25, 1828. S. R. Roberts,
J.P. Baker Walsh, BM.
Claibourne Cavitt & Nancy Cornelius, April 7, 1828, by Scaton
Turner, J.P. James Briley, BM.
William Coley & Rosey Perry, June 2, 1828. Benjamine Brews, BM.
James Cook & Mary Duvall, Jan. 2, 1828. Sam'l Gwin, J.P.

Joseph Corbett & Agnus Biggers, Dec. 30, 1828, by F. E. Pitts. Mason Carr, BM.

James L. Corder & Elizabeth Trout, March 15, 1828. Samuel Trout, BM.

Willis Crews & Nancy Thurmond, Sep. 2, 1828.

John Covington & Polly Crews, March 29, 1828, by Josiah Walton, J.P. Joseph Bloodworth, BM.

Samuel Day & Arena Day, Oct. 22, 1828. John Rawlings, BM.

Thomas Day & Elizabeth Thomas, Sep. 30, 1828. Stephen Norton, BM.

Michael Derryberry & Mariah McCormack, Feb. 5, 1828, by Josiah Walton, J.P. Josiah Walton, BM.

John R. Dickenson & Elizabeth D. Brown, Nov. 17, 1828, by Richd. Johnsn.

Waller W. Dickinson & Mildred Dickinson, Jan. 9, 1828. Robert Dickenson, BM.

Bowles Dinning & Mahala Kirby, Aug. 11, 1828, by Sam Thackson, J.P.

Harry C. Douglass & Elizabeth Elliott, Dec. 18, 1828, by F. E. Pitts. Edw. Stratton, BM.

Jesse Dorris & Polly Freeland, Aug. 14, 1828, by M. Hodges, J.P. Abraham Brodley, BM.

Lewis Dorris & Mary Bush, Sep. 22, 1828, by Wm. Montgomery.

James Doughty & Elizabeth Brown, March 11, 1828, by Robert Norvell. John Alderson, BM.

William Duncan & Eliza Potts, Feb. 12, 1828.

John D. Dunn & Mary Jane Gilliam, June 12, 1828, by Jonathan Davis, J.P.

Henry Easly & Edy Caldwell, Aug. 25, 1828. James Butler, BM.

Willie Eastas & Nancy McReynolds, May 20, 1828. James Wilson, BM.

Josiah Elam & Elizabeth Catron, Feb. 11, 1828. A. H. Guthrie, BM.

Daniel Fraley & Polly Dillon, March 25, 1828. Jonathan Davis, BM.

John W. Franklin & Mary Yancey, Oct. 17, 1828, by Richard Johnson.

Eli Frost & Katherine Varvel (Norvell), April 19, 1828.

John Ganter & Elizabeth Boyer, March 3, 1828. A. G. Donoho, BM.

John George & Elizabeth Raney, Sep. 2, 1828, by John M. Hall. J. J. White, BM.

George Gillespie & Sarah Day, March 22, 1828. Alfred Shoulders, BM.

Michael Graves & Rachel Richmond, July 17, 1828. William Black, BM.

James M. Gunn & Nancy Wilks, Dec. 13, 1828, by Richard Johnson.

Middleton Hall & Mahala Hall, May 24, 1828. Mitchell Bryant, BM.

Riden R. Hall & Sarah Hefner, Jan. 22, 1828, by Robert Norvell. Jeremiah Sarver, BM.

James Harris & Susan Glen, Sep. __, 1828, by Samuel Cochran, J.P.

James Haw & Sarah Dunagin, Dec. 29, 1828, by Isaac Lindsay.

Jonathan L. Haynes & Mary L. Wood, Sep. 1, 1828, by Stephen R. Roberts, J.P. Henry A. Belote, BM.

Thomas Horton & Casy Jones, Feb. 18, 1828. W. L. Perry, BM.

Pitt M. House & Sally Cape (or Cope), Oct. 6, 1828. Samuel Roney, BM.

Dudley Howell & Cintha Jones, April 4, 1828. Jonathan Jones, BM.

Thomas W. Hughs & Elizabeth Taylor, Nov. 11, 1828, by Richard Johnson.

Henry Hunt & Jannet Slater, Nov. 13, 1828. C. L. Jefferies, BM.

Layton Hunter & Elizabeth Robison, Sep. 29, 1828. John Leek, BM.
Timothy Ingram & Nancy Dorris, Aug. 4, 1828, by John McMurtry, J.P.
    David Ingram, BM.
James Johnson & Sally Bruce, Jan. 12, 1828, by Isaac Reed.
Henry Jones & Elizabeth Hawkins, July 10, 1828. Isaac Meador, BM.
Walker Jones & Polly Stone, Jan. 9, 1828, by John Banks, J.P.
    Anderson Stone, BM.
Mastin Keen & Amanda Jackson, Aug. 27, 1828. John Jackson, BM.
Hugh Kirkpatrick & Pelina Liggett, Dec. 6, 1828, by Josiah Walton.
    William Kirkpatrick, BM.
William Little & Sally Scott, March 28, 1828, by John Banks, J.P.
    Sanford Fitz, BM.
Moses Loman & Marua Eliza Dickinson, Sep. 16, 1828. Samuel Carney,
    BM.
Evans Maberry & Sally Trigg, March 26, 1828. Y.N. Douglass, BM.
Daniel Malone & Margaret Brown, March 28, 1828, by W. C. Mills, J.P.
John Malone & Elizabeth H. Hanna, Dec. 13, 1828.
Thomas F. Malone & Polly Bozeman, Dec. 23, 1828, by Elijah Boddie,
    J.P.
William Marcus & Charlotte Armstrong, Jan. 9, 1828, by Josiah Wal-
    ton, J.P. L. B. Edwards, BM.
John Martin & Lovy Mitchell, April 12, 1828. Turner Vaughn, BM.
Major May & Jane Lee, March 31, 1828. Daniel Ascue, BM.
William May, Jr. & Nancy Lee, Sep. 11, 1828. James Vinson, BM.
Stanford A. McAdams & Sabine Welch, July 27, 1828, by Alexander D.
    Duval, J.P.
George McGuire & Ann H. Barr, May 28, 1828, by W. C. P. Mills, J.P.
Fountain McDaniel & Susan A. Graham, Sep. 27, 1828, by S. R. Ro-
    berts, J.P.
Joseph A. McReynolds & Elizabeth Bloodworth, Jan. 27, 1828, by Thos.
    Anderson, J.P.
Annanias Meador & Sarah Law, Dec. 30, 1828, by Samuel Davis, J.P.
    Patrick Zarry, BM.
John Moody & Judith Railey, Oct. 2, 1828. John Woodall, BM.
George Newman & Nancy Carey, Jan. 31, 1828, by John Banks, J.P.
    John Ward, BM.
Henry Peairs & Judith Kennedy, Oct. 21, 1828. Thomas Kirkham, BM.
Moses Peden & Mahaly Mays, March 26, 1828, by Robert Norvell.
    Pleasant Mays, BM.
Vineyard Pound & Nancy Anderson, March 3, 1828.
John Peteet & Nancy Anderson, March 27, 1828. John Carney, BM.
Joshua Pyle & Mary Parker, March 6, 1828, by C. L. Jeffries.
    Samuel Jopes, BM.
Bevely G. Reed & Elizabeth Wood, May 27, 1828, by John Banks, J.P.
    Robert Robinson, BM.
John Roney & Armand Crafton, Oct. 24, 1828, by A. D. Duvall, J.P.
    A. W. Reese, BM.
Thomas Ross & Martha Bandy, March 4, 1828. Robert Ross, BM.
Albert G. Rule & Elizabeth Blackstone, Jan. 22, 1828.
Benjamine Sadler & Amy Butt, Dec. 9, 1828. Samuel Butt, BM.
David M. Sanders & Jane Dwyer, June 10, 1828.
John B. Scruggs & Nicy Shaver, March 31, 1828. A. G. Blackemore,
    BM.

SUMNER COUNTY MARRIAGES

Albert Shelby & Martha Lewis, April 1, 1828, by C. L. Jefferies.
John R. Desha, BM.
John Spain & Lucinda Gregory, Jan. 18, 1828. James H. Parham, BM.
Theodore B. Stealy & Nancy D. Brown, Sep. 8, 1828, by Stephen R.
Roberts, J.P.
James Stewart & Clarissa Mitchner (Mitchenor), Oct. 28, 1828.
John M. Hanley, BM.
Lyman J. Strong & Martha H. Green, Sep. 8, 1828. Z. Green, BM.
Andrew F. P. Taylor & Clowe Branson, Feb. 15, 1828. Leroy P.
Adams, BM.
B. W. Thompson & Elizabeth Parker, Nov. 3, 1828. J. R. A. Tomkins,
BM.
William Thrower & Fanny H. Head, Dec. 23, 1828, by L. R. Roberts,
J.P. William Thrower, BM.
Samuel Trout & Nancy Black, Oct. 23, 1828. William Rippy, BM.
Joseph W. H. Townsend & Tervesa Booker, Dec. 15, 1828. Geo. L.
Booker, BM.
William Tucker & Ann T. Rickman, Jan. 2, 1828. Robert Seawell, BM.
Elihu Henry.
Burell Vaden & Lucindy Parker, Oct. 21, 1828, by John F. Carr, J.P.
John P. Erwin, BM.
John Walton & Charity Perry, Jan. 19, 1828. Thomas Perry, BM.
John Ward & Nancy W. Cardwell, May 15, 1828. John W. Franklin, BM.
Robert West & Margaret Towell, Sep. 8, 1828. Isaac Towell, BM.
Albert Westbrooks & Mary Ann Lefler, Sep. 19, 1828, by _____
Youree, J.P. David Lefler, BM.
Henry Williams & Mariah Thompson, Dec. 24, 1828, by John McMurtry.
Thomas H. Frazer, BM.
Robert Wilson & Louisa Null, Dec. 3, 1828, by James Charlton, J.P.
William Wilson, BM.
James P. Yandall & Locky Meador, Sep. 25, 1828. William McGloth-
lin, BM.
John W. Adams & Sarah J. Durin, March 16, 1829.
William Appling & Mary Ann G. Nemo, Dec. 19, 1829, by Seaton H.
Turner, J.P. James Anderson, BM.
Egleston Austin & Amanda Stealy, Oct. 12, 1829, by Lewis M. Wood-
son. V. D. Austin, BM.
Wilkenson D. Austin & Amanda M. Booker, July 31, 1829, by John
Wiseman, M.G. David Padgett, BM.
Nathan Barker & Priscilla Meallias, May 27, 1829. Thomas Jordan,
BM.
William C. Barns & Nancy Curry, July 7, 1829, by W. Walton. Al-
fred M. Beard, BM.
Henry Beard & Tabitha Malone, Jan. 20, 1829. Carson Dobbins, BM.
William E. Beard & Eoline Vinson, Aug. 20, 1829, by Thos. Ander-
son, J.P. A. F. Yound, BM.
Henry H. Belote & Martha M. Goodall, May 4, 1829, by S. R. Roberts,
J.P. Nathnaiel Herndon, BM.
Jeremiah Belote & Nancy M. Wilson, Dec. 22, 1829. R. T. Wraner,
BM.
George Black & Eliza Anderson, Dec. 8, 1829, by Jonathan David,
J.P. Jesse Rippy, BM.
David L. Bledsoe & Elizabeth Moore, Nov. 26, 1829. Solomon Shoul-
ders, BM.

James Bradley & Susan H. Davis, Oct. 8, 1829, by Wm. Smith, J.P.
Solomon Davis, BM.
Joel Brigance & Matilda Hollis, Dec. 19, 1829. Ruben Hunter, BM.
Bernard Brown & Elizabeth Franklin, Dec. 14, 1829, by John Parker,
J.P. George T. Brown, BM.
Widen Byram & Eliza Whitworth, Aug. 31, 1829, by Isaac Lindsay,
M.G. Lemuel Byram, BM.
Peter J. Byran & Evaline Harper, Nov. 30, 1829. Thomas Byson, BM.
Z. P. Cantrell & Mary M. Sanderson, May 12, 1829, by Wm. Hume,
V.D.M. J. J. Franklin, BM.
Darby H. Cantrell & Elmira W. Gillespie, Jan. 14, 1829. Wm. Mont-
gomery, BM.
Samuel Carney & Mary Frack, Oct. 2, 1829. John Carney, BM.
Jordon Carr & Lucy Ann Burnley, Dec. 19, 1829. Alexander Brown,
BM.
Thomas Carr & Mahala Donelson, Dec. 19, 1829. Willam Shaw, BM.
Ouseley Claibourne & Frances H. Robertson, Sep. 5, 1829. David
Robertson, BM.
John Clendenning & Margaret Frazor, Aug. 24, 1829, by Wm. Mont-
gomery. Wm. Kirkpatrick, BM.
Samuel Coles & Sally Walker, July 2, 1829, by Elijah Boddie, J.P.
John James, BM.
Thomas Combs & Anna Anderson, May 30, 1829. John Anderson, BM.
William Combs & Elizabeth Luton, April 19, 1829. John J. King, BM.
Iddoa Cope & Nancy Lambuth, Dec. 30, 1829. (Also listed as 1830,
see in 1830 list of marriages). Pitt M. House, BM.
William Cummins & Peggy Stalcup, Jan. 22, 1829. Joseph Pitt, BM.
Volentine E. Cunningham & Mary P. Steel, April 20, 1829. R. L.
Warner, BM.
Thomas Darrington & Sarah Laurence, Sep. 24, 1829, by Robert Nor-
vell, M.G. Daniel Oxford, BM.
Lewis Davenport & Mary Harris, April 25, 1829. Edward Sanderson,
BM.
Edward Davidson & Polly King, Oct. 24, 1829, by Demcey Ashford,
J.P. Anderson King, BM.
Anthony Dinning & Sarah Webb, June 17, 1829, by Sam Cochran, J.P.
William Dinning, BM.
Albert S. Donoho & Cynthia A. Wynne, Oct. 24, 1829, by H. Joyner.
C. Hart, BM.
Wilie Dugger & Cynthia Stanley, Oct. 29, 1829. Flood Dugger, BM.
James B. Elizer & Mary Garrett, Sep. 14, 1829, by N. Patton.
Daniel Sample, BM.
Michael Ellis & Leona Moore, Dec. 24, 1829, by J. P. Hogan, J.P.
Granville Moore, BM.
Robert Fairless & Arena Buchanan, Dec. 29, 1829, by James Hogen,
J.P. Robt. Fairless, BM.
Greenberry Ferguson & Polly Mabry, Aug. 28, 1829. William Mabry,
BM.
William D. Ferguson & Margaret D. Neely, Sep. 15, 1829, by John
Wiseman, M.F. F. B. Reed, BM.
Sanford Fitts & Frances F. Higgason, April 24, 1829, by John
Banks, J.P. William Harper, BM.
John Fonville & Mary H. Green, Dec. 31, 1829, by Wm. Walton, J.P.
Wm. L. Laurie, BM.

SUMNER COUNTY MARRIAGES

S. H. Fowler & Louisiana Exom, Sep. 29, 1829. C. Sheeke, BM.
Walter Fowler & Mary Willerford, June 6, 1829, by Meredith Hodges,
    J.P. John Fowler, BM.
John J. Franklin & Sophia Cage, Dec. 16, 1829. Josiah R. Franklin,
    BM.
Henry Gains & Maria Biggers, April 29, 1829. James Key, BM.
William A. Garth & Elizabeth Saffarrns, Oct. 20, 1829, by H. W.
    Hunt. Thos. Roberts, BM.
Gomer Garrison & Priscilla Johnson, July 4, 1829, by D. Latimer,
    J.P. John Garrison, BM.
John Giles & Hannah Garrison, July 31, 1829. Wm. Montgomery, BM.
Allen Gillespie & Charlotte Robb, Dec. 17, 1829, by H. W. Hunt.
    A. F. Young, BM.
Richard Graham & Martha Blythe, May 2, 1829, by Henry W. Hunt.
    Wm. Montgomery, BM.
Lewis Green & Elizabeth P. Guarrant, Nov. 21, 1829. John J.
    Franklin, BM.
Parris Green & Margaret Capps, Oct. 5, 1829, by Robert Guthrie,
    M.G. Joseph Exum, BM.
James M. Hadley & Emiline Blackmore, July 23, 1829, by John R.
    Bain. Y. N. Douglass, BM.
George Hall & Hannah Garrison, July 6, 1829. Dickerson Austin, BM.
Clabourne W. Hamilton & Lucinda E. Parson, Feb. 23, 1829, by John
    R. Bain. S. L. McCall, BM.
Felix G. Hanes & Margarett Logan, Nov. 18, 1829. John D. Hanes,
    BM.
Greenberry B. Harris & Mary Bryson, Dec. 29, 1829. George W.
    Thompson, BM.
William M. Harris & Lucinda Groves, June 9, 1829. Robert T. Brad-
    ley, BM.
Leonard Hickerson & Minerva Ogles, Oct. 24, 1829, by Jonathan
    Davis. A. F. Young, BM.
Ramon L. Hodges & Mary Ann Murphy, Dec. 29, 1829, by S. Cochran,
    J.P. John Alderson, BM.
Rowland Horsley & Elizabeth Shaver, Feb. 8, 1829. Wesley Blake-
    more, BM.
James House & Ann C. Baker, Sep. 24, 1829, by F. E. Pitts. Gran-
    ville P. Morris, BM.
Green Jackson & Betsey Harris, Oct. 13, 1829, by Robert Norvell.
    James Alderson, BM.
Josiah E. Jackson & Jane H. Johnson, Jan. 27, 1829, by Luke P.
    Allen. Michael E. Johnson, BM.
Richard Jackson & Mary Gregory, March 11, 1829. John Spain, BM.
Washington B. Jackson & Sally Lathan, Aug. 28, 1829. Benj. Sea-
    well. Jacob Reese, BM.
Asa Johnson & Francis Bruce, Sep. 14, 1829, by Benj. Seawell. J.
    H. Balton, BM.
Austin Johnson & Rosadell B. White, Sep. 20, 1829, by Lewis M.
    Woodson. Andrew W. Johnson, BM.
Thomas S. Jones & Edy Austin, Jan. 5, 1829, by Reuben Searcy. John
    Austin, BM.
William Jones & Darcus Gibson, Jan. 3, 1829. Reuben Forest, BM.
Thomas Kirkham & Susan Justice, Dec. 21, 1829, by S. Cochran, J.P.
    Ashley Stanfield, BM.

Daniel Kizer & Jane Blair, Aug. 25, 1829, by Wm. Montgomery.
George Frazer, BM.
George W. Lane & Frances Lane, Oct. 3, 1829. Isaac Lane, BM.
Alexander Latimer & Eunice J. Guthrie, Oct. 1, 1829, by Robert
Guthrie, M.G. James Guthrie, BM.
John Latimer & Harriett Underwood, Aug. 24, 1829, by Josiah Walton,
J.P. Wm. Shaw, BM.
Samuel H. Lauderdale & Mary Hall Winchester, Sep. 29, 1829, by S.
A. Robert, M.G. Baylie Payton, BM.
Horace Lawson & Tabitha M. Alexander, Oct. 29, 1829, by Thos. Joy-
ner. Britton Parker, BM.
John Lay & Nancy Watkins, Sep. 24, 1829. Philip Watkins, BM.
John Lee & Melissa Keergin, Aug. 20, 1829. James Escue, BM.
Charles Lewis & Mary Lewis, Feb. 6, 1829. Wm. Montgomery, BM.
George Lowry & Jane Minter, Nov. 18, 1829. John T. Dismukes, BM.
James Luton & Anny Stone, Jan. 24, 1829. William W. Combs, BM.
George W. Mabry & Mary B. Seawell, Sep. 11, 1829. John W. Chil-
dress, BM.
William McClung & Fanny Rutledge, Oct. 30, 1829. Lawson Patterson,
BM.
Fountain L. McDaniel & Nancy G. Belote, Dec. 12, 1829, by S. R.
Roberts, J.P. James L. Hawkins, BM.
Hugh McGee & Rachel Murry, April 14, 1829, by James Wallace, J.P.
Y. N. Douglass, BM.
Joseph A. McReynolds & Elizabeth Bloodworth, Jan. 27, 1829. M.
Parks, BM.
James Meador & Malinda Kelly, Dec. 11, 1829, by Jonathan Davis,
J.P. Josiah Wilson, BM.
Jesse Miller & Milly Ball, Feb. 17, 1829. John F. Carr, BM.
David Mires & Sarah Bloodworth, Aug. 25, 1829, by Elijah Boddie,
J.P. Webb Bloodworth, BM.
Newberry Mann & Betsy Short, Feb. 10, 1829, by W. Smith, J.P.
Jeremiah Fisher, BM.
Joseph R. Morris & Eliza Tomkins, Aug. 4, 1829, by J. R. Bain.
John H. Turner, BM.
F. G. Moseley & Ann Kirkpatrick, Nov. 28, 1829. W. B. Johnson, BM.
Edward Newman & Hannah Hicks, July 7, 1829. R. J. Brown, BM.
Benjamine Newton & Priscilla Butt, July 25, 1829, by Stephen R.
Roberts, J.P. John Butt, BM.
Edwin L. Payne & Elizabeth A. Haynes, Dec. 19, 1829, by Richard
Johnson. Martin F. Dickinson, BM.
John Pearson & Elizabeth Cruise, Sep. 11, 1829, by Josiah Walton,
J.P. Richard J. Thomson, BM.
Allen Perdue & Aynthia Norvell, May 20, 1829. Joseph Spradlin, BM.
Ward Perdue & Fanny Henson, Sep. 18, 1829, by Sam Cochran, J.P.
Jonathan Johnson, BM.
William Phipps & Rutha Bailey, Aug. 31, 1829, by Jonathan Davis,
J.P. Humphrey Mires, BM.
Henry Pitt & Elizabeth Cummings, May 14, 1829. William Pitt, BM.
Ambrose Porter & Hannah D. Hall, Aug. 27, 1829. W. Trousdale, BM.
John B. Pullum & Nancy Horsley, April 29, 1829. Jacob Hunter, BM.
Elijah Puryear & Patsey Mitchell, Aug. 17, 1829. James Walton, BM.
John Ragland & Susannah Parker, Feb. 17, 1829. Elias Adkerson,
V.D.M.

David Redditt & Elizabeth M. Moore, March 2, 1829. David Padgett, BM.

James Roney & Catherine Perry, Sep. 25, 1829, by Alex D. Duval, J.P. A. W. Reese, BM.

Thomas Rutherford & Dorindo Pierce, Aug. 31, 1829. Benj. Rutherford, BM.

William W. Rutledge & Clarissa Belote, March 12, 1829. John H. Derr, BM.

David Saffarns & Malvina Gardner, May 13, 1829, by F. E. Pitts. John Bell, BM.

William Sanders & Eliza A. Woods, July 27, 1829, by John Wiseman, M.G. A. F. Young, BM.

William Scoggins & Milley Hale, Dec. 16, 1829, by John Banks, J.P. Talbot Horsley, BM.

Edmund Short & Patsy Bell, Feb. 26, 1829, by Robert Norvell. Elizabeth M. Clark, BM.

Thomas Short & Beatey Anderson, Dec. 11, 1829. Peter Miers, BM.

Solomon Spann & Matilda Miflin, March 11, 1829, by Robert Norvell. Stuart Miflin, BM.

William Spears & Isable Gillmore, April 8, 1829, by Jonathan Davis, J.P. Edward Simmons, BM.

Peter Stalcup & Saviah Bradley, Aug. 31, 1829. Wm. Bradley, BM.

Pleasant Stalcup & Dovey A. M. Roney, April 15, 1829. A. D. Duval, J.P. Page Stalcup, BM.

Coleman Stark & Lucy Holloway, Dec. 23, 1829, by Isaac Lindsey, L.E.M. Thomas Stark, BM.

Woody Stewart & Narcissa McCormack, Nov. 28, 1829. Jo. C. Guild, BM.

Edward Stratton & Sarah C. Tyree, July 16, 1829, by John R. Bains. David M. Fulton, BM.

Peter Stubblefield & Sarah Badgett, April 27, 1829. Green L. White, BM.

John L. Swaney & Nancy G. Gibson, Jan. 20, 1829. James M. Swaney, BM.

Shadrick Talbot & Hannah Hays, April 9, 1829. Jo. C. Guild, BM.

Chrislly Taylor & Mary Hardeman, Dec. 25, 1829. James Gorley, BM.

James Tinnell & Ann Thacker, Sep. 22, 1829. Henrt Tinnell, BM.

James A. Tinnin & Menerva Hannah, Dec. 9, 1829. David Johnson, BM.

John Giles Trusty & Hannah Garrison, July 31, 1829, by Wm. Montgomery.

Alexander Turnage & Martha Bently, April 14, 1829. S. C. Bruce, BM.

Terisha Turner & Priscilla Parrish, Dec. 24, 1829, by Jas. Wallace, J.P. Stokely Vinson, BM.

William Turner & Eliza Robertson, Sep. 26, 1829, by Stephen R. Roberts, J.P. Richd. M. Allen, BM.

Levi Warner & Elizabeth Cartwright, May 11, 1829, by Henry W. Hunt, BM.

Reubin T. Warner & Sophia G. Moss, May 14, 1829, by Henry W. Hunt. Y. N. Douglass, BM.

Miles Selden Watkins & Sally B. D. Shelby, May 15, 1829, by William Humes, D.M. James Collingsworth, BM.

John Warner & Sarah Brock, Feb. 10, 1829. John T. Carr, BM.

SUMNER COUNTY MARRIAGES

Thomas G. Watson & Martha Sanders, Feb. 25, 1829. William Glover, BM.

Armstead Webb & Jane Hamilton, Nov. 4, 1829, by Y. N. Douglass. Wm. Shaw, BM.

James G. Webb & Amy D. Hawkins, Nov. 28, 1829. Henry L. Jones, BM.

Theophilus Webb & Rebecca Stephens, Aug. 10, 1829, by M. Hodges, J.P. Mathew Perdue, BM.

John J. White & Kitty Ann Waide, March 17, 1829. Wm. H. Turner, BM.

Montilion W. Wilson & Elizabeth Young, Nov. 11, 1829, by F. E. Pitts, M.G. A. F. Young, BM.

Zacheus Wilson & Mary Clark, Jan. 15, 1829, by F. E. Pitts, M.G. Addison Wilson, BM.

Lewis M. Woodson & Lucinda Hanna, Oct. 21, 1829. H. W. Hunt, BM.

Jesse Wyatt & Elizabeth Cavitt, Jan. 2, 1829, by Ed. Edwards, M.G.

Alphonso Young & Nancy Robinson, Feb. 21, 1829. John Robinson, BM.

Robert Alderson & Elizabeth Clark, May 24, 1830, by Robert Norvell. Wm. Alderson, BM.

Elijah Allen & Nancy Whitesides, Nov. 16, 1830, by John Parker. Luke P. Allen, BM.

Richard W. Allen & Sally Brown, March 22, 1830, by Frances Johnston, M.G. Levin Bradley, BM.

Marcey Anderson & Frances Turner, March 29, 1830, by Sam'l Lewis, J.P. Enoch Martin, BM.

John Ashford & Jane Pippin, Oct. 12, 1830. John W. Blakemore, BM.

James Austin & Nancy Bandy, Sep. 27, 1830. John Austin, BM.

Porter Baker & Martha H. Looney, Feb. 16, 1830. Jas. B. Garrison, BM.

Woodford Bandy & Nancy Austin, Jan. 12, 1830. James Austin, BM.

Alexander Banks & Ann Daniel, March 11, 1830. Hill Cryer, BM.

Robert Barns & Joanna Leffler, July 23, 1830. Albert Westbrooks, BM.

James W. Barr & Martha Miers, Oct. 14, 1830, by Barton Brown. Wm. McElruath, BM.

James C. Barrow & Susan Boon, Feb. 10, 1830. Barrel Tisdale, BM.

Thomas Barry & Sarah Peyton, Nov. 16, 1830. A. F. Young, BM.

A. L. Bell & Rebecca Patton, July 26, 1830. John Priestly, BM.

William Bell & Elizabeth Fairless, Oct. 25, 1830, by J. P. Hogan, J.P. Wm. Bell, Sr., BM.

Stephen C. Bowers & Nancy Lasiter, June 8, 1830. Wm. Womack, BM.

Jesse Bracken & Rebecca Woodall, June 18, 1830. Joseph Kelly, BM.

Joshua Bradley & Elizabeth Kirkman, Aug. 4, 1830, by Samuel Cochran, J.P. David Bradley, BM.

John Brigance & Catherine Loving, Dec. 22, 1830, by Wm. Walton, J.P.

Athy Brooks & Letha Gibson, April 15, 1830, by Thomas Anderson, J.P. John Pyle, BM.

Christopher Brooks & Betsey Bender, Feb. 11, 1830, by C. Crain. James McCollock, BM.

Alexander Brown & Sarah Miller, Jan. 15, 1830. John Ball, BM.

Barton Brown & Elizabeth Parker, Aug. 10, 1830, by John M. Holland. Samuel R. Anderson, BM.

SUMNER COUNTY MARRIAGES

William G. Brown & Nancy Steele, Nov. 22, 1830, by James Charlton, J.P.
James Bruce & Raney Stanley, Sep. 1, 1830, by Isaac Lindsay, M.G. Jefferson Bruce, BM.
Robert Bruce & Hannah Cantrell, Feb. 27, 1830. Wm. Jones, BM.
James Butler & Matilda Bell, Dec. 24, 1830, by Samuel Davis, J.P. Wm. Caldwell, BM.
John Capps & Patience Barry, May 21, 1830. Thomas Frazor, BM.
John Carr & Sarah Parsons, Nov. 29, 1830, by J. Higgason, J.P.
William C. Carr & Minerva Willis, Dec. 16, 1830, by Thomas Joyner. A. F. Young, BM.
William Carson & Margaret Brazell, Sep. 28, 1830, by Wm. Walton, J.P. J. L. Warner, BM.
Joseph W. Carter & Nancy White, Sep. 20, 1830. Wm. Carter, BM.
David Clark & Susan Bain, May 25, 1830, by John Parker, J.P. Joshua Hichmond, BM.
John Chapman & Sally Durnall, June 30, 1830, by Robert Norvell. Solomon Shoulders, BM.
Lebbins Cobb & Margaret L. Simpson, Sep. 20, 1830, by J. Davis, J.P.
Valentine L. Cook & Ann Martin, May 24, 1830, by Barton Brown, M.G.
Iddoce Cope & Nancy Lambert (see also listed as Dec. 30, 1839), Dec. 30, 1830.
Note: Gallatin, Jan. 6, 1830. Since my first acquaintance in Gallatin, I have always understood and have never heard it denyed that Nancy a woman of color who has lived with David Richardson is a free woman. This I believe to be the general understanding in the County.
Signed,
D. M. Saunders.

Hugh Cotton & Patience Edwards, Jan. 26, 1830. John Strother, BM.
James Curry & Elizabeth White, Jan. 7, 1830, by James Walton, J.P. Sam'l McGee, BM.
John H. Dalton & Latitia McConnell, Jan. 5, 1830. R. Dalton, BM.
Washington Durnal & Betsey Gibson, June 30, 1830. Solomon Shoulders, BM.
Wilson C. Davis & Nancy G. Key, July 27, 1830. Geo. C. Thurmond, BM.
William Dewey & Elizabeth Mitchell, Jan. 25, 1830. Solomon Shoulders, BM.
Edward G. Dickens & Sarah Sulivan, Jan. 18, 1830, by Frances Jarrett, J.P. L. Kimbrough, BM.
David M. Dickerson & Elizabeth Bently, Aug. 3, 1830, by James Charlton, J.P. Thomas Hughes, BM.
Martin D. Dickerson & Elizabeth L. Cloar, Dec. 23, 1830, by L. M. Woodson. Clifton R. Jones, BM.
Elias Dorris & Martha Rippy, July 19, 1830, by John Stone, M.G. Abram Bradley, BM.
Robert G. Douglass & Elizabeth Blythe, May 20, 1830, by John R. Bain. John P. Tyree, BM.
Allen Dugger & Susan Looney, July 28, 1830. Flood Dugger, BM.
Isreal Dye & Elizabeth Anderson, March 8, 1830, by Robert Norvell. John Alderson, BM.
John W. Ellis & Cherry Parker, Dec. 9, 1830. John J. Ellis, BM.

William Evans & Peggy Smith, April 14, 1830. Abraham Green, BM.
James Escue & Elizabeth Hondershell, March 3, 1830. Wm. U. Lee, BM.
John Ferrell & Harriett Sanders, Feb. 6, 1830, by D. Ashford, J.P.
Warner Beasley, BM.
John Ferrell & Maria Caster, Oct. 15, 1830. William Hannah, BM.
James Foster & Elenor Harris, June 3, 1830. William Bohanon, BM.
Anderson Franklin & Mariah Hodges, June 7, 1830. Elias Strange,
BM.
John Garrett & Nancy Murry, Nov. 25, 1830. Joab Dorris, BM.
William Garrison & Elizabeth McCrary, March 4, 1830, by Wm. Mont-,
gomery. Thomas Frazor, BM.
Michael Gates & Caty Ann Cline, May 28, 1830. Valentine Gates, BM.
Valentine Gates & Anna May, July 1, 1830, by D. Ashford, J.P.
Pleasant May, BM.
James Gillum & Eliza Davis, April 19, 1830. James Webb, BM.
William Glasgow & Elizabeth Tomblin, June 7, 1830. John Wilson, BM.
John M. Goldson & Louisa Stovall, Dec. 2, 1830, by John Parker, J.P.
Calvin Sarver, BM.
Clifford Gray & Dulcena Gregory, May 25, 1830, by Jacob Banks, J.P.
George Stublefield, BM.
John L. Hadley & Elizabeth Bledsoe, May 11, 1830, by J. W. Hall.
Wm. Blackmore, BM.
Carter T. Hall & Roxody Pitt, Oct. 28, 1830. J. L. Swaney, BM.
Samuel B. C. Hall & Malvina Hall, Dec. 31, 1830. Lawson Lane, BM.
John Hanna & Jane Laffata, Dec. 11, 1830, by L. M. Woodson.
Richard Hanna, BM.
David Hatch & Betsey Ann Bison, Jan. 20, 1830, by Thomas Joyner.
P. Jefferson, BM.
Ezekiel Hickerson & Elenor Reed, May 15, 1830. N. Perry, BM.
Robert Hodge & Eunice Lindsey, June 23, 1830, by John R. Bain. Wm.
Glover, BM.
Brantley Honeycutt & Malinda Williams, Aug. 23, 1830. Edward
Latimer, BM.
John J. Horton & Nancy Jouett, Aug. 10, 1830. Isaac Perry, BM.
William Hunter & Sally Goff, July 8, 1830. Porter Marcus, BM.
Alfred Ing & Nancy Miller, Sep. 2, 1830. Knight Crabb, BM.
Jesse Jackson & Mary Ann McCormack, April 27, 1830. Michael Dery-
berry, BM.
A. G. Jefferson & Elizabeth Graves, Dec. 13, 1830. Thos. Jeffer-
son, BM.
David Johnson & Thankful Anderson, Sep. 7, 1830, by J. W. Hall.
John Turner, BM.
Stephen Jones & Betsy Spure (Spurs), Oct. 14, 1830. James Butler,
BM.
William Jones & Delia Ring, Feb. 19, 1830. Walker Jones, BM.
Absolom Joyner & Catherine Perry, Oct. 11, 1830. Wm. Montgomery,
BM.
James Kelly & Malinda Martin, Sep. 20, 1830. Warren Kelly, BM.
Joseph K. Kent & Jane Trigg, Oct. 11, 1830. Thos. Byson, BM.
James Kerley & Ann Brown, Nov. 23, 1830. John Ball, BM.
James Key & Lucinda Thurmand, April 24, 1830. Peterson Key, BM.
Peterson Key & Martha Meador, May 29, 1830. H. Henry, BM.
Anderson King & Martha Ann Fulgum, Oct. 14, 1830, by Demcy Ashford,
J.P. Frederick Wise, BM.

James B. King & Elizabeth A. Blythe, Aug. 5, 1830, by J. W. Hale.
Samuel M. Blythe, BM.
Philip Kiser & Sally Perry, May 17, 1830, by R. Patton, J.P. Wm.
Walton, BM.
Thomas Lomax & Polly Dickason, Sep. 28, 1830. George Dunavin, BM.
Izzor Lambert & Peggy Conway, no date shown. James Cartwright, BM.
Oliver J. Latimer & Caroline Garrett, March 3, 1830, by Daniel
Latimer, J.P. Jonathan Latimer, BM.
Thomas Latimer & Nancy Webb, Jan. 5, 1830. Joseph Webb, BM.
Ira Ledbetter & Lucy Brown, Dec. 13, 1830, by Thomas Joyner. Joel
Algood, BM.
Fulceny Lewis & Lydia Preston, Dec. 21, 1830, by Isaac Lindsey, J.P.
Howell Lewis & Sarah Askey, Jan. 16, 1830. Albert King, BM.
Isaac Lindsey & Mary D. Warren, June 15, 1830. Lewis Lindsey, BM.
William Lyon & Nancy Hall, Dec. 11, 1830. Absom Martin, BM.
Richard Marshall & Ann Hamilton, April 17, 1830. Wm. Shaw, BM.
James Martin & Elizabeth Garrison, March 30, 1830. John J. Trusty,
BM.
Pleasant Mays & Sarah Lovell, Dec. 17, 1830, by Demcy Ashford, J.P.
William Mays, BM.
William McCall & Delia Wood, Nov. 25, 1830. Wm. S. Laurie, BM.
Wm. P. McCallon & Mary Morgan, July 1, 1830. Thomas Freeland, BM.
Samuel McDaniel & Ann Winchester, Oct. 14, 1830. V. P. Winchester,
BM.
William McGammon & Edney Kerby, Sep. 25, 1830. Wm. Blackemore,
BM.
Alexander McGlothlin & Mary Durham, Feb. 14, 1830. Wm. McGlothlin,
BM.
Archibald A. Meador & Rachel Skeen, Feb. 6, 1830. K. S. Skeen, BM.
John Meador & Malinda Bell, Aug. 2, 1830. James Gilliam, BM.
Benjamine F. Miers & Mary Taylor, Dec. 30, 1830. Robt. Barns, BM.
Samuel H. Mills & Martha Ann Turner, June 25, 1830, by James Mar-
tin. R. R. Dalton, BM.
Alfred Mitchell & Minerva Stuart (Colored), Sep. 21, 1830.
John Mitchell & Susan Hunt, Oct. 17, 1830. John H. Henry, BM.
Jefferson Montgomery & Mary Joruth, Jan. 11, 1830. Daniel Sample,
BM.
John Morris & Martha Josey, Jan. 1, 1830. Wright Barnes, BM.
James Motheral & Susan Burnly, Jan. 7, 1830, by Wilson Hedin.
Harris Walton, BM.
Stephen Nelson & Lavina Garrott, Feb. 17, 1830. G. Garrison, BM.
Daniel Osburn & Lucy Bandy, Jan. 19, 1830. Reubin Bradley, BM.
Peter Owins & Henrietta Minter, Feb. 28, 1830. H. L. Wallington,
BM.
George W. Parker & Rebecca Payton, May 18, 1830. Thomas Barry, BM.
Milton Parker & Caroline M. Sullivan, Nov. 17, 1830, by John Wise-
man. John Turner, BM.
Hamilton Parks & Martha Beasley, Sep. 30, 1830, by Geo. Edwards.
Wm. Winham, BM.
Claiborne Parrish & Sally Saunders, Oct. 20, 1830. Reubin Saunders,
BM.
Isaac Perry & Elizabeth Franklin, Sep. 8, 1830. John Bell, BM.
William Perry & Cathron Key, Sep. 1, 1830. John Rider, BM.
George Preston & Lavica Vaughn, Oct. 26, 1830. John Preston, BM.

Clayton Ray & Rebecca Justice, Dec. 11, 1830, by James Wallace, Jr.
Elias Rains & Jane Gray, Sep. 3, 1830, by Samuel Cochran. Wm.
  Harrison, BM.
John Rickman & Malvina Meador, Sep. 12, 1830, by John Baker. Thos.
  Meador, BM.
L. H. Ritchey & Mariah Stark, Oct. 13, 1830. M. L. Meens, BM.
John Robinson & Margaret White, Dec. 8, 1830, by Austin Johnson.
  Thomas Day, BM.
William Roseton & Elizabeth Hale, July 20, 1830, by John Banks, Jr.
  Murrell Ring, BM.
William Rutherford & Karen Pearce, Nov. 23, 1830. D. Cartwright,
  BM.
Cornelius W. Sails & Lucinda M. Adams, Aug. 3, 1830. James Adams,
  BM.
Edward B. Sanders & Cina Stublefield, June 16, 1830, by Frances
  Jarrett, J.P. Joseph B. Winston, BM.
John Sanders & Emiline Pharr, Sep. 14, 1830. Henry Williams, BM.
Henry Satterfield & Mary Garrison, April 12, 1830. Reubin Satter-
  field, BM.
William T. Saunders & Martha A. Colliers, July 28, 1830. Wm.
  Rutherford, BM.
John Scott & Polly Redditt, Nov. 29, 1830. Jno. B. Dickerson, BM.
John W. Shaver & Maranda Stone, Oct. 2, 1830, by Stephen R. Roberts,
  J.P. James C. Shaver, BM.
John L. Smith & Isabella Kirkpatrick, Feb. 17, 1830, by Robt.
  Guthrie, M.G. Robt. Taylor, BM.
Joseph M. Smith & Margaret Allen, July 6, 1830. Wm. Lannel, BM.
Rue Smith & Tennessee Tilly, July 27, 1830. Wm. Downs, BM.
John C. Spillers & Adaline Covington, Oct. 19, 1830, by Thomas
  Anderson, J.P. Wm. P. Allen, BM.
Obedium Stalcup & Dianna Chaney, Aug. 9, 1830, by J. McGlothlin,
  J.P. George Stalcup, BM.
John Stanly & Hannah Cunningham, July 10, 1830. Thos. Jourdan, BM.
Thomas Stone & Malinda H. Walker, July 25, 1830. A. F. Young, BM.
Thomas Stovall & America Bennet, Nov. 29, 1830. Wm. Smith, BM.
Hugh Taylor & Polly Gregory, Feb. 11, 1830. Alfred Beard, BM.
Willis Thompson & Jane Daniel, Oct. 23, 1830. Wesly Easter, BM.
Hastin D. Thurman & Ann Miller, Feb. 26, 1830, by James Charlton,
  J.P. George D. Thurman, BM.
Archibald L. Tombs & Sally Hoffman, Dec. 1, 1830, by ____ Swaney,
  BM.
Benjamine Tribble & Francis Williams, Nov. 15, 1830. Joseph Mc-
  Glothlin, BM.
Garrett Tucker & Jane H. Rickman, Oct. 9, 1830. Samuel Rickman,
  BM.
Samuel R. Turner & Elvira Bracken, Feb. 23, 1830, by Robert Nor-
  vell. Seaton H. Turner, BM.
Samuel Wallace & Elizabeth Brackin, July 21, 1830. John Wallace,
  BM.
Bartholomua Watkins & Eliza M. Robb, Sep. 9, 1830. John Turner,
  BM.
John W. Webb & Polly Wright, May 29, 1830, by S. Turner, J.P. Wm.
  Wright, BM.

SUMNER COUNTY MARRIAGES

Barney Wells & Elizabeth Alvice, Sep. 25, 1830, by James Martin,
    J.P. J. L. Martin, BM.
Charles Wesly Williams & Harriett Northam, Nov. 20, 1830. John
    Williams, BM.
Americus White & Amanda C. Bridges, Sep. 28, 1830. John Bell, BM.
Green L. White & Rachel Caroline Shepherd, Feb. 24, 1830, by Austin
    Johnson. A. G. Blakemore, BM.
Thomas E. White & Pamelia B. H. Jefferies, April 18, 1830. A. F.
    Young, BM.
William White & Elizabeth Evans, April 8, 1830. E. E. Wallace, BM.
Davis Williams & Mary Henderson, Nov. 18, 1830. William Caldwell,
    BM.
John Williams & Pheby Williams, Aug. 24, 1830. George Stalcup, BM.
John L. Williams & S. B. Gordon, Dec. 20, 1830. James Charlton,
    J.P.
Ashby Wilson & Martha Waggoner, July 26, 1830. James Freighly, BM.
Benjamine Wilson & Letha Turner, March 10, 1830. Wm. Duffer, BM.
Lucileus Winchester & Amanda Bledsoe, April 10, 1830. H. B. Stan-
    field, BM.
James F. Wood & Sarah A. Rawlings, Jan. 21, 1830. Wm. Lauderdale,
    BM.
George A. Wyllie & Elizabeth M. Elliott, Dec. 23, 1830.
Josiah A. Alexander & Susanna Gourley, May 4, 1831.
Josiah Archer & Gracy Burgess, March 7, 1831. James N. King, BM.
Ashley L. Austin & Susan H. Booker, March 13, 1831. A. F. Young,
    BM.
James C. Barrow & Susan E. Boon, Feb. 10, 1831, by F. E. Pitts.
Reason Barrow & Caroline White, Aug. 4, 1831, by Isaac Lindsey,
    E.M.C.C. John Bell, BM.
Elisha Barton & Cynthia Bowman, May 24, 1831. Edwin Folk, BM.
Simpson Biggs & Sally Cochran, Sep. 6, 1831. Henry Pitt, BM.
William C. Black & Caroline N. Hall, Oct. 25, 1831. Stephen C.
    Chitwood, BM.
Peyton R. Bosley & Catharine Mary Jane Sanders, Oct. 8, 1831, by
    John M. Holland, M.G. Josiah R. Franklin, BM.
Charles H. Boyd & Harriett Cage, Dec. 7, 1831. David M. Fulton,
    BM.
Edmond Bracken & Margaret Cline, March 12, 1831. Michael Cline, BM.
Jesse Bridges & Mary King, Oct. 12, 1831. John T. Carr, BM.
William H. Brigance & Ann Demcy, Feb. 15, 1831.
John Brown & Eliza Wood, June 2, 1831. Zaph Green, BM.
Squire Brown & Martha B. Flipping, Jan. 3, 1831. William Caldwell,
    BM.
Robert Bruce & Hannah Cantrell, Feb. 27, 1831.
John M. Burney & Emily Kenedy, July 25, 1831, by Greenberry Garrett,
    M.G. Joshua Pyles, BM.
James Burnly & Rachel Vance, Dec. 19, 1831. Abraham Vance, BM.
John L. Butler & Caroline Skeen, Jan. 29, 1831, by Archibald B.
    Duval. Kinion Skeen, BM.
David P. Byrn & Martha C. Kilpatrick, Dec. 14, 1831. Geo. M.
    Bledsoe, BM.
Richard G. Byrne & Agnes Hanna, Aug. 15, 1831. Allen Byrne, BM.
Edward Cage & Malissa Young, Dec. 27, 1831.
William Caldwell & Mary Butler, Jan. 3, 1831. Squire Brown, BM.

SUMNER COUNTY MARRIAGES

Richard Carr & Barbary Miller, Jan. 15, 1831.
William H. Carr & Eliza H. Jones, Dec. 7, 1831. A. Mills, BM.
Richard Carter & Dolly Ann Norvell, Feb. 8, 1831.
Philip Cheek & Lucinda Acre, Oct. 13, 1831. A. C. Gains, BM.
William F. Clark & Emma Douglass, March 22, 1831. David M. Fulton,
    BM.
John Cline & Lydia Hunter, Feb. 7, 1831.
Lebbicus Cobb & Margaret Simpson, Sep. 20, 1831. Samuel McCann,
    BM.
Stephen Cooly & Eliza Ann Cuffman, Dec. 22, 1831. John Bell, BM.
Hugh Cotton & Patience Edwards, Jan. 26, 1831, by Josiah Walton,
    J.P.
Daniel Cowgill & Eliza Stephens, Oct. 3, 1831. James Kingsley, BM.
William Crook & Susan Rutledge, Aug. 15, 1831. John Scoggins, BM.
Matthew Davenport & Lydia Preston, June 25, 1831, by Isaac Lindsey.
    Felix R. Chenault, BM.
William T. Davis & Louisa F. Curley, June 9, 1831, by Caleb Crain.
    John Curley, BM.
William Demcy & Elizabeth Mitchell, Jan. 25, 1831.
Thomas J. Dickenson & Lucinda L. Walker, Oct. 10, 1831, by Austin
    Johnson. David Padgett, BM.
Elijah Dickinson & Sarah Blackemore, Jan. 3, 1831, by Austin John-
    son.
Dempsy Elliott & Levina Cage, Jan. 2, 1831. Y. N. Douglass, BM.
Peleman Fair & Sally James, June 1, 1831. E. E. Wallace, BM.
James L. Fugerson & Elizabeth Mabry, Dec. 7, 1831. Wm. Mabry, BM.
Edmund Forester & Susan Porester, Dec. 29, 1831, by Thomas R.
    Anderson, J.P. John Wilson, BM.
Smith C. Franklin & Elizabeth Cage, May 23, 1831. D. L. Cage, BM.
Thomas Frost & Matilda Wygal, Sep. 25, 1831. James Alderson, BM.
William Galbreath & Adeline Adams, March 2, 1831, by James Latimer.
John Garrison & Nancy Preston, Dec. 7, 1831, by Daniel Latimer,
    J.P. Comer Garrison, BM.
Jacob Gillespie & Elmira Hanna, Aug. 1, 1831, by Luke P. Allen.
    Elijah Allen, BM.
Jacob Gillespie & Elmira Hanna, Aug. 1, 1831.
John B. Graves & Amelia Perry, Feb. 26, 1831.
Edward Green & Nancy Parnel, Dec. 14, 1831. Isaac Parker, BM.
Zachariah Green, Jr. & Mary Jane Brown, April 7, 1831, by F. E.
    Pitts.
James Hackett & Mary Ann Saunders, Oct. 17, 1831. David M. Saun-
    ders, BM.
Tobias B. Hall & Margaret A. T. McKindrey, Sep. 11, 1831, by
    Greenberry Garrett, E.M.E.E. Samuel M. Blythe, BM.
Joseph Hardin & Mary Lawhorn, Feb. 24, 1831, by James Wallace, J.P.
James H. Harper & Susan Bradford, Feb. 5, 1831, by Isaac Lindsey,
    BM.
Nathaniel Herndon & Caroline Swayney, July 5, 1831, by John Banks,
    J.P.
John O. Hickerson & Nancy Stone, Aug. 23, 1831, by Richard Johnson.
    John Gregory, BM.
John B. Hill & Nancy R. Parker, Sep. 27, 1831, by William Barr,
    J.P. Asa McNeely, BM.

SUMNER COUNTY MARRIAGES

James W. Hoggatt & Mary Ann Saunders, Oct. 17, 1831, by H. M. Hume,
V.D.M.
James Holoway & Polly Williams, Jan. 5, 1831, by Isaac Lindsey,
E.M. James R. Boyles, BM.
John M. Hooper & Mary C. Curley, Aug. 18, 1831, by Caleb Crain.
John Curley, BM.
Daniel S. Hudson & Caroline Caruthers, Nov. 17, 1831. Joseph D.
Sullivan, BM.
Thomas Hudson & Elizabeth M. Dew, June 2, 1831, by Thomas Joyner.
Zac F. Green, BM.
Arthur Isham & Elenor D. Goodall, Oct. 4, 1831, by John Wiseman.
Robert H. Jewel & Emily Whitworth, Dec. 28, 1831. W. Byram, BM.
George Keeling & Mary I. Byser, Aug. 2, 1831. Thos. Byser, BM.
Samuel J. Kent & Elednder Harper, Dec. 30, 1831, by Peter Ketring,
J.P. James Bell, BM.
John Kilpatrick & Sally Neal, Dec. 7, 1831. W. T. Hodge, BM.
William King & Fanny Hunter, Jan. 4, 1831. Hugh Cotton, BM.
Sampson Lane & Arena Hall, Jan. 4, 1831. Samuel H. Bugg, BM.
James T. Leath & Martha D. Anderson, March 16, 1831. V. P.
Winchester, BM.
Jefferson May & Arminta Weaver, June 2, 1831, by James Charlton,
J.P.
Wesly McAdams & Polly Robertson, March 2, 1831. William Galbreath,
BM.
Winfrey McConnell & Emeline King, Dec. 13, 1831. Thomas J. Wood-
son, BM.
James McDaniel & Mildred A. Miers, Dec. 14, 1831. Solomon Shoul-
ders, BM.
Alexander McGlothlin & Mary Durham, Feb. 14, 1831.
James McClothlin & Lucinda Baird, Sep. 30, 1831, by Francis John-
son, M.G. Joseph McGlothlin, BM.
James K. McGoodwin & Amanda Baker, Dec. 28, 1831. Y. N. Douglass,
BM.
John McNeil & Henrietta B. Jones, Nov. 26, 1831, by Rich. Johnson.
Jno. H. Turner, BM.
John Mitchell & Cinthia Langford, Oct. 1, 1831, by L. W. Woodson.
William Stewart, BM.
James Norman & Sarah M. Wallace, Nov. 28, 1831. James Butler, BM.
Macijah C. Penn & Mary Asky, July 9, 1831, by Chas. Watkins, J.P.
John Asky, BM.
Elisha Pritchett & Nancy Ashly, Nov. 22, 1831. W. Smith, BM.
Shedrick Quarles & Isabella Eneas, Aug. 18, 1831. Anthony Butcher,
BM.
William Ralston & Elizabeth Montgomery, Sep. 30, 1831. James S.
Morris, BM.
James Rice & Mary Barnard, Jan. 7, 1831. Randolph Mabry, BM.
Henry Rippy & Mary C. Hamilton, Aug. 8, 1831, by Robert Norvell.
Roland T. Hodges, BM.
Frances Rogan & Martha L. Reed, March 21, 1831, by F. E. Pitts.
R. Parker, BM.
Jefferson Rogers & Eliza Martin, July 15, 1831. Edward Kelly, BM.
William Rumley & Jane Butler, July 2, 1831. John T. Carr, BM.
William A. Saunders & Sarah Johnson, Jan. 17, 1831, by Lewis M.
Woodson, M.G. Thomas Saunders, BM.

Joseph Shaw & Minerva Cole, Feb. 16, 1831.
Benjamine Smith & Ann L. Bradford, Aug. 19, 1831, by Thos. Joyner. James Cross, BM.
James Stalcup & Nancy Stubblefield, Oct. 12, 1831, by Josiah Caruthers, BM.
David Taylor & Louisa M. Durham, March 7, 1831, by Lewis M. Woodson.
John K. Taylor & Manerva Rutherford, Dec. 31, 1831, by Alexander Taylor, BM.
Nicholas Thompson & Mary Yancy, Jan. 4, 1831, by Austin Johnson.
Richard Thompson & Mary Ann Moore, Dec. 17, 1831. John Wilson, BM.
Isaac Towel, Jr. & Mary Whitworth, Dec. 14, 1831, by Isaac Lindsey. Samuel Towell, BM.
John H. Trigg & Catherine Shepherd, Sep. 8, 1831. E. G. McKain, BM.
William Trusty & Elizabeth Lester, Jan. 27, 1831. Thos. B. Clendening, BM.
John H. Turner & Sarah Wiseman, May 27, 1831. Jno. W. Carter, BM.
James B. Turner & Margaret Turner, Feb. 24, 1831, by J. W. Hall.
Wilson Turner & Martha Hickerson, Oct. 18, 1831. Sanford Fitts, BM.
David Twopence & Nancy Hobert, Jan. 6, 1831. D. M. Sanders, BM.
James M. Walker & Sarah Holaway, Dec. 22, 1831. John Boyers, BM.
Charles G. Watkins & Eliza W. Tally, Feb. 16, 1831. William S. F. Clark, BM.
Charles White & Elizabeth Peek, March 23, 1831. Turner Taylor, BM.
Russell Whitesides & Elizabeth G. Henry, Feb. 14, 1831, by Luke P. Allen.
Alexander Williams & Martha J. W. Belote, July 25, 1831. Robert H. Lewis, BM.
Stewart Williams & Emily Ambrose, _____ 26, 1831. John H. Williams, BM.
Jonathan Wilson & Elizabeth Moore, Nov. 17, 1831. Solomon Shoulders, BM.
William H. Wims & Sarah Coker, July 21, 1831. John F. Carr, BM.
William L. Winston & Mary F. Brown, Dec. 19, 1831. R. C. Goodall, BM.
John Wood & Polly Hicks, Aug. 10, 1831. Jerry Alsup, BM.
John Woodall & Catharine Reese, Feb. 5, 1831, by James L. Martin, J.P.
R. S. Wynne & Elizabeth Townsend, March 11, 1831. James McKoin, BM.
Merry C. Abston & Mary Ann Douglas, April 3, 1832. Edward Stratton, BM.
Alvin Baldridge & Margaret Barr, Aug. 18, 1832. Richard J. Thompson, BM.
Woodford Bandy & Martha Busby, July 2, 1832, by Seaton H. Turner, J.P. James H. Busby, BM.
William Barrow & Marian Cartmell, July 3, 1832, by Burrell Tisdale. Elijah Boddie, BM.
Thomas H. Barton & Nancy Austin, June 16, 1832. John H. Turner, BM.
Amzi L. Bell & Rhoda McCall, Nov. 28, 1832. Franklin Potts, BM.
Pleasant Bell & Lucinda Gaines, June 26, 1832. Sam'l Escue, BM.
Wm. M. Blackmore & Rachel J. Barry, June 26, 1832. J. Y Blythe, BM.

SUMNER COUNTY MARRIAGES

Spyway E. Blackwood & Cathrine Garret, April 26, 1832, by Dan'l
   Latimre, J.P. Thomas W. McMurtry, BM.
Bayley Boyles & Elizabeth Pentacoat, Sep. 30, 1832, by Luke P.
   Allen. Thomas Meadow, BM.
Randal Branham & Susan Horsly, April 30, 1832, by Austin Johnson.
   David Dickinson, BM.
William Briggance & Jemima D. Briggance, July 14, 1832. Reuben
   Hunter, BM.
Augustin Brown & Cinthia Warren, Oct. 13, 1832, by John Parker, L.D.
   James M. Steel, BM.
Jefferson Bruce & Mary Wallace, Sep. 19, 1832. Frederick Dugger,
   BM.
William Bruce & Elizabeth Buchannon, Nov. 6, 1832, by Peter Ketring,
   J.P. James Benton, BM.
William A. Butt & Emily Boren, June 12, 1832. Alexander Pirkle,
   BM.
E. F. Calhoun & Lydia E. Brown, July 9, 1832. C. P. McDaniel, BM.
John Carter & Lithey Morris, March 7, 1832, by Wm. M. Carter, J.P.
   John Morris, BM.
David Cartwright & Sarah Pitt, Sep. 17, 1832. Richard G.Thompson,
   BM.
William Carroll & Jenoma Flowers, May 8, 1832. William F. Lind-
   sey, BM.
Reuben M. Cather & Charlotte K. Collier, March 1, 1832, by Wm.
   Edwards, J.P. Wm. Solomon, BM.
George Chaney & Susan Dickens, Dec. 30, 1832, by Robert Norvell.
   Hardin T. Garretson, BM.
James Christa & Sarah Speers, April 8, 1832, by Samuel Davis.
   James W. Speers, BM.
Granville Christie & Margaret Crawley, Sep. 6, 1832. James W.
   Speers, BM.
William R. Clawger & Mary Lambeth, March 6, 1832, by Arch B. Duval.
   Wm. Lambuth, BM.
Charles Clendenning & Cauley Honeycut, Oct. 15, 1832, by Peter
   Ketring, J.P. Hugh Johnston, BM.
William Cline & Hetty Rippy, Feb. 2, 1832. Edward Brackin, BM.
James Coleman & Leather Shoemaker, March 28, 1832, by Daniel Mc-
   Auley, J.P. Edward Lee, BM.
Tarlton Crews & Jane Day, Feb. 28, 1832, by Wm. C. Carter, J.P.
   Willis Crews, BM.
Willis Crews & Margery Byrn, Feb. 28, 1832. William B. Stovall,
   BM.
Wright W. Croslin & Catharine Byron, Dec. 17, 1832. Joseph Hondy-
   shell, BM.
Larkin T. Crowder & Fanny Lawhorn, Sep. 27, 1832. Addison
   (Addision) Wilson, BM.
Roisdon R. Dalton & Jane Bell, Jan. 9, 1832, by J. Talley, J.P.
   Jas. L. McKoin, BM.
Thomas Day & Mary A. Hart, March 19, 1832. John Parker, BM.
Griffith Dickinson & Mary Badgett, Oct. 13, 1832. Richardson
   Dickinson, BM.
Olive Dickinson & Sarah Stubblefield, Sep. 17, 1832. William Burn-
   ley, BM.
James Dilley & Elizabeth Stark, Jan. 14, 1832. Wm. H. McInger, BM.

SUMNER COUNTY MARRIAGES

Samuel Dobbins & Minerva Bowls, Dec. 3, 1832, by D. Ashford, J.P. John Dobbins, BM.
Roland A. Dorris & Jane Garret, March 26, 1832, by Peter Ketring, J.P. Absolom H. Dorris, BM.
Joshua Doss & Jemima Turner, Feb. 1, 1832. Benjamine Wilson, BM.
Henry Doughty & Mary Axum, Dec. 25, 1832. William Stratton, BM.
Stephen E. Douthet & Anne Brizendine, Sep. 13, 1832, by Robert Norvell. John P. Douthat, BM.
Joel Dunnegan & Mary Harrison, Aug. 30, 1832, by Peter Ketring, J.P. Jese Harrison, BM.
Samuel Edmunds & Elizabeth Butler, Dec. 18, 1832. Oscar Staley, BM.
Richard Eidson & Martha Crews, Nov. 11, 1832. Nathan Crews, BM.
Archie S. Elam & Sarah Cheek, July 25, 1832, by Daniel Latimer, J.P. Wallace Honeycut, BM.
Josephus Elam & Averilla Turpin, Feb. 8, 1832, by Robt. Patton, J. P. Joel Elam, BM.
Daniel Iscue & Malinda Rice, Feb. 14, 1832, by Charles Watkins, J.P. Leonard C. Escue, BM.
John Escue & Elizabeth Smith, June 23, 1832. James Escue, BM.
John Forester & Rebecca P. Fowler, Oct. 24, 1832, by L. M. Woodson. Isaac Robertson, BM.
Hardy Forrester & Martha Crumply, Oct. 11, 1832. Philip Brown, BM.
Moses Furguson & Malinda Goff, July 19, 1832, by H. K. Winbourn, M.G. Daniel Gossadge, BM.
Richard Garrison & Minerva Looney, July 27, 1832, by Josiah Walton, J.P. Comer Garrison, BM.
William B. Gilliam & Lucinda Davis, July 21, 1832, by Samuel Davis, J.P. Thomas Meador, BM.
Richard N. Graham & E. C. Gwin, Nov. 11, 1832. Thos. Bunton, BM.
Chas. H. Gray & Catharine L. Hassel, Dec. 20, 1832. J. Y. Blythe, BM.
William Gray & Margaret Howdyshell (Houndshell), Oct. 19, 1832, by Elisha Vaughn. Joseph Johnston, BM.
John Gourly & Harriett Giles, Feb. 22, 1832, by Thomas Anderson, J.P.
Bluford Hallum & Minervi Davis, April 17, 1832. Marcus W. Cage, BM.
William Hanna & Julia Ann Harris, Feb. 6, 1832. Enoch Simpson, BM.
Asa Harper & Rutha Huddleston, July 11, 1832. Wm. M. C. Barrm, BM.
Moses Harris & Lucy Jackson, Jan. 5, 1832. Robert Harris, BM.
Reuben W. Hay & Cynthia Wren, Dec. 20, 1832. Beverly Miller, BM.
Thomas N. Henly & Sally Gibbs, Jan. 25, 1832. Solomon Shoulders, BM.
William C. Holman & Sarah Rogers, Sep. 11, 1832. Thos. H. Turner, BM.
Henry M. Holloway & Martha B. Hannah, Aug. 27, 1832.
Seth Holt & Elizabeth M. Markham, May 17, 1832. John M. Phillips, BM.
Reuben Hunter & Lucinda Goff, Oct. 23, 1832. Robert Dorris, BM.
Henry Harrel & Harriett Davis, March 24, 1832, by Samuel Davis. Cato Moss, BM.
Hugh Jackson & Elizabeth Preston, Oct. 29, 1832, by Samuel Latimer, J.P. Jese Jackson, BM.

John R. Jackson & Julia B. Watwood, March 15, 1832. Eli G. McKain, BM.
Thomas James & Agnis L. Weathered, Aug. 14, 1832. J. B. Howard, BM.
Ethelred H. Johns & Nelly Woods, Sep. 18, 1832. Frances J. Montero, BM.
Daniel Johnson & Francis R. Graham, Aug. 1, 1832. G. R. Morris, BM.
Alfred Jones & Rebecca Partee, Oct. 25, 1832. Isaac N. Parker, BM.
David H. Jones & Isabella Carr, Feb. 17, 1832. William B. Lawson, BM.
James Jones & Laurinda Ambrose, Jan. 21, 1832. James Boyles, BM.
James B. Jones & Mary Ann Allen, Nov. 1, 1832, by Robert Patton, J.P. James Perkins, BM.
Elisha Keen & Barbary Justice, April 3, 1832, by Samuel Cochran, J.P. John P. Avent, BM.
James Keen & Mary Boykin, Feb. 1, 1832, by Jas. L. Martin. Wm. M. Woodall, BM.
Alfred Key & Elizabeth White, Oct. 1, 1832. Thomas Meador, BM.
James Kirby & Ann Furgeson, June 2, 1832. John H. Turner, BM.
Hiram Lacy & Charlotte Haslet, Oct. 22, 1832. Peter Wall, BM.
Nimrod Langford & Mary Ann Sanford, Nov. 20, 1832. James Martin, BM.
William A. Lauderdale & Penelope Head, Oct. 31, 1832. B. H. Lauderdale, BM.
Whitmill Liggett & Matilda Loony, June 4, 1832. Jonathan Latimer, BM.
William Lester & Virginia J. Bralie, March 7, 1832. R. M. Potts, BM.
Abram Macky & Sally Matherly, June 20, 1832. Wm. Shane, BM.
Reason A. Mahu & Jane Asply, July 14, 1832, by Luke P. Allen. Wm. Asply, BM.
William M. Marshall & Harriett M. Stewart, July 26, 1832. James C. Mosby, BM.
Mathew Mays & Peggy Lovell, Sep. 4, 1832. William Mays, BM.
George McCorkle & Eliza Maxy, Sep. 7, 1832. William Towpence, BM.
David McElwrath & Lucinda S. Bottom, Sep. 26, 1832. James Stratton, BM.
A. N. NcFerson & Sarah McNeely, March 12, 1832. Samuel Barr, BM.
James R. McGavock & Louisa C. Chenault, Nov. 1, 1832, by Wm. Hume, V.D.M. Wm. R. Saunders, BM.
Eli. G. McKoin & Sebella C. Walton, Nov. 20, 1832. Wm. M. Blakemore, BM.
Asa McNeely & Sarah R. Jones, Dec. 13, 1832. John Wilson, BM.
Pleasant Mifflin & Elizabeth Richardson, Oct. 22, 1832, by Henry Anthony. Mathew Turner, BM.
William Morris & Nancy Davis, April 12, 1832. John Morris, BM.
Andrew Nix & Elizabeth Murry, Nov. 29, 1832, by Peter Ketring, J.P. Rolan A. Dorris, BM.
William S. Normant & Mary Hart, Oct. 17, 1832, by Daniel Latimer, J.P. William Hart, BM.
David Ormand & Elizabeth Wilson, May 10, 1832. John Wilson, BM.
Robert Patton & Elizabeth Beaird, Jan. 11, 1832. Alfred Patton, BM.

Daniel Perdue & Harriett Wyatt, Jan. 26, 1832, by Daniel McAuley,
J.P. Joshua Wyatt, BM.
James Perkins & Nancy Ward, Nov. 1, 1832. James B. Jones, BM.
Richard Pond & Anna M. Guthrie, Aug. 13, 1832. Andrew H. Guthrie,
BM.
James A. Potts & Jane A. Anderson, Nov. 19, 1832, by J. W. Hall.
Thomas Barry, BM.
John Preston & Elizabeth Fibbs, April 14, 1832, by Isaan Lindsey,
M.G.
Daniel Pursley & Elizabeth Murry, Nov. 15, 1832, by L. M. Woodson.
James Rice & Mary Barnard, Jan. 7, 1832, by Samuel Cochran, J.P.
Samuel Cochran, BM.
James Richardson & Lavina Ganes, Feb. 8, 1832. Henry Druham, BM.
Daniel T. Sanders & Hannah E. Canfield, June 27, 1832. Wright
W. Crosslin, BM.
David W. Scoby & Tabitha Parnell, Feb. 16, 1832. John McClenon,
BM.
William P. Searcy & Mehetelen Stark, Dec. 31, 1832, by Isaac Lind-
sey, E.M.G. Thomas J. Everett, BM.
James Senter & Nancy Phillips, Aug. 6, 1832, by James L. Martin,
J.P. Seaton Duffer, BM.
Mark Senter & Susannah Louisa Jones, Dec. 17, 1832. David Allen,
BM.
James Slaton & Lucinda Acre, March 14, 1832. Solomon Shoulders,
BM.
John H. Smith & Malvina D. Weathered, Nov. 7, 1832. James H. Bates,
BM.
Perrin S. Smith & Mary Turner, Sep. 24, 1832. Wm. Cothran, BM.
Edwards Spears & Jincy Dalton, Aug. 8, 1832. James M. Spears, BM.
James Steel & Martha Baily, Oct. 15, 1832. John Wilson, BM.
Joseph Stephens & Amelia Perdue, Feb. 21, 1832, by Jos. McClothlin,
J.P. E. J. Bracken, BM.
Barnet Stewart & Sally Archer, July 9, 1832. David Richardson,
BM.
Jeremiah Stewart & Matilda Bernard, April 30, 1832. Wm. Maberry,
BM.
Jese Stewart & Malinda Stewart, Sep. 2, 1832. Turner Mitchell, BM.
John L. Stratton & Frances Clay, Jan. 28, 1832, by J. N. Ralston.
James C. Mosby, BM.
Ira Strother & Nancy Edwards, Oct. 8, 1832. Jas. L. McKoin, BM.
Richard Strother & Permillian Donoho, Oct. 27, 1832. John L.
Griffin, BM.
Isaac Sullivan & Frances H. Gilham, April 7, 1832, by James L.
Martin. John Kerley, BM.
John Summers & Marthena Witt, July 11, 1832, by Ed. Edwards. Jo-
seph Ing, BM.
Thomas Summers & Nancy Milton, Dec. 5, 1832, by S. H. Turner, J.P.
Cornelius Summers, BM.
Absolum Tinsley & Eliza McCormick, April 4, 1832.
Isaac T. Tinsley & Mary Ann Turner, June 4, 1832. John H. Turner,
BM.
George W. Tunnage & Nancy Bentley, Aug. 4, 1832, by James Charlton,
J.P. Albert Dickason, BM.

John E. Turner & Rachel Garrett, April 11, 1832. Samuel D. Reed, BM.

Jacob Tyree & Frances Clardy, March 12, 1832. George M. Tyree, BM.

Douglas Walton & Nancy Prier, Feb. 21, 1832. Olive Dickerson, BM.

William A. Weaver & Amelia Evans, May 16, 1832. John Parsons, BM.

Joseph Webb & Elizabeth Zaricor, Dec. 15, 1832. John Zaricor, BM.

John White & Ann Burns, Oct. 19, 1832. Thomas Bledsoe, BM.

Purvey Wilkerson & Rody Strate, June 15, 1832. Samuel H. Jopes, BM.

William H. Wilkinson & Georgett C. Witte, Jan. 14, 1832. William A. Weaver, BM.

George P. Williamson & Elizabeth Ann Horton, March 3, 1832, by R. Pattomn, J.P. Thomas Flack, BM.

Jeremiah H. Wilson & Elizabeth White, March 16, 1832. John Gilbert, BM.

John B. Wilson & Nancy R. Lunsford, April 9, 1832, by Luke P. Allen, J.P. Mumphord L. Sneed, BM.

Stephen Winham & Mary Rule, Sep. 27, 1832. J. L. Warren, BM.

John Wood & Sarah Alsup, Jan. 2, 1832. Jeremiah Alsup, BM.

John Balch & Sophia Stone, Jan. 17, 1833.

Thompson Baldridge & Susan Armstrong, July 13, 1833, by Charles Watkins, J.P.

John Bentley, Jr. & Martha Ann Bunton, July 29, 1833.

Benjamine V. Berryman & Elizabeth F. Bracken, Jan. 21, 1833, by Robert Norvell.

Thomas J. Bledsoe & Mahala White, Sep. 28, 1833, by James Wallace.

Thomas Buckingham & Elizabeth Talbot, Dec. 21, 1833.

Robert A. Burney & Delila Stalcup, March 2, 1833.

John Burnley & Levisa Carr, Oct. 23, 1833, by John T. Carr.

William Burton & Elizabeth Williams, Nov. 11, 1833, by Henry R. Winbourn.

John Campbell & Minerva Jones, Jan. 3, 1833.

James Carroll & Eleanor Gregory, Aug. 28, 1833, by James Charlton.

Elijah Clack & Myrum Alderson, April 12, 1833, by Robert Norvell.

Charles F. Clendenning & Polly Frazier, Nov. 16, 1833, by Chas. Watkins.

Andrew Cline & Polly Sikes, Dec. 3, 1833, by Henry S. Anthony.

A. J. Crenshaw & Amy Lathum, Dec. 19, 1833, by B. C. Seawell, J.P.

John Culbreth & Mary Burton, Jan. 3, 1833. Arthur B. Duval, BM.

Ezekiel Davis & Jane Lee, July 18, 1833, by Henry S. Anthony.

Richardson Dickerson & Matilda Black, Feb. 20, 1833, by Austin Johnson.

William Dickerson & Elizabeth Blakemore, Oct. 19, 1833, by Francis A. Jarrett.

John B. Dickinson & Lucy Epperson, Nov. 20, 1833.

Francis R. Dirt & Jane Latimer, Aug. 12, 1833, by Ed. Edwards.

Robert C. Dodd & Sally C. Holt, Oct. 1, 1833, by Francis A. Jarrett, M.G.

Robert Donnell & Mary I. Wallace, Oct. 9, 1833, by J. W. Hall.

William Downs & Elizabeth Soper, Feb. 11, 1833, by Elijah Boddie.

Joel Driver & Louisa I. Winn, Dec. 27, 1833, by Richard Johnson.

Peter Elam & Margaret King, March 7, 1833, by Peter Ketring.

Edward P. Gaines & Margaret Ellis, March 24, 1833, by Henry R. Winbourn.

John R. Greer & Nancy Allen, Sep. 3, 1833, by Amzi Bradshaw.
Cyrus B. Hale & Eliza P. Taylor, Dec. 10, 1833, by Richard Johnson.
Wm. G. Hardy & Ann T. Wren, April 17, 1833, by John Wiseman.
Madin D. Harper & Sarah Malone, July 30, 1833, by John Rankin.
Solomon H. Harris & Matilda Simmons, Oct. 24, 1833, by Samuel Davis.
John H. Hicks & Elizabeth Spears, April 24, 1833, by Jonathan Davis.
Asa W. Hodges & Mary Brown, Dec. 7, 1833, by Robt. Norvell.
Joseph Houndershell (Houdershell) & Lucinda Kelly, Sep. 25, 1833,
   by S. H. Turner.
Anthony M. House & Lidia Boyle, Nov. 16, 1833, by Jas. McGlothlin.
Benjamine Hutson & Eliza Dorris, Jan. 14, 1833, by Daniel Latimer.
Robert Jackson & Margaret Zaricor, July 31, 1833, by Josiah Walton.
Joseph Johnson & Cynthia Shepherd, April 3, 1833, by Robert Patton.
John Keen & Chloe Hodges, Aug. 17, 1833, by Samuel Cochran.
John King & Mary R. Bowen, Oct. 29, 1833, by E. Alexander.
William Lewis & Elizabeth Honeycutt, Dec. 2, 1833, by Daniel Lati-
   mer.
Isaac Litton & Pamelia Parker, Dec. 26, 1833, by G. V. Henderson,
   E.M.E.C.
William Loafman & Elender Pulliam, Jan. 6, 1833.
William Lockett & Louisa E. Horsley, Dec. 20, 1833, by N. Brown.
Rilman D. Lovell & Edy Hunter, July 13, 1833, by D. Ashford.
Fendel Lowhorn & Mirandia D. Foster, Feb. 20, 1833, by James L.
   McKoin.
Elisha Marcum & Harriet Gaines, March 4, 1833, by Samuel Davis.
Friley Martin & Martha Crenshaw, March 12, 1833, by L. M. Woodson.
Jonathan McCrady & Mary Ann Wheeler, March 27, 1833, by Jonathan
   Davis.
Pleasant Mitchell & Sarah Hunt, Dec. 17, 1833, by Thomas Gilmore.
John Mounton & Catharine Lefler, Oct. 30, 1833, by S. H. Turner.
Thos. I. Norman & Ophelia Skippeth, Oct. 19, 1833.
John Oglesby & Nancy W. Rickman, April 3, 1833, by Wm. E. Potts,
   M.G.
James Piles & Nancy Smothers, Jan. 19, 1833, by John T. Carr.
Lee Perdue & Polly Benson, May 30, 1833, by D. Ashford.
Cheatham Pucket & Catharine Jones, March 9, 1833, by Isaac Lindsey.
George W. Ray & Frances Gregory, Oct. 1, 1833, by James Charlton.
James Robertson & Nancy Mathis, May 4, 1833, by Peter Kelving.
Marcus Robertson & Margaret Horsley, Jan. 28, 1833, by Austin
   Johnson.
James Rogers & Polly Brazil, April 23, 1833.
John Rush & Susanna Brown, Dec. 20, 1833.
James F. Sacra & Mary G. Johnson, Aug. 28, 1833, by Francis Johnson.
John Sanderson & Martha Carroll, Feb. 28, 1833.
James Sullivan & Nancy Wims, Dec. 15, 1833, by James L. Martin.
Joshua Smith & Nancy Panky, July 24, 1833, by James L. McKoin.
David Thompson & Elizabeth G. Young, Oct. 24, 1833.
William Thornhill & Pamelia Roberts, Jan. 21, 1833, by James L.
   McKoin.
John D. Topp & Malinda Harrell, Nov. 8, 1833, by Freeman Senter.
Samuel S. Turner & Martha C. Goodall, April 30, 1833.
John Walton & Lorana Spears, Jan. 15, 1833.
Wilson Watts & Amanda Newton, Sep. 26, 1833, by James Charlton.
William S. Webb & Tabitha Zaricer, Oct. 31, 1833, by James T.

Tompkins.
Austin Wells & Elizabeth Harrison, Dec. 14, 1833, by Robert Joyner.
Joseph West & Frances Dorris, June 2, 1833, by Giles L. McKoin.
Alfred Williford & Mary Perkins, June 14, 1833, by James McGloth-
lin.
Thomas J. Woodson & Clarissa B. Scurry, May 1, 1833.
James R. Youree & Mary Ann Belote, Nov. 2, 1833, by Archd. B. Duval.
James Alderson & Palsey Morgan, May 24, 1834, by J. Hobday, J.P.
George W. Allen & Louisa F. Douglas, June 26, 1834, by Geo. Don-
nell, V.D.M.
Mabin Anderson & Maria McCall, Dec. 4, 1834, by Geo. Donnell,
V.D.M.
Jordon Austin & Lucy Patton, Oct. 1, 1834, by William Barr, J.P.
Morgan W. Baker & Elizabeth Hurt, Nov. 6, 1834, by S. H. Turner.
William Bates & Susan Wright, Nov. 3, 1834, by Samuel Cochran, J.P.
Geo. W. Bledsoe & Martha Ann Lauderdale, Aug. 29, 1834, by J. W.
Hall.
Thomas B. Bookerville & Eliza Ball, Oct. 27, 1834, by Richd. John-
son.
Zacharia Bowles & Minerva Harper, Oct. 13, 1834, by Henry K. Win-
bourn.
Mathew J. Boykin & Nancy Kean, July 19, 1834, by Jas. L. Marlin,
J.P.
Elijah Bradley & Mahala McCormack, April 30, 1834, by Jesse Gamb-
ling, J.P.
Reuben Bradley & Susan Woodall, Jan. 20, 1834, by Henry K. Winbourn.
James Bray & Mary Lovin, Oct. 4, 1834.
Willis Brown & Lucinda S. Meador, Feb. 25, 1834.
John Burchet & Susan Shepherd, April 14, 1834, by Robt. Patton,
J.P.
Oliver Bush & Eliza Paul, Dec. 11, 1834, by J. Hobady, J.P.
Allen Byrn & Nancy Gillespie, Dec. 9, 1834, by Richard Johnson.
William G. Cage & Julia G. Franklin, May 13, 1834, by J. W. Hall.
Elkainer Cain & Martha Pyle, Feb. 4, 1834, by Jas. L. McKoin, J.P.
Charles Caldwell & Eliza Patton, Aug. 12, 1834. Geo. Donnell,
V.D.M.
Alanson Cannon & Elizabeth C. Sharp, May 16, 1834.
Alason G. Carr & Eliza Young, Feb. 18, 1834, by Archd B. Duval.
John R. Chaney & Missouri Gregory, May 8, 1834, by Elisha Vaughan,
M.G.
Phillip Chapman & Celia C. Hamilton, Feb. 25, 1834.
James Cheek & Margaret Ann Carroll, July 16, 1834, by John McMurtry,
J.P.
Henry Clenny & Martha Bugg, Oct. 8, 1834.
Calvin Cloar & Ann Woodson, Sep. 10, 1834.
James Collins & Elizabeth Keane, May 10, 1834.
John Crenshaw & Mary Stewart, May 14, 1834, by Thos. Joyner.
William Curless & Permelia A. Dorris, Dec. 16, 1834.
George W. Dew & Mary Ann Ward, Aug. 16, 1834.
Thomas G. Dinning & Susan Busby, Aug. 14, 1834.
Robert D. Dobbins & Nancy C. McLin, March 1, 1834.
John Z. Dobbs & Mary A. S. Toombs, April 1, 1834.
Young N. Douglas & Bennetta E. Rawlins, Jan. 16, 1834.
Williams Downs & Nancy Ferguson, May 6, 1834.

James Dunn & Margaret Seawell, July 12, 1834.
James Evans & Mary A. Barr, Dec. 2, 1834.
Zachariah C. Fagg & Mary Turner, Nov. 8, 1834.
John B. Foster & Susan Gwin, Oct. 14, 1834, by G. V. Henderson, E.M.E.E.
John Gray & Mary Ann Townsend, Aug. 4, 1834.
James Gourley & Elizabeth Simpson, Dec. 30, 1834.
Jacob Garrett & A. C. Conner, Dec. 15, 1834.
Archibald Gregory & Mary Laytham, April 14, 1834.
James Hamilton & Jane Taylor, Nov. 4, 1834, by Archibald B. Duval.
James A. Harkreader & Elizabeth A. Bradford, Dec. 22, 1834.
Jesse Harper & Mariah Watson, Feb. 24, 1834.
Thomas M. Harrell & Francis A. Willis, July 3, 1834.
George Hornsby & Susan Shaver, May 20, 1834, by Nimrod Brown, J.P.
Benjamine R. Howard & Mary M. Baker, June 19, 1834.
John B. Howard & Margaret Grimm (or Gwin), Nov. 20, 1834.
Joseph Hudspeth & Amanda M. Hudspeth, April 21, 1834.
Jerry Hullet & Zilpha Hradley, Aug. 16, 1834, by Jesse Gambling, J.P.
James Hunt & Nicy D. Tuner, Oct. 4, 1834.
Burnice B. Jones & Mary Youree, Oct. 29, 1834.
Stephen M. Jones & Catharine C. Bracy, June 21, 1834, by Wm. Bradford, M.G.
Abner G. Johnson & Mary Burkett, Dec. 20, 1834, by Alex Graham.
Francis A. Jordon & Lydia Jackson, Oct. 18, 1834, by G. V. Henderson, E.M.E.C.
Jonathan Knight & Margaret Burke, June 28, 1834.
Benjamine A. Latimer & Rozena Stratton, Sep. 29, 1834, by G. T. Henderson, E.M.E.C.
Harry B. Lauderdale & Jane Malone, Jan. 14, 1834.
Charles H. Ledsing & Nancy T. Brown, Nov. 26, 1834.
Edward C. Loony & Sarah Dewey, Jan. 1, 1834, by Jesse Hambling, J.P.
George Love & Melissa Elliott, Jan. 9, 1834, by James Wallace, J.P.
Charles B. Luton & Sarah Lambeth, July 26, 1834.
Robert W. Ming & Lydia B. House, March 10, 1834, by Jas. McGlothlin, J.P.
John G. Newton & Milly Pruett, Dec. 27, 1834.
Hezekiah Oneal & Sarah Colia, Dec. 23, 1834, by John Parker, L.D.
Robert H. Parks & Maria A. Harder, Dec. 3, 1834.
Thos. Payne & Susan Payne, Nov. 3, 1834.
John Perdue (or Pardue) & Mary Saunders, March 28, 1834.
Gilbert Perrigan & Milly Carroll, Feb. 22, 1834.
Hosea Phelps & Sally King, Aug. 15, 1834.
John Philips & Sarah Hunt, Aug. 19, 1834.
William Plummer & Eliza Boyle, Feb. 22, 1834, by Jos. McGlothlin, J.P.
John Rice & Margaret Love, Dec. 9, 1834.
Benjamine Roney & Rorotha Busby, April 12, 1834.
James Roney & Mary Bradley, Nov. 3, 1834.
John Roney & Edna Spradline, Feb. 22, 1834.
Pleasant Ryan & Betsy Caldwell, Sep. 30, 1834.
Wm. R. Saunders & Elizabeth R. Bowen, Sep. 1, 1834.
James F. Schluter & Emily Winchester, Oct. 7, 1834.
Wylie B. Seawell & Malinda E. Rickman, Sep. 8, 1834.

William Smothers & Mary Cook, Aug. 16, 1834.
Wm. A. Starret & Mary Linsey, Nov. 3, 1834.
Hamblin Stewart & Amarilla McCormick, April 25, 1834.
James Stone & Mahalia Edwards, Dec. 19, 1834.
Levi Stone & Elizabeth Gains, May 3, 1834.
Wilkerson Sutton & Barberry Weeks, Feb. 11, 1834.
Enoch Thomas & Abby Ann McElurath, Nov. 4, 1834.
Epperson Thornhill & Polly White, Jan. 2, 1834.
William C. Tomson & Hellen L. Bressie, May 1, 1834.
Haden S. Trigg & Elizabeth Wilson, July 28, 1834.
Elias E. Vinson & Elizabeth Turpin, Feb. 28, 1834.
Seathmead Warren & Mary Donelson, Aug. 18, 1834.
John West & Sally B. Browning, Oct. 22, 1834.
Thomas Wethers & Sally Troudale, March 17, 1834.
James Woodall & Sarah House, July 2, 1834.
Ransum S. Wynn & Elizabeth H. Townsend, March 11, 1834.
Francis M. Youree & Mary Ann Jones, Sep. 8, 1834.
John Zaricor & Mary Ann Jackson, Jan. 11, 1834.
Benjamine Adams & Sarah P. Brown, Oct. 21, 1835.
Reuben Alderson & Sally Stephens, April 28, 1835.
James Allen & Mary H. Wyllis, Jan. 14, 1835.
Jackson Alley & Louisa Perkins, May 30, 1835.
Henderson Ally & Elizabeth Perdue, Jan. 14, 1835.
James Anderson & Charlotte E. Old, July 4, 1835.
Dickson Austin & Emily Anderson, March 23, 1835.
Daniel Barbour & Sally Wyatt, Aug. 15, 1835.
Henry Biggs & Margaret Brylie, Nov. 3, 1835.
Henry Blackburn & Thedocia A. Bandy, Sep. 19, 1835.
Zachariah Blalock & Frances Vanover, Dec. 28, 1835.
Isaac N. Bledsoe & Nancy Lee, Aug. 3, 1835, by John Parker, M.G.
William Borders & Polly Groves, Dec. 10, 1835.
John W. Bracy & Nancy Wooten, Nov. 14, 1835.
Nathan Bradley & Ally Boren, March 11, 1835.
John Bloodworth & Mary Bloodworth, Dec. 23, 1835.
Thomas Bridges & Lucinda Berry, March 21, 1835.
Elisha R. Brown & Nancy Rush, Feb. 14, 1835.
James Brown & Polly Tuttle, Aug. 15, 1835, by Thomas Gilmore.
Joseph W. Brown & Susanna Markrum, June 8, 1835.
John W. Bruce & Eliza Kenedy, July 7, 1835.
Samuel Brylie & Nancy Summers, Dec. 29, 1835, by T. Y. Turner, J.P.
Hiram Brylie & Patsey Wilet, Dec. 19, 1835.
Samuel Butler & Mary Hunt, Jan. 12, 1835.
Wilson Cage & Polly Cunningham, Jan. 1, 1835, by G. W. Morris.
Alfred F. Campbell & Polly Huston, Jan. 7, 1835, by John McMurtry,
    J.P.
George Cannon & Lucinda Gaines, Jan. 15, 1835, by Jesse Gambling,
    J.P.
Ewing S. Capps & Polly Pitt, July 18, 1835.
Nelson Cardwell & Polly Bennett, (no date).
John Carr & Phoebe Marshall, Dec. 19, 1835.
Corum Cummings & Susan Irby, Feb. 7, 1835.
Moses M. Donelson & Jane Zedacher, March 5, 1835.
James Donoho & Nancy Johnson, March 17, 1835, by Joseph Pitt.
Robert B. Douglas & Delia Mitchell, Dec. 14, 1835, by A. K. Duval.

Ambrose Downs & Eliza Lassiter, Sep. 8, 1835, by Stokley Vinson.
James M. Garrot & Edith Chaina, Aug. 20, 1835.
Joseph H. Garrot & Elizabeth Nickens, Sep. 26, 1835, by John
   Holiday, J.P.
Israel Greenhalgh & Susan Parker, Jan. 26, 1835, by H. B. Hill.
Micajah Griffin & Melinda Hardin, Oct. 28, 1835, by Joseph Pitt.
Thomas T. Hall & Susan Fisher, Nov. 16, 1835.
F. S. Haynes & Mariah E. Swaney, Jan. 14, 1835.
J. D. Harper & Lydia Harper, March 24, 1835.
Joseph Harper & Hannah Rankins, July 16, 1835, by John Parker, J.P.
Beverly Head & Evelina D. Wiseman, Dec. 19, 1835, by Daniel Smith,
   M.G.
Nathaniel Hicks & Elizabeth Finn, Nov. 4, 1835.
Hugh B. Hill & Mary Read, Oct. 29, 1835, by Geo. Donnell, V.D.M.
John Hobdy & Elizabeth C. Hodges, Sep. 22, 1835, by Jos. McGloth-
   lin, J.P.
Joseph H. Holdman & Nancy Settle, Dec. 22, 1835, by Thomas Gilmore,
   J.P.
Robert Horton & Isereania Pitt, May 5, 1835, by Joseph Pitt.
Rich'd Hyden & Martha Allsup, Nov. 9, 1835.
John Inman & Evelina Turpin, Dec. 21, 1835, by John McMurtry, J.P.
John W. Judd & Lydia Starkey, Nov. 9, 1835. Robert Patton, J.P.
John J. James & Rhoda Ball, Aug. 12, 1835.
Bartholomew Kelly & Elizabeth Woods, Dec. 21, 1835.
Edward Lee & Emily Garrot, June 5, 1835.
John Legg & Elizabeth Brylie, Oct. 3, 1835.
J. M. Litton & Matilda K. Doxey, Feb. 4, 1835, by W. B. Bowles.
James Love & Mariah Elliott, Jan. 8, 1835, by James Wallace, J.P.
Nathan Mandrell & Malinda Trout, Sep. 2, 1835, by Thomas Gilmore,
   J.P.
Anderson Martin & Margaret Satterfield, Oct. 31, 1835, by Thos.
   Gilmore, J.P.
C. R. Martin & Nancy Mayberry, June 19, 1835, by John Hobdy, J.P.
William Mayberry & Elizabeth Barnard, Jan. 17, 1835.
Henry Mayhew & Mahalia Meador, Dec. 12, 1835.
Isaac McGlothlin & Sinia House, Dec. 8, 1835.
Murdock McLean & Elizabeth McCalley, June 15, 1835.
John McWrath (McElarath) & Lucretia M. Bottom, Jan. 15, 1835, by
   W. P. Rowles.
Amaziah Morgan & Mary Parker, Aug. 24, 1835, by Wm. Bransford, M.G.
Jeremiah L. Murrah & Anna Jernigan, April 11, 1835.
John A. Nealy & Mary Langsford, Dec. 18, 1835, by Luke P. Allen.
Henry Newman & Elizabeth Hunter, July 25, 1835, by Nathan Hunter,
   BM.
Nelson Parker & Cinthia Whitesides, Feb. 9, 1835, by John Parker,
   J.P.
Calvin W. Pearson & Cansiah Loving, Aug. 20, 1835.
John Perry & Susan Sadler, Oct. 22, 1835, by Thomas Gilmore, J.P.
John A. Reddick & Sarah A. Hodges, July 30, 1835.
John Richmond & Martha Carter, June 4, 1835.
John A. Robeson & Jane Hughes, Oct. 6, 1835.
George W. Roney & Amanda Hutchenson, March 3, 1835.
Allen Ross & Margaret Taylor, March 3, 1835.
Charles Simmons & Jane Hunt, March 21, 1835.

SUMNER COUNTY MARRIAGES

John Smothers & Elizabeth V. Davis, Dec. 16, 1835.
Wm. Smothers & Polly Hunt, Aug. 6, 1835.
James Spears & Martha Wolf, March 16, 1835.
Willis Spilman & Elizabeth Spilman, Feb. 2, 1835.
Wm. Stephenson & Malinda Weathers, May 9, 1835, by C. Woodall, J.P.
Benjamine B. Sutton & Therissa Carter, Jan. 2, 1835.
Colby Sutton & Leticia Vaughn, Nov. 21, 1835.
George Swaney & Aramitti Lowery, Nov. 3, 1835, by Freeman Senter.
James P. Taylor & Elizabeth A. Franklin, March 16, 1835, by Hall
   Cryer, M.G.
Orren Tisdale & Emily Moore, Aug. 27, 1835, by Elijah Boddie, J.P.
J. J. Underwood & Jane A. Clopton, Sep. 9, 1835.
Joseph Vance & Mary Leath, Sep. 21, 1835.
Philip Vance & Mary Erwin, March 14, 1835.
Samuel A. Williams & Sarah A. Clark, Jan. 13, 1835.
Curry Watson & Charity Downs, Nov. 21, 1835, by Stokley Vinson,
   J.P.
John Wilson & Francis Williams, Sep. 8, 1835.
James H. Wray & Mary L. Graham, Nov. 4, 1835.
Moses Walker & Catherine Phons, June 11, 1835.
James Abbott & Mariah Stone, June 20, 1836, by L. B. Laurence.
   George Love, BM.
William Allen & Elenor Willis, Feb. 15, 1836. Robert Williams,
   BM.
William C. Alvis & Lucinda Simmons, Oct. 11, 1836, by Taylor G.
   Gilliam. Abraham Muce, BM.
Joseph Aston & Clarissa B. Reed, July 30, 1836. Daniel Safferan,
   BM.
Ishmael H. Baile & Jane M. Adams, Oct. 29, 1836, by L. M. Woodson.
James M. Baker & Polly Harrel, July 26, 1836, by Freeman Senter.
   Joseph W. Harrel, BM.
Thomas Barnard & Sally Williams, Aug. 9, 1836, by J. H. House.
   Benjamin Gribble, BM.
Joseph Barr & Mary Taylor, June 1, 1836, by Elijah Boddie. Solo-
   mon Shoulders, BM.
John C. Beasly & Mary Allen, Jan. 4, 1836. Joseph Barbor, BM.
Jeremiah Bentley & Nancy Patton, Jan. 12, 1836.
Isaac Beldsoe & Sally W. Hanner, Nov. 23, 1836. M. B. Turner, BM.
James Bledsoe & Harriet Higgins, Dec. 24, 1836. Allin Carter, BM.
Absolum Brady (or Bradley) & Polly Mayberry, April 12, 1836. Ran-
   dal Mayberry, BM.
H. T. Brassell & Louisa Evans, Sep. 5, 1836, by L. B. Evans.
Zachariah Brazier & Mary S. Stone, Dec. 3, 1836. Josiah Rascoe,
   BM.
Ishamel H. Briley & Jane M. Addam, Oct. 29, 1836. Henry Volentine,
   BM.
John H. Brown & Sarah A. Houndershell, March 2, 1836, by Elisha
   Vaughan. William Gray, BM.
Joseph Brown & Edy Brown, July 1, 1836, by Thomas Gilmore. Levi
   Richmond, BM.
Volentine H. Brown & Mary Pyle, March 1, 1836. James L. McKoin,
   BM.
William P. Browning & Mary Brown, Nov. 12, 1836, by Luke P. Allen.
   James Oglesby, BM.

97

Archibald Bruice & Martha Leath, Oct. 6, 1836. Shelton Dalton, BM.
James H. Bushby & Malinda Roney, Jan. 25, 1836, by S. H. Turner.
James Dinning, BM.
William Butler & Susan Patton, Aug. 23, 1836, by Jesse Harper.
William Twopence, BM.
Robert Button & Susan Davidson, June 28, 1836. William P. Branch,
BM.
R. W. Donnell & Lucy Ann Green, Oct. 26, 1836, by Arch B. Duval.
Elkainer Coin & Martha Pyles, Feb. 4, 1836. V. H. Brown, BM.
John O. Cage & Sarah Robb, Jan. 12, 1836, by J. W. Hall. John T.
McClain, BM.
Isiah Carman & Martha Eagan, Feb. 3, 1836, by Francis Johnson.
Thomas Tiller, BM.
Jesse Carr & Maria E. Sanford, March 14, 1836. H. F. Anderson, BM.
J. A. Carr.
Thomas H. Carr & O. S. Mathew, Dec. 26, 1836, by James Charlton.
Andrew J. Graham, BM.
John Chapman & Winny Abel, Sep. 25, 1836. Stephen A. Gilliam, BM.
Benjamine Clardy & Lucinda A. Avrett, Sep. 5, 1836, by John Wise-
man. John G. Averitt, BM.
W. B. Chilton & E. A. Baird, Dec. 23, 1836, by John Beard. Aron
S. Neel, BM.
John T. Coker & Anna Kirley, Sep. 24, 1836, by Taylor G. Gilliam.
Dan'l Griggs, BM.
Lewis Cook & Synthia Stratton, Jan. 4, 1836. Joseph Barber, BM.
Henry F. Cotton & Elizabeth Cotton, March 26, 1836, by Jesse Gam-
bling. William Rice, BM.
John Cron & M. C. Johnson, Dec. 19, 1836. Abner Luckadoo, BM.
Thomas D. M. Crumpton & Eliza A. Doxey, Jan. 17, 1836. Willie
Vinson, BM.
James Dempsey & Elizabeth Hutson, Aug. 3, 1836. Charles Mathis,
BM.
Robert Desha & E. Garrett, June 24, 1836, by W. Hall. Thomas
Donoho, BM.
William T. Dickason & Janette Watts, May 25, 1836, by James Charl-
ton. Samuel K. Henderson, BM.
James Dinning & Mary Hollis, March 24, 1836, by Jesse Gambling,
J.P.
R. W. Donnell & Lucy Ann Green, Oct. 20, 1836. Robert T. Moore,
BM.
H. L. Douglas & M. B. Hall, July 5, 1836. G. C. Pitts.
John Dowell & Frances Stewart, March 19, 1836. Demcy Ashford, BM.
Elvin Dugger & Amanda Jorey (or Josey), Aug. 17, 1836. John
Morris, BM.
James Duke & Celia Garrett, May 12, 1836. John Duke, BM.
James Dunning & Mary Hollis, March 14, 1836. John Grainger, BM.
Gatewood H. Durham & Sarah Grissum, Jan. 30, 1836. Joseph Key, BM.
Jobe Edens & Patsey Douglass, Sep. 28, 1836, by Samuel Laurence.
Samuel Edens, BM.
W. A. Edwards & Amelia Huffman, Sep. 27, 1836, by Jas. Tompkins.
Isaac W. Harris, BM.
Ananias Epperson & Elizabeth Davis, Oct. 26, 1836. William Simp-
son, BM.
Robert Evins & Emily Heughes, June 20, 1836, by Joseph Spradling.

E. R. M. Reynolds, BM.
Albert C. Franklin & Henrietta E. Watkins, March 30, 1836. William McElurath, BM.
Isaac Freeland & Nancy Ann Gra-(?), Oct. 31, 1836. Elijah Stalcup, BM.
Hardin Garretson & Permilia Griggs, Jan. 20, 1836. Samuel Bugg, BM.
Henderson P. Grainger & Sarah Durham, Oct. 31, 1836. Elijah Stalcup, BM.
William Grainger & Lucilla Polk, Nov. 16, 1836, by J. H. House. Peter W. Martin, BM.
Andrew Graves & Rachel Mandrall, March 12, 1836, by Thomas Gilmore. David Mandrall, BM.
Humphrey Griffin & Mary Weems, Nov. 30, 1836, by John H. Robertson, (Preacher). William Carr, BM.
Daniel Griggs & Elizabeth Read, Oct. 23, 1836, by Elisha Oglesby. Henry Griggs, BM.
Andrew H. Guthrie & Jane S. Kirkpatrick, March 7, 1836, by John McMurtry. Robert Patton, BM.
R. C. Haile & Susan C. Seawell, Nov. 15, 1836. B. W. Mills, BM.
James Hall & Nancy Morgan, July 16, 1836. William Link, BM.
R. W. Hammond & Mary P. Clayton, Sep. 27, 1836, by J. H. House. William Solomon, BM.
Willis (also William) Harrison & Elizabeth Wiatt, Dec. 9, 1836, by Freeman Senter. King Wiatt, BM.
William Harrison & Nancy Morris, July 1, 1836, by Thomas Gilmore. Joseph Brown, BM.
John Haynie & Mary Patton, Jan. 20, 1836. Nathan Underwood, BM.
Alfred Head & R. A. Vinson, Sep. 19, 1836. James M. Head, BM.
Peter M. Hendricks & Jane May, July 13, 1836. Richard May, BM.
Joseph Hodge & Ritty Harpool, June 23, 1836, by B. S. Rutherford. James Kirkpatrick, BM.
Griffin Hodges & Martha E. Bruise, May 17, 1836. A. J. Rutherford, BM.
William Horton & Malinda Hains, Sep. 19, 1836. Geo. Townsend, BM.
James House & Anne P. Crenshaw, June 22, 1836, by Elijah Boddie, J.P. Z. W. Baker, BM.
William Hutchinson & Lucinda Coats, Oct. 15, 1836, by E. L. Martin, (L.D. of M.E.CH). James Stratton, BM.
W. B. Jennings & Mary Ann J. Lasiter, Dec. 19, 1836, by B. B. Brown. Alexander Britt, BM.
Lewis D. Jetton & Mildred B. Saunders, May 19, 1836, by Thos. Joyner.
John Jocey (or Gocey) & Harriett Cotton, Dec. 21, 1836, by Jesse Gambling. Robert White, BM.
Edmund Jones & Catherine Richardson, Feb. 18, 1836, by Daniel McAuley, J.P. J. A. Browning, BM.
John W. Jordan & Sally P. Walker, July 25, 1836, by I. R. Bain. Andrew J. Hamilton, BM.
Thomas M. Joyner & F. E. McKendree, Nov. 22, 1836, by O. E. Ragland. Wm. Ragland, BM.
O. L. Kaine & Elizabeth Night, Aug. 4, 1836. Jas. C. Drew, BM.
John Keen & Sally Nix, Dec. 25, 1836, by Taylor G. Gilliam. Samuel Boykin, BM.

Edward Kelly & Rhody Perkins, Feb. 1, 1836, by J. B. Bracken. Thomas Sommers, BM.

William Key & Rachel Graves, March 4, 1836. Macklin Key, BM.

William F. Kirkpatrick & Mildred Wright, May 23, 1836, by Francis Johnson, June 23, 1836. R. T. Warner, BM.

Henderson King & Eliza Ashford, July 26, 1836, by Robert Norvell. Josiah Ashford, BM.

John Lauderdale & Matilda Jones, March 12, 1836. David Carr, BM.

John W. Lauderdale & Eliza B. F. Seawell, Oct. 31, 1836, by Thomas Joyner, Dec. 31, 1836. James N. Malone, BM.

Coalman Leath & Mary Coal, Jan. 18, 1836, by Thos. Gilmoer. Carrol Shrum, BM.

Thomas Loyd & Mrs. Charlotte C. Chambers, March 26, 1836.

Reddick Maddry & Sarah E. Jackson, May 23, 1836, by B. S. Rutherford. Hubbard H. Sanders, BM.

John Main & Tennessee Smith, Aug. 20, 1836, by Jesse Harper. Jefferson May, BM.

C. B. Malone & L. Summerman, June 8, 1836, by H. B. Hill. Thomas W. Epson, BM.

Henry Mandrill & Elizabeth Morris, Jan. 28, 1836, by Thomas Gilmore. Nathan Mandrill, BM.

James Mason & Elizabeth Staley, Sep. 2, 1836, by Freeman Senter. Volentine Austin, BM.

James M. May & Susan Watson, April 5, 1836. Marcus W. Laurence, BM.

John Murphy & Mary Jackson, July 24, 1836. James McBride, BM.

John Mayberry & Charity Taylor, May 2, 1836, by J. Brackin. J. B. Brackin, BM.

Joseph McGlothlin & Milly C. Hamblin, July 18, 1836, by J. H. House. James McGlothlin, BM.

Wm. C. Meador & Mary Jane Martin, Feb. 6, 1836, by Thomas Gilmore. I. T. Blythe, BM.

Bluford Meador & Perlina Meador, Sep. 12, 1836, by J. B. Brackin. William McGlothlin, BM.

William Miller & Jane Brasher, Jan. 13, 1836. Sanford Beckenstaff, BM.

Addison Mitchell & Mary Ann Hodge, Oct. 25, 1836, by I. R. Bain. L. P. Black, BM.

Daniel H. Murry & Harriet H. Swift, May 28, 1836, by B. S. Rutherford. Dobin Davis, BM.

Abraham Neece & Jane Stower, Dec. 25, 1836, by Taylor G. Gilliam. Washington Jacobs, BM.

Thomas Oneill & Elizabeth Morris, Dec. 30, 1836. Jesse Skeen, BM.

James M. Owen & G. A. E. Dismukes, Sep. 8, 1836. R. M. Boyers, BM.

James T. Penny & Martha Patton, Aug. 8, 1836, by George Donnell, V.D.M. B. D. Hawkins, BM.

John Perkins & Sally Ally, March 19, 1836. Wooddy Martin, BM.

John Pogue & Polly Storm, April 23, 1836. Henry White, BM.

David Prock (or Brock) & Flora (Flava) Love, Nov. 11, 1836, by Taylor G. Gilliam. Tilman Cannon, BM.

Thomas Puryear & Perlina Bressie, June 6, 1836. Alexander Liggon, BM.

William Puryear & Mary E. Pierce, April 12, 1836, by James M. Gray, BM.

E. R. M. Reynolds & Lucy Dinkins, Sep. 6, 1836. Joseph Spradlin, BM.

David H. Rickman & Mary Tucker, Oct. 10, 1836, by John Parker. Jesse Tucker, BM.

Samuel Rippy & S. E. Mattocks, Sep. 21, 1836, by J. B. Brizendine. Joseph West. BM.

L. H. Ritchey & Mariah D. Starke, Oct. 13, 1836.

Nathaniel Robinson & Nancy Padget, July 18, 1836, by Hiram Duty. Thomas M. White, BM.

William Roney & Mary Granger, Oct. 10, 1836. P. M. House, BM.

W. P. Rawles & Emily May, May 5, 1836, by Wm. M. McFerrin. W. Cothran, BM.

Lorenzo Sanders & Susan Anderson, April 19, 1836, by Peyton Welch. John W. Eustice, BM.

Peter T. Sanders & Martha A. Mills, Jan. 11, 1836, by G. W. Morris. James H. Sharp, BM.

Luke Senter & Zorita Durham, Feb. 15, 1836, by Wm. Barr. Joseph McNeil, BM.

Hardy Silber (Silbur) & Mary Steel, Nov. 9, 1836, by Ben Gray. Robert Bugg, BM.

James Simmons & Martha D. Jacobs, March 14, 1836. Joel Simmons, BM.

John Sloan & Susannah D. Harris, April 26, 1836, by P. Winn. Charles Burnley, BM.

James Smith & Mary Brooks, July 7, 1836, by Robert Joyner. Flood Dugger, BM.

Jackson Snead & Sally Jenkins, Dec. 5, 1836, by Thomas Gilmore.

Samuel Spears & Mary Brown (Jr.), July 20, 1836. Jesse R. Brown, BM.

John W. Spradlin & Margaret Cope, Sep. 6, 1836, by J. H. House. Joseph Spradlin, BM.

Hamilton Stainback & M. E. Judd, Nov. 2, 1836, by Robert Patton. D. T. Hatch, BM.

Luther Stamps & Mahala Login, April 11, 1836, by Freeman Senter. John Jackson, BM.

Solomon (Solo.) Stapleton & Jemime Richardson, Nov. 9, 1836. Mathew Morgan, BM.

Harbert Stewart & Martha Archy, Nov. 2, 1836, by Elisha Oglesby. Turner Mitchell, BM.

William Stewart & E. C. Parker, July 13, 1836, by L. M. Woodson. Minor B. Hanes, BM.

Stephen Stone & Sarah Schabell, Dec. 23, 1836. James Stratton, BM.

William Stone & Jane Ashford, Jan. 1, 1836, by Henry S. Anthony. Isaac Baker, BM. Solomon Shoulders.

Edward Stratton & Lavinia Walton, Aug. 2, 1836. Richmond C. Tyre, BM.

Peter Stubblefield & Milly Badget, Sep. 6, 1836. Thomas Donoho, BM.

Sandy Subtle (Subttle) & Matilda Dinning, Jan. 5, 1836. John Graves (see 1837 list). Jesse Hollis, BM.

George A. Swift & Mary Jones, Sep. 8, 1836. Sidney C. Swift, BM.

Allen Tilley & Clarinda Stamps, March 20, 1836, by Freeman Senter. John D. Norvell, BM.

Robert Thompson & Elizabeth Finn, Oct. 25, 1836, by Samuel Laurence.

Henry D. Young, BM.

Friar Trail & Elizabeth Hobday, Jan. 30, 1836. Rowland Hay, BM.

Charles W. Turner & Mary Ann Graves, Jan. 16, 1836. Wm. G. Durham, BM.

William Turner & Virginia Underwood, Feb. 24, 1836. Walter L. Bugg, BM.

James Vaugn & Oneida Sutton, June 25, 1836, by Elisha Oglesby. Richard A. Carr, BM.

James F. Walch & Sara Ann Moss, Nov. 29, 1836. Edwin A. Moore, BM.

Erasmus D. Walker & Mary C. Cook, April 14, 1836. Thomas C. Douglass, BM.

William P. Walton & Jane M. Tyree, Feb. 29, 1836. I. M. Baldridge, BM.

James G. Webb & Mary Evans, July 16, 1836. William Turner, BM.

John Weeks & Delila Sutton, Aug. 13, 1836. David Prock (or Brock), BM.

Albert Westbrook & Mary Stewart, Dec. 7, 1836, by Jesse Gambling. Night Crabb, BM.

William White & Sarah E. Wilson, June 8, 1836. Robert Moore, BM.

Thomas Whitesides & Elizabeth Palmer, April 9, 1836, by Luke P. Allen. Robert C. Ellis, BM.

Charles D. Wiatt & Mary T. Callas, April 2, 1836. Robert Taylor, BM.

John L. Williams & S. B. Gordan, Dec. 20, 1836. Andrew J. Hamilton, BM.

Robert P. Willmott & Nancy Stone, March 21, 1836, by Joanthan Davis. Austin C. Atwood, BM.

James Wims & Nancy Gailbreath, Feb. 9, 1836, by John Carr. William Wims, BM.

Peter Yount & Ann Elizabeth Ailor, Jan. 1, 1836, by Jesse Gambling. John Sadler, BM.

James Alexander & Jane C. Stewart, April 13, 1837.

P. L. Anderson & Mary Carter, May 8, 1837.

R. G. Armfield & Betsey McDaniel, May 23, 1837.

Mathew Armstrong & Nancy Marquess, Nov. 2, 1837, by L. B. Edwards.

Robert Armstrong & Malinda Strother, Feb. 1, 1837.

Josiah P. Ashford & E. Anthony, Jan. 11, 1837, by Robert Norvell.

John G. Avritt & Mary Dalton, Feb. 7, 1837.

Elisha Barnard & Polly Bradley, April 25, 1837.

William H. Bates & Elizabeth Hawkins, Dec. 9, 1837, by J. B. Brizendine.

James Bell & Martha Marcum, Dec. 18, 1837. Mathew Hutchinson, BM.

Isaac Bland & Parlie Saunders, Feb. 16, 1837.

J. W. Bradley & T. G. Cardwell, May 22, 1837, by C. G. Browning.

Jesse Bradley & Mary Kirby, Nov. 19, 1837, by William Woodall.

Samuel Boykin & Deborrah Pike, March 28, 1837, by Taylor G. Gilliam.

William Brandon & Jane Cooper, Dec. 14, 1837.

J. M. Brigance & E. E. George, Oct. 26, 1837.

James Brigham & Priscilla Crabb, Oct. 28, 1837, by Joseph Pitt.

S. C. Bruice & M. O. Smith, Aug. 15, 1837, by H. B. Hill.

John W. Buck & Emiliza Garrett, April 4, 1837, by John McLin.

Embry Buckley & Susan Martin, Nov. 4, 1837.

John W. Bunton & Mary H. Howell, Feb. 5, 1837.

SUMNER COUNTY MARRIAGES

William Butler & Ellen Ellis, March 29, 1837, by J. H. House.
Terry H. Cahal & Ann Saunders, March 9, 1837, by James P. Smith.
David Carr & Leannah Bell, Sep. 9, 1837.
Landon I. Carter & Nancy Carter, April 5, 1837, by Thomas Gilmore.
A. M. Caruthers & Martha Robinson, July 20, 1837.
John Cheek & Patsey Perdew, April 26, 1837, by Robert Norvell.
J. W. Clark & Nancy Chapman, Oct. 19, 1837.
James Cockran & Margaret Grainger, March 15, 1837, by John Graves.
James Cole & Jane Underwood, Sep. 2, 1837, by Lewis Hiett.
William Cooley & Eliza Hassell, April 27, 1837.
David Culwell & Malinda Davis, Oct. 1, 1837, by Bartlet Turner.
D. R. Curle & A. E. Jefferson, Oct. 12, 1837, by Lewis Hill.
John Dearin & Elizabeth Holloway, Feb. 27, 1837, by Thomas Gilmore.
James Dinning & Sally Cooper, July 4, 1837, by Freeman Senter.
Thomas C. Douglas & F. A. Contrell, July 13, 1837.
John H. Dowell & Elizabeth S. Weatherhead, Oct. 30, 1837.
Ambrose Duffer & Mildred Flipping, Nov. 9, 1837, by John H. Robertson.
Edward Duffer & Emily T. McClary, March 30, 1837, by Taylor G. Gilliam.
Felming W. Duncan & Lucy Greer, June 25, 1837, by Elisha Oglesby.
M. D. Duncan & Caroline T. Chambers, April 6, 1837, by Elisha Oglesby. F. A. Duncan, BM.
William Empson & Margaret Freeland, Feb. 16, 1837. William Empson, BM.
Daniel Escue & Henrietta Donnell, Feb. 9, 1837, by Elisha Vaughan. Samuel Gourly, BM.
David O. Fenix & Mary Meador, July 10, 1837, by Freeman Senter.
R. M. Field & Mary D. Smith, Feb. 6, 1837. Joseph Thompson, BM.
James Frazor & Ann Shaws, Nov. 21, 1837, by B. S. Rutherford.
Alexander Graham & Adaline Saunders, Feb. 9, 1837, by B. B. Brown.
Benjamine Griffin & Lucy Gregory, Feb. 19, 1837, by R. M. Potts. William Smothers, BM.
Abner L. Hanna & Mary I. Parker, Nov. 6, 1837, by John W. Hanner.
Elvis Harden (Harder) & L. K. Guthrie, Jan. 18, 1837, by S. H. Turner.
Ezekiel Harper & Sarah Ellis, April 25, 1837, by J. H. House.
William C. Harper & Mary R. Haslet, July 11, 1837, by John Graves.
Giles C. Harris & Catharine Meador, Feb. 15, 1837, by Taylor G. Gilliam. James Hawkins, BM.
John Hawkins & Elizabeth Leffler, Jan. 16, 1837, by S. H. Turner.
B. J. Henley & M. A. Counts, Nov. 14, 1837, by L. B. Edwards.
Henry Highton & Frances H. Gilliam, Oct. 19, 1837. Bartlett Turner, BM.
H. W. Hill & S. W. Robeson, Aug. 21, 1837.
German Hodges & Eliza Ann Jourdan, Sep. 4, 1837.
R. T. Hodges & Nancy Brewer, June 6, 1837.
James Hollis & Frances Smith, June 17, 1837, by Lewis Hitt.
John Hope & Mary Renser, April 4, 1837, by Joseph Spradlin.
A. G. Hudson & Malinda Stone, June 26, 1837, by W. P. Rowles.
Geo. W. Hughes & Elizabeth Walker, May 20, 1837, by Hiram Duty.
Crawford Hughs & Catharine Wilks, May 6, 1837.
Lion (Sion) Hunt & Eliza Brown, Nov. 28, 1837, by F. Johnston.

Thomas C. Hurt & Winifred Underwood, Oct. 23, 1837, by B. S.
  Rutherford.
Nelson Johnson & Mildred Mabry, Nov. 29, 1837, by William Barr.
Judithan Jones & Levicy Carr, Feb. 13, 1837, by William P. Taylor.
Moses Jordan & L. Buchanan, Jan. 26, 1837, by Robt. Joyner.
Thomas Keefe & Jane Barr, Oct. 12, 1837, by A. B. Duval.
William Kenedy & Elizabeth Leffler, June 20, 1837, by Joseph Pitt.
King Kerley & Elizabeth Brown, March 14, 1837, by Taylor G. Gilliam.
  John Kerley, BM.
B. S. Kirk & V. E. Jones, Nov. 9, 1837, by E. B. Brown.
Alexander Lavisky & Harriet Lockhart, April 12, 1837.
Owen Lee & Jolene Fry, March 30, 1837, by Robert Joyner.
John M. Lewis & F. A. J. Wilks, Dec. 11, 1837.
William Little & Elizabeth Lunsford, Aug. 17, 1837.
Louis Loney & Nancy Merryman, Nov. 11, 1837.
S. W. Malone & Elizabeth E. Williams, Sep. 2, 1837.
Charles Matthews & Francis Bell, March 15, 1837.
Bennett Marshall & Mary Fisher, Oct. 2, 1837.
Andrew McConnell & Sarah Stone, March 13, 1837, by L. B. Edwards.
J. M. McMurry & Elizabeth Anderson, Dec. 27, 1837.
Nathaniel Meador & Cathrine Perdue, Sep. 25, 1837, by Freeman
  Senter.
Lewis N. Meadors & Lucinda M. Condon (or Cowdon), Feb. 9, 1837, by
  Samuel Laurence. William C. Simpson, BM.
William Meadow & Izabella Hannah, June 2, 1837, by Thomas Gilmore.
William Meadows & Elizabeth Williams, Oct. 30, 1837, by B. S.
  Rutherford.
Thomas Mitchenor & Parky Locket, Oct. 3, 1837, by Thos. Mitchenor.
Maclin Moody & Cinthia A. Morris, March 27, 1837, by John Graves.
William Morris & Martha Gilbert, Oct. 5, 1837.
A. H. Moser & Nancy Pullam, Dec. 5, 1837, by T. Horsly.
Samuel Neel & Sarah Neel, Feb. 24, 1837, by Francis Johnson. Joseph
  W. Beard, BM.
Thomas Neel & Polly Baird, May 8, 1837, by John Beard.
John Neighbors & Elizabeth Childers, Oct. 23, 1837, by Isaac Lind-
  say.
Christian Nix & Mildred Keen, Sep. 14, 1837, by Isam Cron.
John C. Payne & Jane West, Sep. 2, 1837.
Reason E. Perdue & Nancy Pardue, Nov. 2, 1837.
William Proctor & Nancy Slate, May 30, 1837.
J. A. Rickman & M. T. Seawell, Aug. 28, 1837.
A. Richmond & Nancy Key, Aug. 24, 1837.
Berry Right & Nancy Nemo, Dec. 23, 1837.
Thomas G. Roney & Elizabeth Lambert, Dec. 21, 1837.
Gail Sanders & Martha A. Malone, Feb. 2, 1837.
James Scoggins & Mildred Woodson, Jan. 4, 1837.
James Scott & Elizabeth Slate, July 29, 1837.
W. N. Seawell & S. A. Rickman, June 26, 1837.
R. S. Shaw & Mary Harder, Oct. 23, 1837.
John G. Skeen & E. Harrold, Sep. 13, 1837.
William L. Sloan & Malinda Jones, March 21, 1837. James Story, Jr.
  BM.
James K. Smith & Priscilla Hiett, March 20, 1837, by Lewis Hiett,
  Esq.

SUMNER COUNTY MARRIAGES

Thomas Somers & Polly Alley, Feb. 15, 1837.
Wm. W. Somerset & Rozena Barr, April 17, 1837.
J. Somerville & Sally Roney, June 27, 1837.
Z. A. Stone & Jane Cox, March 26, 1837, by Ben Gray.
James Story & Jane M. Lauderdale, Sep. 11, 1837.
W. R. Stovall & L. I. Bradley, May 22, 1837, by C. G. Browning.
Sandy Subttle & Matilda Dinning (see list 1836 also), Jan. 5, 1836
    (1837). Jesse Hollis, BM.
William Taylor & L. Neely, Dec. 2, 1837.
John S. Tucker & Malvina Rickman, Nov. 27, 1837.
J. H. Turner & M. J. Johnson, Oct. 5, 1837, by Nathan S. Johnson.
I. B. Vinson & L. T. Harper, Oct. 5, 1837.
Thomas Walsh & Lucy T. Martin, Jan. 14, 1837.
David Warner & E. F. Hensley, Oct. 5, 1837.
Thomas M. White & Lucy A. Jackson, Dec. 21, 1837.
W. W. Weathered & Lucy V. Brown, Aug. 14, 1837.
H. L. Wilson & Evlind Barber, Oct. 3, 1837.
R. S. Winn & M. A. Taylor, May 13, 1837.
F. G. Wormington & Lucy A. Bell, Nov. 6, 1837.
Joel Yancy & Celia Davis, Jan. 10, 1837.
W. S. Alexander & Mary Ann Rickman, May 4, 1838.
W. W. Angel & Delany Love, April 19, 1838, by L. B. Canard.
Armstead Alderson & Eliza Bradley, Aug. 19, 1838. John Jackson,
    BM.
Samuel Archer & Elizabeth Parker, Jan. 13, 1838. Joel Richardson,
    BM.
Young Ball & Mary Dalton, Aug. 31, 1838, by Z. G. Goodall.
Sanford Barnard & Sarah Bradley, May 25, 1838. Randolph Maberry,
    BM.
John Bayne & S. J. Dodd, Oct. 6, 1838, by H. A. Belote.
Edward Benson & Miram Harrison, May 10, 1838. Alexander Benson,
    BM.
Bob Bugg & _____ Seany _____, June 4, 1838, by Ben Gray. Wil-
    liam Twopence, BM.
John M. Bugg & Sarah Taylor, Feb. 14, 1838.
Shapman Bloodworth & M. L. Forrester, Oct. 30, 1838, by B. S.
    Rutherford.
A. G. Blackmore & Harriet Sanders, Jan. 31, 1838.
William Bloodworth & Malvina Straton, Dec. 9, 1838, by P. Bradford.
A. Brigance & Nancy Ann Hollis, Feb. 10, 1838, by R.D. Hobday.
Hazel Green Butt & Mary Ann Barker, March 12, 1838, by Freeman
    Senter.
O. L. Cage & L. E. Douglass, Oct. 17, 1838.
Thos. Cardwell & B. Lewis, June 25, 1838, by J. A. Browning.
William Caruthers & Sally Giles, Aug. 30, 1838, by John McLin.
William Caveness & Rhody Walker, May 26, 1838, by John W. Spradlin.
Claborn Chumbley & Judith Hale, March 7, 1838. William Hale, BM.
Jordan P. Coleman & Senith Turner, Dec. 25, 1838.
James Croseday & Winnie Joyner, Sep. 3, 1838. Abram B. Joyner,
    BM.
Robert H. Crump & Lydia M. Bledsoe, Jan. 9, 1838.
W. H. Crump & E. J. May, Oct. 4, 1838.
William C. Dinkins & Lucinda Harrison, Aug. 30, 1838. John W.
    Dinkins, BM.

Izaiah Dixon & Margaret Hains (or Harris), Nov. 20, 1838, by Francis Johnson.
R. B. Durham & Mary Senter, Oct. 16, 1838. William G. Durham, BM.
William G. Durham & Malinda Rippie, Oct. 16, 1838, by Rodney B. Durham.
James A. Edmunds & Tobitha M. Brackin, Dec. 6, 1838. James Butler, BM.
Geo. W. Farris & Mary E. King, Nov. 28, 1838.
Ezekiel Flemming & Elvira McGaha, Dec. 12, 1838.
T. I. Flowers & Martha Ann Johnson, May 5, 1838, by Luke P. Allen.
James Franklin & Mariah Cage, Oct. 14, 1838.
William Fulgum & Matilda King, Nov. 14, 1838.
J. H. Gambill & Mary T. Slate, Aug. 8, 1838.
M, P. Gentry & E. Sanders, Feb. 17, 1838.
James Gloover (Glover) & Y. E. Tyree, April 3, 1838.
Andrew J. Green & Mahala Graham, April 2, 1838.
W. C. Gregory & L. P. McAnnis, Oct. 20, 1838.
Jesse Goodman & Elizabeth Epperson, Oct. 29, 1838. Annanias Epperson, BM.
W. H. Hall & C. D. Barry, Nov. 19, 1838.
John O. Hamilton & Eliza Gourley, Feb. 21, 1838.
W. F. R. Hamilton & Amanda Latimer, June 14, 1838. Isaac W. Luton, BM.
Thomas S. Harden & Ann Hunter, June 18, 1838.
Skelton T. Harris & S. G. Thurmonde, June 11, 1838.
Nathaniel Harrison & Emily Sanders, Sep. 24, 1838.
C. F. Harvey & M. W. McKendree, May 16, 1838.
Abel Hicks & Jemima Lovell, July 28, 1838.
Shirley Hodges & Jemima Marlin, Nov. 20, 1838.
J. G. Hollis & Levicy Hall, Jan. 15, 1838. Wiley Birdsell, BM.
William Holt & Sarah Kelly, Dec. 12, 1838.
Samuel Huskin & Fiajah Jones, Feb. 21, 1838.
Isaac T. Jackson & Mary Moore, June 22, 1838.
William Johnson & Martha J. Odle, Dec. 22, 1838.
Clifton A. Jones & Margaret Garret, Nov. 15, 1838. Mark Senter, BM.
T. J. Jordan & Ann M. Kent, Jan. 30, 1838.
Elisha Keen & Sally Woolf, March 4, 1838. James Gilliam, BM.
Anderson Kirkham & Jane Barker, Nov. 8, 1838. Joseph H. Garret, BM.
Hugh A. Kirkpatrick & P. O. Hamilton, Jan. 17, 1838. William F. R. Hamilton, BM.
J. D. Kirkpatrick & Socky Joiner, March 12, 1838, by B. S. Rutherford.
J. T. Kirkpatrick & Mildred Garrett, Sep. 23, 1838, by James N. Rea.
M. W. Laurence & Rebecca Poteet, Aug. 7, 1838, by Francis Johnson.
Jones Locket & L. B. Smith, Dec. 21, 1838.
George Long & Sophrony Cotton, Jan. 15, 1838. John R. Jiley, BM.
Harvey Lovell & Elizabeth Egnue, March 20, 1838.
J. N. Malone & K. Hannah, Oct. 15, 1838. H. B. Lauderdale, BM.
William Marcum & Charlotte Bell, Feb. 8, 1838. Joseph Dalton, BM.
Andrew Martin & Nancy Lefleer, Dec. 1, 1838.

SUMNER COUNTY MARRIAGES

Levi Matherly & Betsey Mathews, May 28, 1838, by Lewis Hiett.
Levi Matherly, BM.
Mathew Moore & Charity Guthrie, Dec. 21, 1838. Joseph Pitt.
James McBride & C. Lockhart, Jan. 6, 1838.
Meridy McCormack & Anny Stewart, Jan. 4, 1838, by Taylor G. Gilliam.
Willie Morris & Susan Roney, Jan. 8, 1838. Solomon Shoulders, BM.
Tilford Morris & Nancy Hunter, Nov. 20, 1838. John Hunter, BM.
B. T. Morton & E. S. Tompkins, Oct. 16, 1838. A. McAuley, BM.
H. I. Murry & Mary Harper, Oct. 19, 1838.
David Myers & Nancy Potts, Sep., 25, 1838. Elvis Rippy, BM.
Alsey Oniell & Mary Crumplin, March 12, 1838. Isaac Forest, BM.
John N. Patton & Martha King, March 5, 1838. John Patton, BM.
J. B. Pearce & Francis Wyatt, Dec. 26, 1838, by B. S. Rutherford.
Lorenzo D. Peck & Mary M. Hammet, Feb. 2, 1838. James Groom, BM.
Jefod Perry & Nancy Carter, Aug. 8, 1838, by Thomas Gilmore.
Thomas Perry & Sarah Morrison, Feb. 10, 1838.
John Pike & Elizabeth Phillips, Sep. 20, 1838. Joseph G. Tooley,
BM.
William Prichard & N. E. Liggan, May 28, 1838. James M. Brown, BM.
William Read & Nancy Joanes, July 24, 1838, by William P. Taylor.
John W. Reese & Nancy S. Latham, Nov. 5, 1838.
William Rider & Margaret Draper, Dec. 11, 1838.
Wesley Savely & Harriet Harper, Sep. 8, 1838.
J. P. Seawell & M. M. Cobb, May 21, 1838. H. B. Lauderdale, BM.
Joseph Sevier & Sally Hudson, Feb. 27, 1838. Benj. Hudson, BM.
Obadiah Smith & Ann Wethers, June 28, 1838.
Elihu Smothers & Mary Ann Jacobs, Feb. 11, 1838. John L. Stinson,
BM.
John Smothers & Elizabeth Smothers, March 8, 1838.
Drury Spillman & Nancy Devasure, Oct. 10, 1838.
Jesse Spradling & Susan Allin, Dec. 13, 1838. Obadiah Spradling,
BM.
Christopher Staley & L. Burns, Sep. 18, 1838.
Thos. Stewart & Ritty McCormack, Jan. 3, 1838.
James Stone & A. T. Carter, Dec. 20, 1838.
Stephen Stone & Sarah Schabell, Dec. 23, 1838.
Bartholomus Stovall & Betsey Avetts, May 16, 1838. Robert Stovell,
BM.
William S. Stowers & E. S. Parrish, Jan. 31, 1838.
M. M. Taylor & C. I. Taylor, April 24, 1838.
Pleasant Taylor & Peggy Curry, March 16, 1838.
Granderson Terry & Delpha Dice, Sep. 29, 1838.
Bartlett Turner & Margaret Foster, Jan. 23, 1838.
Henry Volentine & Martha Steele, Feb. 5, 1838.
S. S. Wallace & S. M. Carr, Aug. 23, 1838.
Marcus Watts & Mary Newton, Jan. 19, 1838.
Reuben White & Harriet Briley, June 26, 1838.
Byram Whitson & Hannah Gourley, May 28, 1838.
John Williamson & Elizabeth Thompson, Feb. 20, 1838.
Isaac Wood & Mary Satterfield, Jan. 1. 1838.
William F. Wood & S. E. Vinson, Jan. 13, 1838.
William Wright & M. J. Patton, Dec. 18, 1838.
Benjamin Wyatt & Sarah Murdock, Jan. 10, 1838.
A. E. Wallace & M. C. Crenshaw, Nov. 29, 1838.

ADDITIONS

Ezekiel C. Hodges & Rebecca Dorris, Oct. 17, 1823, by Meredith
   Hodges, J.P. Wm. Hodges, BM.

Anderson, (cont.)
Jane 6
Jane A. 90
John 53, 74
John B. 27
Jonathan 25
Kezina 6
M. 46
Mabene 46
Mabin 93
Mahalah 34, 38
Marcey 78
Margaret 35, 37
Martha D. 85
Mary 23, 43
Mebane 56
Miles 12
Milley 15
Nancy 25, 72
P. L. 102
Polly 23
Rebeccah 13
Robert 13, 32
Sampson 66
Samuel 20, 22, 32
Samuel R. 78
Sarah 25
Stephen 2, 4
Susan 101
Thankful 80
Thomas 7, 16, 43, 44, 45, 46, 51
Uriah 1
William 2
William F. 63
William H. 31, 43, 64
Andrews, James 39
Angel, John 39
W. W. 105
Walthett 39
Angela, John 50
Angle, Patsey 9
Anglea, James 53, 62
John 50
Polly 53
Anthony, E. 102
George 66
Henry 57
Jacob 57
Julia Jane 36
Joseph 21
Matilda 46
William 32
Appling, William 73
Archer, Josiah 83
Sally 90
Samuel 105
Archy, Martha 101
Armfield, Isaac 23
John 51
Mary 51
R. G. 102
Sally 35
Violet 47
Armstrong, Archibald C. 39
Charlotte 72
Elizabeth 42
James L. 8, 9
Mary Ann 64
Mathew 102
Robert 45, 102
Susan 91
Thomas 57
Arnold, Daniel 70
Ebenezer 49
Arrington, Susannah 1

Ascue, Daniel 72
Ashford, Demcy 64, 98
Eliza 100
Frances 66
Jane 101
John 78
Josiah 100
Josiah P. 102
Ashley, Elizabeth 39
Ashlock, Benjamine 23
Fanny 14
Nancy 43
Philip 27
Ashly, Nancy 85
Askew, Allen 18
Elisha 45
Isaac 25
Askey, Sarah 81
Asky, John 85
Mary 85
Aspley, Betsey 50
John 27
Lemuel 51
William 27
Asply, Jane 89
Patsy 55
Wm. 89
Aspy, Polly 26
Asque, Elizabeth 13
Aston, Joseph 97
Atcheson, Nathan 12
Atchinson, John G. 46
William 15
Atchison, Adam 8
Nathan 8, 16
William 16
Willis 27
Atherly, John 16
Atkins, Dicy 17
Isaac 17
Philip 23
Winny 17
Atkinson, Willis 18
Atwood, Austin C. 102
Aust, Frederick 70
Joseph 70
Austin, Ashley L. 83
Diana 65
Dickerson 75
Dickinson 66
Dickson 95
Edy 75
Egleston 73
James 78
John 75, 78
Jordon 93
Nancy 78, 86
Polly 60
V. D. 73
Volentine 49, 100
Wilkenson D. 73
William 43, 62
Avent, Dolly H. 32
Harris 16
Herbert 22
John P. 89
Averitt, John G. 98
Avetts, Betsey 107
Avrett, Lucinda A. 98
Avritt, John G. 102
Axcum, Sally 25
Axum, Mary 88
Sally 25
Babb, B. 63
Baber, Benjamine 46
Charity 36
Badget, Jane 27

Badget, (cont.)
Milly 101
Thomas 27
Badgett, Jonathan 17
Mary 87
Polly 11
Sarah 77
Tabitha 19
Baile, Ishmael H. 97
Bailess, Polly 22
Bailey, Jememiah 52
John 14
Rutha 76
Sally 40
Samuel A. 49
Baily, Harriett 60
Martha 90
Bain, John R. 52
Susan 79
William N. 64
Bains, Moses 14
Baird, E.A. 98
Isham 3
Lucinda 85
Polly 104
Baker, Amanda 85
Ann C. 75
Eliza W. 43
Isaac 14, 20, 26, 101
James 49, 52
James M. 97
John 20, 23
Jourdan 53
Levi A. 57
Malvina 58
Martin 16
Mary M. 94
Matilda 39
Morgan W. 93
Mourning 48
Porter 78
William 32
Z. W. 99
Zach. W. 62
Balch, John 91
Baldridge, Alvin 86
Charity 25
I. M. 102
J. W. 65
Jane 18
Josiah W. 51
Peggy 49
Thompson 91
Baldrudge, Josiah W. 66
Baldwin, William 1
Bale, James 20
Bales, David 57
Balir, Nancy 64
Ball, Abner 10
Eliza 93
Elizabeth 10
James 5, 49
John 78, 80
Milly 76
Polly 46, 47
Rhoda 96
Richard 15
Young 105
Ballard, C. 34
Washington G. 34
Balthrop, Willie 39
Balton, J. H. 75
Bandy, Betsey 38
Charlotte 53
Edward 66
Epson 49
Ferrin 53

Bandy, (cont.)
  Horatio 38
  Jamason 49
  Jamison 25, 32, 43
  Jane 32, 65
  John 51
  Lucy 81
  Martha 72
  Mossy 56
  Nancy 56, 78
  Perrin 65
  Polly 38
  Richard 32
  Sally 45, 49
  Thedocia A. 95
  Woodford 78, 86
Bane, Edwin 51
Banks, Alexander 78
  Elizabeth 32
  Emaline 54
  Samuel M. 70
Banton, John 18
  Lewis 36
Barber, Evlind 105
  Joseph 98
Barbor, Joseph 97
Barbour, Daniel 95
Baren, Francis 46
Barham, Elizabeth 59
  John 21, 32, 46
  Thomas 46
Baringer, Jonathan 23
Barker, Isreal 16
  Jane 106
  Joshua 27
  Mary Ann 105
  Nathan 73
  Polly 9
  William 21
Barkley, Caty 3
Barlow, Lewson 61
Barnard, Darcus 16
  Dorias 40
  Elisha 48, 102
  Elizabeth 96
  Jacob 27, 40-41
  James 25, 49
  Jenny 48
  Lucusia 16
  Mary 85, 90
  Nancy 18
  Sally 44
  Sanford 105
  Thomas 97
  Zadoch 25
Barnes, Ezekiah Collum 33
  Kinchen 12
  Nancy 58
  Nathan 62
  Patsey 4
  Polly 3, 12
  Sally 19
  Solomon 21, 38
  Turner 32
  Wright 23, 34, 47, 57,
    81
Barnet, Casander 12
  William 12
Barnett, James 20
  John 8, 39
  Lucy 35
  Peggy 19
  Thomas 12
Barns, Betsey 49
  Celia 5
  John 4
  Polly 8

Barns, (cont.)
  Rebecca 8
  Robert 78, 81
  Samuel 4
  William C. 73
  Zachariah 70
Barr, Ann H. 72
  Caleb 62
  Esther 2
  Hugh 25
  James W. 78
  Jane 104
  Jane P. 59
  John 16, 33, 38, 40,
    44
  Joseph 97
  Margaret 86
  Mary 59
  Mary A. 94
  Nancy 48
  Polly 36
  Robert 51
  Rozena 105
  Samuel 60, 89
  Silas 16
Barret, Thomas 6
Barrett, Daniel 22
  David 25, 47
  George 25
  James 36
  Josiah 46
  Nancy 35
  Polly 67
  Thos. 9
Barrm, Wm. M. C. 88
Barron, Joseph 21
Barrot, Thos. 14
Barrott, David 21, 33
  Polly 50
Barrow, Edmond 57
  James C. 78, 83
  Nancy 51
  Peggy 23
  Reason 83
  William 86
Barry, C.D. 106
  Evaline 20
  Francis 25
  James 17, 20, 31, 34
  Mary 53
  Patience 79
  Rachel J. 86
  Red D. 24
  Thomas 78, 81, 90
Barton, Dosha 52
  Elijah 33
  Elisha 83
  Elizabeth 33
  James 46, 49
  Thomas 39
  Thomas H. 86
Baskerville, Jane L. 62
  Martha J. 20
Bason, Barbary 14
Bass, Gilford 42
  Hastey 5
Batcheldor, John 21
Bate, Humphrey 47
Bateman, Asail 36
Bates, Anny 40
  Any 43
  Humphrey 61
  Humphreys 15
  James H. 90
  John 40
  Olive 34
  Polly 15, 43

Bates, (cont.)
  William 93
  William H. 102
Bathey, Matthew 33
Bauldright, Anny 16
Bayne, John 105
  Mathew 42
Baynes, Elsworth 12
  Sally 4
  Susan 63
Beacham, Susan 50
Beaird, Elizabeth 89
Beard, Adam 3, 23
  Alfred 82
  Alfred M. 53, 73
  Ann 63
  Anny 13
  Betsey 3
  David 5, 57
  David, Sr. 13
  Henry 52, 56, 64, 73
  Henry N. 59
  Joseph W. 57, 104
  Martha 64
  Polly 24
  Rebecka 4
  Sally 22
  Thos. 22
  Thomas C. 24, 36
  William E. 73
Beardin, John, Jr. 42
Beardon, Fanny 25
  Harriett 19
  Solomon 36
Bearnard, Jacob 8
  Nelly 8
Beasley, Martha 81
  Patsey 25
  Warner,80
Beasly, Ann 18
  John C. 97
Beason, David 70
  Henry 70
  Mary Ann 55
Beaver, Jesse 46
  Pincey 51
Beckenstaff, Sanford 100
Beckman, Polly 36
Beeler, Betsy 50
  John C. 21
Beldsoe, (See also Bled-
  soe)
  Isaac 97
Bell, A. L. 78
  Alfred 46
  Amzi L. 86
  Ann 2
  Betsey 60
  Charlotte 106
  David 21
  Francis 104
  Isaac 42
  James 14, 85, 102
  Jane 10, 87
  John 32, 33, 35, 36,
    38, 52, 56, 61, 67,
    77, 81, 83, 84
  Joseph M. 36
  Leannah 103
  Levesta 39
  Lucy A. 105
  Malinda 81
  Margaret 69
  Matilda 79
  Micajah 36
  Nancy 49
  Patsy 77

Bell, (cont.)
Patton 66
Pleasant 86
Polly 1, 21
Robert 10, 27, 69
Samuel 1
William 8, 78
Wm., Sr. 78
Bellew, Peter 5
Bellmay, Jan 20
Belote, Anny 14
Clarissa 77
Harriett 67
Henry 46
Henry A. 71
Henry H. 73
Jeremiah 73
John 46
Martha J. W. 86
Mary Ann 93
Nancy G. 76
Benas, Molly 2
Benbrook, Daniel 66
Elbert 70
Nathan 27
Bender, Betsey 78
Burl 58
Bennet, America 82
Bennett, Elizabeth 26
Elizabeth C. 66
Griffin 31
Nancy 37
Patsey 22
Polly 95
Richard 21
Benson, Alexander 105
Edward 105
Josiah 59
Polly 92
Benthal, Rhody 17
Susannah 17
Willis 51
Benthall, Daniel 49
Franky 57
Mary 8
Bentley, James 5
Jeremiah 97
John 12, 14, 25, 40
John, Jr. 91
Nancy 90
William 57
Bently, Betsey 46
Elizabeth 79
Martha 77
Sally 62
Benton, James 87
John 3, 5, 6
Berdin, Mary 37
Bernard, David 51
Elisha 53
Jacob 53
Matilda 90
Susanna 15
Valentine 44, 48
Zadeck 32
Berry, Lucinda 95
Molly 6
Polly 35
Berryman, Benjamine V. 91
Beson, David 70
Susannah 4
Best, Keziah 39
Bevard, Lawrence 27
Bever, James 57
Bickert, Elizabeth 2
Biddle, Elizabeth 64
Biggers, Agnus 71

Biggers, (cont.)
Joshua 49
Maria 75
Biggs, Adam 27, 40
Henry 95
James 57, 63, 70
John 51
Joseph 6
Margaret 40
Simpson 83
Bilbo, Mary H. 70
Billings, John 8, 12
Bingham, Alvan 18
Binley, Patsey 39
Biram, Moses 43
Bird, Abram 29
Polly 2, 4
Wm. 4
Birdsell, Wiley 106
Bishop, Joseph 5
Bison, Betsey Ann 80
Biter, Betsey 2
Bitner, Betsey 2
Black, Caty 17
Elizabeth 49
Gabriel 2, 14
George 73
John 14'
L. P. 100
Matilda 91
Michael 49
Nancy 47, 73
Polly 48
Sam'l P. 12
Sarah 25
William 70, 71
William C. 83
Blackamore, Cena 14
Blackard, Betsey 47
Polly 39
Sarah 44, 56
Thomas 44, 51
Blackburn, Henry 95
Blackemore, A. G. 72
John 21
Matilda 47
Reuben 57
Sarah 84
Wm. 81
Blackman, Elizabeth 33
Leaner 25
Blackmore, A. G. 105
Anny 18
Emiline 75
Fieldon N. 43
Frances S. 35
George 1
Geo. D. 1
George D. 46
J. D. 26
James 8
John 18
Reuben 46
William 80
Wm. M. 86
Blackston, Sally 65
Blackstone, Elizabeth 72
Blackwell, Betsey 4
Fanny 21
John L. 58
Thos. 25
Blackwood, Spyway E. 87
Blain, George 36
Blair, Ellenor 8
Fanny 44
Jane 76
John 64

Blair, (cont.)
Joseph 23
Mary 68
Peter 8
Polly 63
Sally 63
Blakard, Job. 46
Blake, Thomas E. 70
Blakemore, A. G. 83
Catharin 63
Edward 62
Elizabeth 91
Geo. D. 45
Geo. W. 65
Jefferson 53
John 62
John W. 78
Lee C. 51
Susan 24
Wesley 65, 70, 75
Wm. M. 89
Blalock, Zachariah 95
Bland, Isaac 102
Blankenship, Prudence 30
Blar, Nancy 64
Blasangam, William 21
Bleason, Prudence 11
Bledsoe, (See also Beld-
soe)
Abraham 10, 17
Amanda 83
Anthony 1
Betsy 1
Caty 20
David 70
David L. 73
Elizabeth 80
Geo. M. 83
George W. 93
Henry 10, 23
Isaac 8
Isaac M. 7
Isaac N. 95
Isaac W. 8
James 97
Lydia M. 105
Mary 2
Mildred 63
Peggy 1
Polly 3
Polly Ann 65
Prudence 11
Rachel 1
Sally 4
Suckey 2
Thomas 91
Thomas J. 91
Wm. 20
William L. 23, 29, 36,
48
Bloodworth, Betsey 22
Elizabeth 72, 76
Henry 12, 22
John 95
Joseph 71
Lemuel 53
Mary 95
Patsey 59
Priscilla 12
Rushia 58
Sarah 76
Shapman 105
Thomas 14
Web 8
Webb 12, 17, 25, 30,
45, 55, 76
William 53, 105

Bloodworth, (cont.)
Zelpha 31
Blythe, Andrew 3, 48
Elizabeth 79
Elizabeth A. 81
I. T. 100
J. Y. 86, 88
Martha 75
Rachel 3
Richard 23
S. H. 38
S. K. 23, 45, 46
S. W. 36
Samuel E. 16
Samuel K. 17, 25, 26, 59
Samuel M. 81, 84
Boaz, Edmond 25, 34
Edmund 18
Boddie, Elijah 26, 35, 86
Body, Elijah 27
Bogin, Edward 1
Bogle, Hugh 49
James 49
Rachel 49
Bohann, Polly 35
Bohanon, William 80
Boiles, Patsey 40
Boles, Anne 24
Isaac 24
Bond, Allen 32
John B. 39, 48
Bonds, Polly 9
Bone, James 2
John 38
Susannah 2
Bonner, Thomas 51
Williamson 39
Booker, Amanda M. 73
Dalton 43
Geo. L. 73
John 62
Mary 42
Susan H. 83
Tervesa 73
Bookerville, Thomas B. 93
Boon, Harriett 46
Nathan 14
Susan 78
Susan E. 83
Booth, Lewis 8
Boothe, Chas. 9
Salley 9
Borders, Peter 24
Polly 24
William 95
Boren, Ally 95
Emily 87
Francis 10
John 10
Richard 53
Stephen 46, 53
Tarlton 12
William 23
Borene, Caty 22
Francis 22
Borrin, Francis 66
Nancy 66
Bosley, Peyton R. 83
Boswell, Fanny 26
Bottom, Lucinda S. 89
Lucretia M. 96
Merry S. 53
Bough, Sally 15
Bowen Catherine 12
Celia Wilson 22
Elizabeth R. 94

Bowen, (cont.)
Frances 48
John 35
John H. 16, 21, 22, 34, 41
Levisa 27
Mary R. 92
Bower, John H. 33
Bowers, Jeremiah 17
Stephen C. 78
Bowlen, Matthew C. 21
Bowler, Elizabeth 25
Bowles, John 23
Martha 39
Rachel 29
Zacharia 93
Bowling, George 51
Bowls, Minerva 88
Bowman, Celia 67
Cynthia 83
Elizabeth 27
James 27
James A. 51
Jane 62
John T. 27
Joseph 12
Patsey 24
William H. 69
Bowyer, Reason 3
Boyce, Nichl. 6
Boyd, Anna 40
Charles H. 83
John 2, 46
Robert 43, 62
Sally 43
Siras 57
Boyer, Elizabeth 71
Henry 14
Margaret 66
Nancy 39
Richard 6
Sally D. 42
Boyers, Charlotte 30
David 23
John 86
John M. 41
Lucresia 15
R. M. 34, 46, 100
Robert M. 24, 32, 41
Robert Morris 34
Sidney 41
Boykin, Hannah 68
Mary 61, 89
Mathew J. 93
Samuel 65,.99, 102
Boyle, Eliza 94
Hugh 46, 51
James 32
John 32
Lidia 92
Rachel 42
Boyles, Bayley 87
Elizabeth 48
James 53, 89
James R. 50, 85
Nancy 23
Richard 66
Susan 67
Boyman, Caleb 34
Boze, Edmond 30
Bozeman, Polly 72
Bracken, E. J. 90
Edmond 83
Eliza 53
Elizabeth F. 91
Elvira 82
James 24

Bracken, (cont.)
James B. 53
Jane 18
Jesse 78
John 23, 42
Rosannah 8
William 8, 9, 34, 39
William, Jr. 57, 62
Brackin, Edward 87
Elizabeth 82
J. B. 100
Malinda 64
Margaret 34
Oina 16
Polly 16
Rachel 25
Tobitha M. 106
William 10, 16, 18
Bracy, Catharine C. 94
John W. 95
Bradford, Ann L. 86
Cecilia M. 25
Cynthia 21
Eliza 43, 47
Elizabeth A. 94
Emisia 46
Francis 43, 62
Henry 3, 25
Susan 84
William 23, 56
Bradley, Abraham 36, 48
Abram 79
Absolum 97
Catherine 56
David 6, 12, 14, 36, 41, 49, 57, 78
Edward 9
Elijah 93
Eliza 105
Henry 21
J. W. 102
James 74
James B. 70
Jesse 27, 102
John 14, 23, 28, 66
John D. 18
Joshua 7, 23, 36, 55, 78
Judith 50
L.I. 105
Levin 78
Luke 28, 53
Mary 94
Nancy 14, 36
Nathan 95
Polly 102
Reuben 93
Reubin 81
Richard 23
Robert 35, 36, 57, 62
Robert T. 75
Samuel 21
Sarah 105
Saviah 77
Susanna 57
Susannah 14
Thomas 21, 28
William 23, 57, 77
Bradly, Isaac 57
Bradshaw, Betsey 16
John 8, 16
Salley 23
William 5, 6
Brady, Absolum 97
Braham, JOhn 43
Brake, Drusilla 22
Bralie, Virginia J. 89

Branch, William P. 98
Brandon, William 102
Branham, John 49
   Randal 87
   Sally 49
Brannon, Joseph 70
Branson, Clowe 73
Brantley, Charles 1
   William 32
Brasher, Jane 100
Brasil, Courtney 9
Brassell, Benjamin 53
   H. T. 97
   Tabitha 36
Braswell, Elizabeth 12
Bratney, Jane 36
Braton, Polly 5
Bratton, James 10, 37
Bray, James 93
Brazel, Judy 49
   William 6
Brazell, Margaret 79
Brazier, Zachariah 97
Brazil, Polly 92
   William 3
Break, Sylva 10
Breedlove, A. B. 39
Breene, Mary C. 57
Bressie, Hellen L. 95
   Perlina 100
Brevard, Alfred A. 49
   Cyrus W. 66
   John C. 70
   Sally 3
Brewer, Nancy 103
Brews, Benjamine 70
Brewster, Martha 36
Brezeal, Biddy 5
Briant, Edward 40
Bridgers, Edmund 10
   John 10
Bridges, Amanda C. 83
   Edmond 22
   Jesse 83
   Sally 26
   Thomas 95
Bridgewater, Amanda 70
Briding, John 42
Brigance, A. 105
   Betsey 30, 40
   Caty 10
   Charles N. 28, 45
   David 7
   Geo. S. 33, 40
   J. M. 102
   James 7, 9, 11
   Joel 74
   John 28, 36, 78
   Lavina 31
   Mahali 40
   Peggy 32
   Polly 2, 7
   Sally 53
   Thankful 50
   Wm. 2
   William H. 83
Briggance, Jemima D. 87
   William 87
Briggs, Adam 32
   Polly 32
Brigham, James 102
Briley, Elizabeth 11
   Harriet 107
   Ishamel H. 97
   James 32, 61, 70
   Nancy 35
   Polly 38

Briley, (cont.)
   Sally 61
   Susanna 53
   William 32
Brily, Elisha 57
Brinkley, John A. 49
   Kendal 32
Brisby, John 13
Brisley, John 10
Britt, Alexander 99
   Martha 69
Britton, James H. 53
   Nancy 8
Brizendine, Anne 88
   J. B. 66
   Richard C. 66
   Young P. 66, 70
Brizindine, Nancy 66
Brock, David 100, 102
   Durham 21'
   Moses 43, 49
   Sarah 77
Broddie, Ledewick 46
Brodley, Abraham 71
Brooke, David 52
Brooks, Athy 78
   Christopher 78
   Edmund 62
   John 18, 21, 62, 66
   Judy 60
   Mary 101
   Packy M. 65
   Pleasant 62
   Sally 46
   Thomas 46, 65
Brookshire, Enock W. 46
   Thomas 28, 30
Brookshires, Thos. 20
Broughton, Abel 66
   Able 67
Brown, Alexander 74, 78
   Ann 80
   Anna D. 47
   Anny 61
   Augustin 87
   Barton 78
   Benjamine 27
   Bernard 74
   Betsey 42, 64
   Edy 97
   Elisha R. 95
   Eliza 103.
   Elizabeth 70, 71, 104
   Elizabeth D. 71
   Eunice 59
   F. 22
   Frederick 14
   George T. 74
   Hanah 23
   Hannah 23, 43
   Jacob 43, 51, 66
   James 10, 18, 57, 95
   James M. 107
   Jane 37, 55
   Jemima 62
   Jeremiah 46, 52
   Jesse 36
   Jesse R. 101
   Joel 22
   John 10, 23, 33, 38,
     41, 42, 50, 62, 66,
     83
   John H. 97
   Joseph 33, 97, 99
   Joseph W. 95
   Lazarus 5
   Leonard 9

Brown, (cont.)
   Lucy 51, 81
   Lucy V. 105
   Lydia E. 87
   Manaweather 49
   Margaret 72
   Mary 5, 41, 92, 97
   Mary, Jr. 101
   Mary F. 86
   Mary Jane 84
   Milly 49
   Nancy D. 73
   Nancy T. 94
   Nimrod 51
   Philip 88
   Polly 17, 42
   R. J. 76
   Rachel 12
   Raney 64
   Reuben D. 51
   Reuben S. 51
   Richard 62
   Robert 23, 47
   Sally 78
   Samuel 17, 59, 62, 66
   Sarah P. 95
   Squire 83
   Stephen 5, 6
   Susan 64
   Susanna 92
   Susanna T. 51
   V. H. 98
   Volentine H. 97
   William 33, 70
   William G. 79
   Willis 93
Browning Clarissa 56
   Clifton G. 62
   Daniel 21
   David 21
   Edmund 20, 23
   Edward 36
   George 12
   J. A. 99
   Jacob A. 36
   James G. 66
   John 48, 49, 51
   Jonathan 62
   Nancy 48
   Sally B. 95
   William P. 97
Bruce, David 14
   Elizabeth 44
   Francis 75
   James 23, 79
   Jefferson 79, 87
   John 33
   John W. 95
   Littleton 46
   Lucy 14
   Mary 49
   Polly 12, 18
   Reuben 62
   Robert 18, 33, 79, 83
   S. C. 77
   Sally 72
   Simon 62
   Thomas 33, 49
   Walter 8
   William 19, 87
Bruice, Archibald 98
   S. C. 102
Bruise, Martha E. 99
Brundige, Stephen 49
Bryan, Dennis 3
Bryant, Charlotte 9
   Levi 62

Bryant, (cont.)
  Lucretia 18
  Mitchell 71
Brylie, Elizabeth 96
  Hiram 95
  Margaret 95
  Samuel 95
Bryly, Polly 69
Bryson, Mary 75
  Peter 17, 33
Buchanan, Arena 74
  L. 104
Buchannon, Elizabeth 87
Buchanon, James 2
  Rebeccah 2
Buck, Elender 2
  John W. 102
Buckham, Andrew 14
Buckhanan, Sarah 32
Buckingham, Thomas 91
Buckley, Embry 102
  Francis 45
  Patrick 55
Buckly, Eliza 70
  Patrick H. 58
Buckner, Eliza 69
  Harriett 47
Bugg, Ansil D. 36
  Arthur D. 46
  Bob 105
  John L. 56, 61
  John M. 105
  Joice E. 36
  Martha 93
  Mary Ann 69
  Richard G. 53
  Robert 101
  Samuel 99
  Samuel H. 85
  Walter L. 102
Bull, Alex. 45
  Betsy 32
  Margaret 51
  Rebecca 67
  William A. 43
Bullers, Joseph M. 38
Bunch, Mariah 57
  Permelia 47
Bunckley, Catharine 9
Bundy, David 49
Bunn, Henry 6
Bunton, Betsey 45
  John W. 102
  Martha Ann 91
  Polly 42
  Thomas 39, 88
Burchet, John 93
Burchett, William 12
Burford, John H. 33
Burgess, Gracy 83
Burk, Elisha 2
  Elizabeth 34
  Frances 44
  Lucy 28
  William 3-
Burke, Lewis 66
  Margaret 94
Burkett, Mary 94
Burney, John M. 83
  Robert A. 91
  William 23
Burnley, Charles 101
  John 91
  Lucy Ann 74
  Sarah 39
  William 87
Burnly, James 83

Burnly, (cont.)
  Susan 81
Burns, Ann 91
  Betsey 49
  George 53
  James 10
  L. 107
  Mary 55
Burris, Dickison 62
  Dickson 66
Burrow, Patsey 56
Burton, Jinny 11
  Lydia 38
  Mary 91
  Maryann 7
  Tabitha 11
  William 91
Busby, Anderson 58
  Ann 64
  Elijah 49, 59
  Elizabeth 59
  Fanny 16
  James H. 86
  John 67
  Lucy 49
  Martha 86
  Nancy 46
  Patsy 70
  Polly 31
  Rorotha 94
  Stephen 18
  Susan 93
  William 46
Bush, Alsa 56
  Benjamin 29, 52
  George 12, 53
  Greenberry 70
  Josiah 58
  Mary 39, 71
  Miley 53
  Oliver 28, 93
  Tenny 70
  William 39, 46, 53,
    55, 58
Bushby, James H. 98
Bushrod, Clarissa 3
Butcher, Anthony 85
Butler, Aaron 18
  Aron 8
  Elijah 57, 62
  Elizabeth 88
  Henry 53
  James 71, 79, 80, 85,
    106
  Jane 85
  John L. 83
  Mary 83
  Samuel 95
  William 98, 103
Butt, Amy 72
  Betsey 30
  Hazel 19
  Hazel Green 105
  John 51, 76
  Phillip 70
  Priscilla 76
  Samuel 70, 72
  William A. 87
Butterworth, Dolly L---?
  62
  Elizabeth H. 68
  Jese 39
  John 39
Button, Robert 98
Byram, Lemuel 43, 62, 74
  W. 85
  Widen 74

Byran, Peter J. 74
Byrd, Abram 19
Byrn, Allen 93
  Charles L. 28
  David P. 83
  George 59
  J. W. 28, 31, 35
  Jno. 19
  John N. 44
  John W. 15, 23, 33, 34
    35, 36, 41, 44
  Margery 87
Byrne, Allen 83
  Richard G. 83
Byrnn, J. W. 43
Byrns, J. W. 21
  James 1
  John 33
  John W. 21, 25
  Martin 46
  Stephen 1
Byrom, Noah 43
Byron, Catharine 87
Byser, Mary I. 85
  Thos. 85
Byson, Elizabeth 44
  Sally 58
  Thomas 74, 80
Caffry, John 43
Cage, Adaline 67
  D. L. 84
  Edward 83
  Eliza D. 62
  Elizabeth 84
  H. 30
  Harriett 83
  James 11, 12
  Jesse 10, 18, 19
  John O. 98
  John Overton 60
  Levina 84
  Loftain 10
  Louisa 57
  Marcus W. 88
  Mariah 106
  Martha T. 60
  Nancy 49
  O. L. 105
  Orville 49
  Patsey 30
  Priscilla 63
  Reuben 5, 19
  Sally 2
  Sophia 75
  William 2, 12
  William G. 93
  Wilson 4, 5, 95
Cahal, Terry H. 103
Cain, Elkainer 93
  James 58, 66
  Josiah 35
  Mary Ann 64
Caine, Joseph 22
Calbert, Mary 33
Caldwell, Anne 4
  Betsy 94
  Charles 93
  David 70
  Edy 71
  Hardy 61
  Isaac 4
  James 17, 20
  Jane M. 52
  William 11, 58, 79, 83
Calhoun, E. F. 87
  Samuel 43
Callas, Mary T. 102

Calvin, Polly 12
Camhorn, Polly 53
Camp, Elizabeth 34
Campbell, Alfred F. 95
  Colin 37, 62
  David 12, 62
  James 51, 60
  Jehosephat 63
  John 91
  Joseph 16, 25
  Mary 63
  Nancy 10, 32, 37
  Robert 3, 10
  Sarah 2
  Thomas 8
  William 17
Cane, Josiah 21
Canedy Dempsey 4
  John 4
Canfield, Hannah E. 90
Cannon, Alanson 93
  David 58
  George 95
  Tilman 100
Cantrell, Darby H. 74
  Hannah 79, 83
  J. P. 34
  James B. 43
  Mary 46
  Ota 18
  Sarah 10
  Stephen 10
  William 27, 34, 36, 42,
    67
  Z. P. 74
  Zebulon 41
  Zebuton 34
Cantrill, William 28, 33,
  37
Cape, Sally 71
Capps, Ewing S. 95
  John 79
  Margaret 75
  William 13, 26
Caps, Elizabeth 59
Car--- ?, James 48
Cardwell, Nancy G. 21
  Nancy W. 73
  Nelson 28, 95
  T. G. 102
  Thos. 105
Carel, Robert 21
Carey, Elizabeth 20
  John H. D. 62
  Nancy 72
  Richard H. P. 62
  Thomas 36
Carless, Benjamine 28
Carman, Isiah 98
  John 44
  Larkin 33, 46
  Phebe 42
Carmon, Larkin 67
Carney, Daniel 49
  Jane 57
  John 72, 74
  Joshua 58
  Samuel 72, 74
  Shelton 53
Carothers, Ezekiel 39
  Hugh 5
  James 5, 8, 10
  Jinny 10
  Majory 29
  Margaret 39
  Thomas 8, 30
Carpenter, Frederick 49

Carpenter, (cont.)
  Wineford 44
Carr, Alason G. 93
  Anna 49
  David 39, 100, 103
  Elisha 63
  Elizabeth 38
  Hannah 1, 17, 50
  Isabella 89
  J. A. 98
  James 6, 13, 37, 38,
    39, 42, 46, 47, 48,
    49, 58, 67
  James C. 67
  Jesse 98
  John 2, 6, 68, 79, 95
  John, Jr. 17
  John F. 76, 86
  John S. 51
  John T. 77, 83, 85
  Jordon 74
  King 1, 2, 5, 9, 17,
    40
  Levicy 104
  Levisa 91
  Mason 71
  Peggy 6
  Polly 48
  Richard 1, 84
  Richard A. 102
  S. M. 107
  Sarah 6
  Sary 59
  Thomas 74
  Thomas H. 98
  William 30, 99
  William C. 79
  William H. 84
  William P. 43
  Wilson L. 62
Carrel, Thos. 21
  Wiley 14
Carroll, Betsey 18
  Elizabeth 42
  Hannah 26, 37
  James 91
  Margaret Ann 93
  Martha 92
  Milly 94
  Polly 34
  Robert 33
  William 25, 87
Carrothers, Esther 19
  William 19
Carson, Betsy 35
  James 2
  Matheen 26
  William 79
Carter, A. T. 107
  Alexander 17
  Allin 97
  Gideon 25, 58
  James 53
  Jarrett 58
  John 87
  Jno. W. 86
  Joseph 25, 69
  Joseph W. 79
  Kinchin 8
  Landon I. 103
  Martha 96
  Mary 102
  Nancy 103, 107
  Richard 84
  Therissa 97
  William 43, 49, 79
Cartmell, Marian 86

Cartwright, Alexander 12
  D. 82
  David 87
  Elizabeth 77
  James 43, 45, 81
  Mary 68
  Patsey 5
  Polly 56
  Robert 18
  Sally 6
  Thomas 2
  Thomas W. 58
  William 21, 23
Caruthers, A. M. 103
  Caroline 85
  Josiah 86
  Robert 67
  William 105
Cary, James 11
  Polly 11
Casney, John 67
Casselberry, Mary 5
Caster, Maria 80
Cather, Reuben M. 87
Cathey, Alex. 12
  Betsey 3
  Elizabeth 10
  Griffith 6
  Hannah 13
  James 15
  Jane 5
  Mathew 60
  Mathew B. 45
  Peggy 7
  Susannah 6
  William 9, 10, 12
Cato, Green H. 67
  Robert 22
Caton, Abner 53
Catron, Elizabeth 35, 71
Cattron, Catherine 22
  Peter 22
  Susannah 26
Cavatt, Peggy 16
Caveness, William 12, 105
Caviatt, Elizabeth 9
Caviness, Tabitha 65
Cavitt, Alexander 56
  Andrew 36
  Claibourne 70
  Elizabeth 78
  Moses 22, 23
  Polly 20
  Richard 23
  Sarah 22
Cavy, Leutitia 60
Center, Any 66
  Lucinda 51
  Richard 14
Chadbourne, John 36
Chaddock,Josa 11
Chaina, Edith 96
Chambers, Anny 11
  Caroline T. 103
  Mrs. Charlotte C. 100
  Joshua 6
  Lucinda 49
  William W. 51
Chance, Polly 13
Chandler, Andrew 46
Chaney, Dianna 82
  George 87
  John R. 93
Chapill, Prudence 53
Chapman, Anna 24
  Archibald 51
  Benjamine 67

Conger, Betsy 19
Congill, Martin 67
Conn, Joseph 9
   Josephus 15
   Octavia 23
Connell, Enoch P. 23
   William B. 62
Connelly, John 43
Conner, A. C. 94
   Lewis 62
Connolly, John 41
Connor, Betsey 49
Contrell, F. A. 103
Conway, Peggy 81
Conyers, Thomas 1
Cook, Benjamine 58
   Dempsey 67
   Elizabeth 58, 68
   J. C. 47
   Jacob C. 23
   James 70
   Lewis 98
   Mary 95
   Mary C. 102
   Rebeckah 41
   Thomas 10, 68
   Turner 33
   Valentine L. 79
   Wiley 49
   Yerby 17
Cooley, William 63, 103
Cooly, Stephen 84
   William 53
Coop, Hannah 13
Cooper, Elizabeth 23
   Hannah 16
   Houston 17
   Jane 102
   Jenny 6
   John 16, 30
   Rachel 3
   Sally 103
Cope, Iddoa 74
   Iddoce 79
   James 54
   Margaret 101
   Richard 39
   Sally 71
   Susan 55
Copland, John 16
Corbett, Joseph 71
Corbin, Charnel 5
Corcle, Elizabeth 16
Corder, Charity 19
   James L. 71
   Lewis 33
   Polly 64
Corkle, William 5
Corley, Austin 51
Cornelius, Nancy 70
   Richard 67
Correll, Sally 47
Cothran, W. 101
   Wm. 90
Cotton, Ann 46
   Arthur 40
   Betsey 40
   Centhia 69
   Elizabeth 98
   Frances 47
   Harriett 99
   Henry F. 98
   Hugh 79, 84, 85
   John 2, 5, 21, 44
   Lazrus 2
   Mary 40
   Moor 54, 58

Cotton, (cont.)
   Moore 5
   Nancy 12
   Sophrony 106
   Telitha 6
Cougher, Sally 11
Counts, M. A. 103
Covention, Washington 67
Coventon, Washington 67
   William 12
Covington, Adaline 82
   John 71
   Polly 48
   Sarah 57
   William 67
Cowan, Margaret 8
   Sally 3
Cowden, William 17
Cowdon, Lucinda M. 104
Cowen, Elizabeth 16
   George 39
   Margaret 28
   Mathew 5
Cowgill, Daniel 84
   Martin 46, 60, 62
Cowin, Hugh 26
Cox, Jane 105
Crabb, Celia 18
   Knight 80
   Nancy 52
   Night 102
   Priscilla 102
   Susan 52
Crabtree, Jacob 39
   Joseph 1, 4
   Nancy 4
Crafford, Jennet 5
Crafton, Armand 72
   Hezekiah 62
   Polly 63
Craighead, T. B. 36
Crain, Ezekiel 43
Crane, Betsey 11
   Ezekiel 47
   Lewis 4, 11, 45
   Polly 50
   Susannah 45
   William 33, 38
Cravatt, Levatha 7
Cravens, Nancy 28
Cravins, John 1
Crawford, Ann 58
   Elender 11
   Elizabeth 43
   Hugh 1, 34, 54
   John 18
   Josiah 39
   William 6, 7
Crawley, Margaret 87
Creenshaw, William 17
Crenshaw, A. J. 91
   Anne P. 99
   Elizabeth 43, 46
   John 23, 93
   M. C. 107
   Martha 68, 92
   Mary 53
   Meredith 28
   Meredith G. 35
   Nancy 69
   Nathan 21, 24
   Nathaniel 18
   Susan 39
   Susanna 52
   William 26
Crewan, Jos. M. 7
Crews, Benjamine 39, 69

Crews, (cont.)
   Edward 62
   Fanny 48
   Jane H. 60
   John 58, 59
   Martha 88
   Nathan 88
   Pleasant 14
   Polly 71
   Sally 40
   Sophia 29
   Tarlton 87
   Willis 71, 87
Cribbins, Curry 1
Crider, Caty 34
Crighton, Robert 44
Crocket, David 31
   Robert 62
Cron, John 98
Crook, William 84
Croseday, James 105
Croslin, Wright W. 87
Crosner, George 8, 10
Cross, Elizabeth 14
   James 86
   Zachariah 1
Crossland, Lucretia 44
Crossley, James 68
Crosslin, Wright W. 90
Crosswaite, Polly 40
Crouder, Janny 20
Crow, John 54
Crowder, Cage 58
   Larkin T. 87
   Lewisa 30
   Terry 59
   Thomas 28, 30
Cruise, Elizabeth 76
   Mary Ann 60
Crump, Adam 21, 24
   Lewis W. 54
   Robert H. 105
   W. H. 105
Crumpler, John 67
Crumplin, Mary 107
Crumply, Martha 88
Crumpton, Thomas D. M. 98
Crunk, John 49
Crutcher, Edmund 5
Crutchfield, Thomas 46, 49
   William 10
Cruze, Drury 46
Cryer, Hardy 46
   Hardy M. 23, 38, 40, 64
   Hill 78
   James 11, 30
   Mary 51
Cuffman, Eliza Ann 84
   Janthe 69
   P. 11
   Pavatt 26
Cufman, Pavatt 14, 15
Culbertson, Thomas 58
Culbreth, John 91
Culwell, David 103
   William 63
Cummings, Corum 95
   Elizabeth 76
   George 5
   Nancy 47
   Sally 49
   Thos. 49
Cummins, Nancy 34
   William 59, 74
Cunning, Patsey 26

Dill, Sally 50
Wm. 8
Dillard, Elizabeth 3
Gabriel 43
Nancy 14
Dilley, James 87
Dillon, Isaac 12, 51
Jesse 32
Polly 71
William 49
Dining, Andrew 39
John 40, 41
Dinkins, John W. 105
Lucy 101
William C. 105
Dinning, Andrew 12, 22
Anthony 74
Bowles 39, 71
James 98, 103
John 12, 62
John Richard 54
Matilda 101, 105
Nancy 22
Peggy 16
Tabitha 62
Thomas G. 93
William 10, 28, 36, 74
Dirt, Francis R. 91
Dishman, Jane 40
John 40
Dismuke, Lucinda 54
Dismukes, G. A. E. 100
John T. 76
Dixon, Anny 4
Ephraim 28
Izaiah 106
Jeremiah 51
Joseph 1
Josiah 12
Keziah 6
Matthew 8
Sarah 4
Dobb, John 25
Dobbins, Alexander B. 50,
51
Anne 4
Carson 11, 17, 23, 37,
49, 73
Henry 51
Isabella 50
John 12, 63, 66, 88
Polly 37
Priscilla 17
Robert 4
Robert B. 36
Robert D. 93
Sally 11
Samuel 88
Thomas C. 63
Dobbs, John Z. 93
Dodd, Marcus 12
Mary 63
Robert C. 91
S. J. 105
Dodson, Elizabeth 40
Evelina 49
Mary 39
Nancy 21
Donalson, Lewis G. 49
Donelson, Ann C. 65
Mahala 74
Mary 95
Molley 14
Moses M. 95
Sam'l. 7, 9
Donnell, A. 36
Adlae 41, 44

Donnell, (cont.)
Eunice 44
Henrietta 103
Jesse 44
Latimer 54
Persis 54
R. W. 98
Robert 91
Susan 54
Donoho, A. G. 71
Albert S. 74
Anthony 28
Clementine 34
Elizabeth 18, 32
Eveline 51
Isaac 5
James 28, 95
John 5, 11, 40, 43
Nancy 37
Noah 63
Permillian 90
Sally 48
Sarah 55
Thomas 98, 101
Walter 8, 40
William 55
Dorr, Henry 10
Dorris, Abegail 41
Absolom H. 88
Betsey 26
Catherine 46
Elias 79
Eliza 92
Elizabeth 9, 52
Frances 93
Isaac 28
Jane 28, 33
Jesse 71
Joab 80
John 28, 33, 51
Levi A. 63
Lewis 70, 71
Margaret 44
Nancy 43, 72
Peggy 46
Permelia A. 93
Rebecca 26, 52, 70,
108
Robert 36, 88
Rolan A. 89
Roland A. 88
Samuel 21, 43
Tabitha 36
Viney 59
William 21, 33, 36,
46, 62
William, Jr. 23
Zelpha 36
Dorsett, Willis 21
Dosit, James 18
Doss, Elizabeth 62
James 21
Joshua 62, 88
Dossett, Betsey 48
Dossit, Betsey 43
Dotson, Nancy 50
Doty, John 54
Dougan, Robert 4
Dougherty, Rebecca 21
Doughtry, Nancy 57
Doughty, Henry 88
James 71
Douglas, Agnes 40
Alfred H. 41
Alfred M. 45
Edw. 28, 40, 43
Elmore 41, 52

Douglas, (cont.)
Ezekiel 6
G. N. 62
George 63
H. L. 98
Isaac 64
James 2, 15, 23, 32,
36, 37
John 67
Louisa F. 93
Martin 67
Mary Ann 86
Norval 63
Patsey 15
Robert B. 95
Sally 6
Thomas C. 103
W. H. 15, 23
Wm. H. 44, 49
Willie J. 43
Young N. 93
Douglass, A. H. 39
Abraham 11
Alfred M. 33
Asa B. 55
Edward 2, 3, 46
Eliza 48
Elmore 3, 36
Emma 84
Evaline 46
Ezekiel 4
George 57
H. H. 69
Harry C. 71
Harry L. 21
Harvey C. 56
Howard 10
Isaac C. 43
James 21
Jesse 26
John 27
L. E. 105
Nancy 55
Patsey 98
Reubin 2
Robert G. 79
Thomas C. 102
William 23
William H. 17, 18, 27,
28
Y. N. 72, 75, 76, 77,
84, 85
Douthat, John P. 88
Douthet, Stephen E. 88
Dowel, David 26
Dowell, John 50, 52, 98
John H. 103
Polly 24
Sarah 50
Susanna 43
Downs, Ambrose 96
Augustine 46
Ballard 67
Charity 97
John 46
Thomas 58
Tilley 51
William 61, 82, 91,
93
Doxey, Eliza A. 98
Hannah 55
Jeremiah 7, 43
John 21
John L. 43
Matilda K. 96
Stephen 21
Doyal, John 12

Doyal, (cont.)
 Sally 12
Draper, Daniel 28
 Dicey 70
 Elizabeth 68
 Joshua 38
 Margaret 107
Drew, Jas. C. 99
Dreweney, Patsey 25
Drewney, Patsey 25
Drewry, Sarah 27
Driver, Joel 91
Druham, (See also Dur-
 ham)
 Henry 90
Drumbhelln, Nicholas 70
Drumheln, Nicholas L. 67
Duff, Jane 46
Duffer, Ambrose 103
 Auston 58
 Edward 103
 Nancy 67
 Seaton 64, 90
 Setan 67
 Seton 67
 Wm. 83
Duffy, Francis 54, 67
Duggar, Flood 21
Dugger, Allen 79
 Avarilla 30
 Charlotte 28
 D. 8
 Dred 8
 Elvin 98
 Flood 18, 74, 79, 101
 Floyd 42
 Frederick 87
 James 8
 Jarroth 21
 Jeremiah 64
 Leonard 5, 25, 28
 Lucy 42
 Luke 5, 30
 Prunetta 55
 Pully 25
 Wesley 28
 Wilie 74
Duke, James 10, 98
 John 98
 Thomas 43, 57
Dukes, Lucy 26
Dulass, William 23
Dunagin, Peggy 64
 Sarah 71
Dunavin, George 81
Duncan, Elizabeth A. 28
 F. A. 103
 Harriett S.A. 62
 Hiram 43, 46, 55, 64
 John 51
 M. D. 103
 Marshall B. 68
 Mary T. 48
 Milley H. 63
 Polly 43
 Sandy P. 16
 William 71
Dunigan, Polly 61
Dunn, Abner 67
 Hugh T. 12
 Hugh Torrence 12
 James 94
 John D. 71
 Joseph B. 54
 Shadrack 10
Dunnegan, Joel 88
Dunning, James 98

Dunning, (cont.)
 Micajah 18
Duren, George 17
 Nancy 17
 Sally 36
Durgess, Jeremiah 57
Durham, (See also Dru-
 ham)
 Betsey 33
 Buckner S. 43
 Gatewood H. 98
 Henry 23
 James 43, 56, 59
 John 21, 43, 47
 Louisa M. 86
 Mary 81, 85
 Nancy 44, 56
 Patsy 22
 R. B. 106
 Rhody 31
 Sally 64
 Samuel 21
 Sarah 99
 Thomas 45
 William 14
 Wm. G. 102, 106
 Zorita 101
Durin, Polly 31
 Sarah J. 73
 Thomas 23
Durlin, Elias 28
Durnal, Washington 79
Durnall, Sally 79
Durning, Susan 47
Durran, Thos. 47
Duty, Betsey 20
 Hiram 54
 John 54
 Nice 38
 Patsey 20
 Polly 23
Duval, Adaline M. 39
 Alex. D. 65
 Alexander D. 36
 Archibald Bowling 39
 Arthur B. 91
Duvall, Mary 70
 Nancy 22
Dwyer, Jane 72
Dyal, Jenny 1
Dye, Isreal 79
 Julian 23
Dyer, Abasuerus 49
 Betsey 4
 Ely 43
 Fanny 28
 Haxin 18
 Lucy 38
 Mary 24
 Thomas 18
Eagan, Hugh H. 49
 Martha 98
Earle, Ezeas W. 33
Early, Elizabeth 53
 Julia 70
Earthman, Isaac 18
Easbery, Betsy 14
Easley, John 26
 Joseph 15
 Milton 40
 Patsey 19
Easly, Henry 71
Eastas, Willie 71
Easten, Margaret 17
Easter, Wesly 82
Echols, Joel 18, 21
 Larkin 21

Echols, (cont.)
 Nancy 56
Eckols, Clounda 14
Edens, Jobe 98
 Samuel 98
Edison, James 64
 Joseph 46
 Samuel 46
Edmunds, James A. 106
 Samuel 88
Edson, Samuel 43
Edward, L. B. 64
 Wm. 66
Edwards, A. 9
 Adonyah 15
 Benjamine 33
 Betsy 2
 Cullen 43
 Darkness 2
 David 17
 Drew 46
 E. 57
 Ed. 67
 Edward 51, 52
 James 5, 16
 John 18
 L. B. 72
 Lovy 58
 Lucithe 21
 Mahalia 95
 Martha 26
 Milly 8
 Nancy 16, 90
 Nathan 26
 Patience 79, 84
 Polly 17
 Priscilla 18
 Richard 12
 Richards 21
 Sally 18, 26
 Seaborn 67
 Simon 15
 Sulley 21
 Thomas 2, 3, 13, 18,
  46, 51
 W. A. 98
 William 46, 49, 65
 William, Jr. 12
Effitor, Archibald 4
Egnue, Elizabeth 106
Eidson, Richard 88
Elam, Archie S. 88
 Joel 88
 Josephus 88
 Josiah 71
 Peter 91
Elder, James 7
Elim, Samuel 43
Eliss, Thornin 26
Elizer, James B. 74
Elliott, Cinthia E. 60
 Dempsy 84
 Elizabeth 25, 71
 Elizabeth M. 83
 George 14, 29, 33, 34,
  40, 42, 66
 Hugh 19
 James 23
 Mariah 27, 96
 Melissa 94
Ellis, Abraham 5, 20
 Betsey 15
 Elender 44
 Ellen 103
 Everard 26
 Isaac 18
 J. G. 48

121

Ellis, (cont.)
Jacob 28
James 26, 35
James T. 28
Jesse 47
John J. 79
John W. 79
L. 37
Levi 21
Levi D. 23
Margaret 91
Michael 74
Nancy 22
Polly 16, 37
Robert C. 102
Sally 14
Samuel 44
Sarah 103
Simeon 14, 15, 16
Smelling 19
Survellen 24
Ellison, Jacob 43
Elliss, Edward 13
Everard 12
James G. 53
John 8
Polly 13
Sibella 13
Elliston, Alexander 54
Joseph T. 33
Emery, John 54
Susannah 54
Emory, Susannah 70
Empson, William 21, 103
Emry, Michael 40
Endsley, Patsey 49
Eneas, Isabella 85
Enox, Elizabeth 6
Epperson, Ananias 98
Annanias 106
Elizabeth 106
Lucy 91
Epson, Thomas W. 100
Ernest, G. Haley 55
Erspy, Robert 1
Ervin, James 15
Erwin, Abner 46
Alfred 46
Elim A. 28
Elim A.A. 63
Geo. 65
George I. 63
John P. 73
Mary 97
Mathew 63
Mathey 49
Escue, Daniel 62, 103
James 76, 80, 88
John 88
Leonard 33
Leonard C. 88
Sam'l 86
Esken, Samuel 63
Eskew, John 54
Esley, Drewry 28
Eson, Gideon 28
Espey, William 7
Espy, Betsey 5
Peggy 8
Essex, Elizabeth C. 36
Sarah 56
Thomas 63
Thomas W. 54
Estes, Richard B. 26
Etheridge, Stephen 40
Etherly, Polly,7
Ethridge, Garrard 15

Eubanks, Patsey 45
Eury, Francis 8
Eustice, John W. 101
Evans, Amelia 91
Barbary 59
Barshaba 62
Cornelius 28, 46
Elizabeth 83
George 4
Isaac 47, 54
James 94
Jesse 46
Louisa 97
Mariah 50
Mary 102
Patsey 11
Peggy 26
Stephen 10
William 19, 80
Everett, Thomas J. 90
Evins, Robert 98
Ewing, Alexander 58
Alexander C. 58
William R. 58
Exom, Louisiana 75
Exum, Arthur 10, 18
Eliza 49
Joseph 75
Martha 18
Polly 34
William 18
Ezell, Benjamine 51
Fagg, Zachariah C. 94
Fair, Peleman 84
Fairless, Charity 48
Elizabeth 78
Lanty 54
Robert 74
Fairly, George 3
Farley, John 17
Farmer, Catharine 56
Thos. 7
Farr, James 3, 4
Jane 35
Farrier, Euridice 20
George 12
John 4
Nathaniel 4
Farris, Geo. W. 106
Phebe 55
Faulk, Aney 9
Orran 23
Wm. 9
Faulks, Orran 24
Fawke, Levi 12
Fenix, David O. 103
Ferguson, Greenberry 74
John 40, 43
Mary 51
Nancy 2, 43, 93
Nelson 28
Pheby 51
Tildy 18
William D. 74
Ferneybough, John 23
Ferrell, Bernard 14
Birrom 15
Birtis W. 58
Cherry 33
Clement 21
John 80
Nancy 19
Peggy 41
Susanna 19
Thomas 12, 29
Fibbs, Elizabeth 90
Field, R. M. 103

Figures, Mathew 43
Fikes, Isabella 49
Fillingan, John 23
Fillingham, John 21
Fin, William 58
Findley, Hugh 16
Finix, John 15
Finley, Hugh 18
Obadiah 21
Wm. 37
Finn, Elizabeth 96, 101
Rebecca 34
Shadrick 15, 49
Fishback, Rosy Ann 64
Fisher, James 16
Jeremiah 76
Mary 104
Peter 3, 14
Susan 96
William 2
Fitts, Sanford 33, 36,
74, 86
Fitz, Sanford 72
Flack, Sally 55
Thomas 91
Fleetwood, Hardy 54
Merina 31
Sally 31, 42
Fleming, Beverly 26
James 26, 54, 60
Robert 12, 36, 46
Flemming, Ezekiel 106
Flipping, Martha B. 83
Mildred 103
Flood, Dolly 17
Flowers, Jenoma 87
T. I. 106
Flynn, George 4
Folk, Edwin 83
Follis, Raven C. 25
Sally 37
Fonvial, James 61
Fonville, John 74
Ford, Betsey 35
Crisia 33
Francis 47
John 50
John W. 36, 50
Joshua 36
Polly 58
Forest, Isaac 107
Reuben 75
Forester, Edmund 84
John 88
Stephen 59
Forrest, Isaac 18, 21
Reuben 23
Forrester, Hardy 88
Jacob 33, 35
Lydia 23
M. L. 105
Rebecca 43
Stephen 50
Foster, Addison 40, 41,
43, 44, 47
B. 47
Clarey 35
David 13
Dovy 43
James 43, 80
John 31, 41
John B. 94
John H. 67
John M. 65
Kitty 24
Margaret 107
Mirandia D. 92

122

Foster, (cont.)
  Nancy 40
  Sara 62
Found, John 4
Fowke, Levi 12
Fowler, Benjamine 67
  John 75
  Rebecca P. 88
  S. H. 75
  Walter 75
Foxall, Thomas 51
Frack, Mary 74
Frail, Solomon 17
Frailey, Daniel 15
  Elizabeth 56
Frainham, William 47
Fraley, Daniel 71
  Jane 62, 66
  Polly 69
Fraly, Polly 65
Franklin, Albert C. 99
  Anderson 80
  Ann 18
  Elizabeth 74, 81
  Elizabeth A. 97
  J. J. 74
  James 2, 12, 106
  James, Jr. 7
  John 56
  John J. 75
  John W. 71, 73
  Josiah R. 75, 83
  Julia G. 93
  Mary M. 52
  Peggy 12, 13
  Polly 36
  Sally 33
  Smith C. 84
  William 46, 52, 56, 70
Frazer, Donald 36
  George 76
  James 1, 2
  Thomas H. 73
  William 1
Frazier, James 1
  Polly 91
Frazor, Alexander 15
  Elizabeth 54
  George 43, 47
  James 43, 103
  Jane 29
  Margaret 74
  Peggy 47
  Thomas 43, 55, 79, 80
Freeland, Isaac 99
  John 13
  Margaret 103
  Polly 71
  Susanna 20
  Thomas 81
Freeman, Anne 20
  Cama 36
  Kidey 19
  Richard 3
Freighly, James 83
French, Benjamine 40
Fronville, Mary 52
Frost, Eli 71
  Sarah 25
  Thomas 84
Frudle, James 67
Fry, Basil 2
  Jolene 104
Fugerson, James L. 84
Fulgum, Martha Ann 80
  William 106

Fulke, Burwell 13
Fuller, John 22, 43
Fulton, David M. 77, 83, 84
  Eliza 36
  Jane 35
  John F. 60, 63
Fuqua, Wm. 48
Furgason, Roxanna 69
Furgerson, Sarah 24
Furgeson, Ann 89
Furguson, Moses 88
Gailbreath, Nancy 102
Gaines, Daniel 47
  Edward 30
  Edward P. 91
  Hannah 48
  Harriet 92
  John 15
  Lucinda 86, 95
  Moses 13, 44
  Nancy 48
  Polly 14
Gains, A. C. 84
  Elizabeth 95
  Henry 75
  Moses 16
  Sally 16
Galbreath, John 19, 58
  William 84, 85
Gale, Betsey 12
Gambell, John 14
  Mary 14
Gambill, Henry 10
  J. H. 106
  John 10, 15
  Martin 15
Gamblin, James 10
  Nancy 18
Gambling, Jesse 40, 46, 69
  Phoebe 13
  Polly 7
Gandy, John 6
Ganes, Lavinia 90
Gant, Betsy 48
Ganter, John 71
Gardner, Abagail 12
  Allen 45, 53
  Celia 15
  Cullen 33
  Cullin 41
  Elizabeth 52
  Hezekiah 8
  James 18
  Jane 67
  John , Jr. 58
  Malvina 77
  Rachel 7
  Robert 18
  Sally 37, 53
Garnder, Sally 13
Garner, Polly 32
Garret, Cathrine 87
  Jane 88
  Jesse 61
  John 7
  Joseph H. 106
  Margaret 106
Garretson, Hardin 99
  Hardin T. 87
Garrett, Betsey 45
  Caroline 81
  Catharine 18
  Celia 98
  David 54
  E. 98

Garrett, (cont.)
  Emiliza 102
  Francis 8
  Francis E. 63
  George 18
  Jacob 94
  John 51, 80
  Mary 74
  Mildred 106
  Polly 57
  Rachel 91
  Smith 51
  Wm. 8
Garrison, Alexander 63
  Caty 23
  Comer 84, 88
  Elizabeth 81
  Ephraim 17
  G. 81
  Gomer 75
  Hannah 75, 77
  Jas. B. 78
  John 29, 34, 59, 75, 84
  John, Jr. 17
  Mary 82
  Mason 15
  Nancy 16
  Polly 33, 36, 38
  Rachel 53
  Richard 45, 88
  Sally 15, 50
  William 26, 80
Garrot, Emily 96
  James M. 96
  Joseph H. 96
Garrott, Lavina 81
Garth, William A. 75
Gates, Michael 80
  Valentine 80
Gathier, John 2
Gentry, M. P. 106
George, Betsey 27
  E. E. 102
  John 71
  Sherwood 29
  Thomas 4
  William 36
Gibb, Mary 69
Gibbs, Sally 88
Gibs, Isbel 5
Gibson, Betsey 66, 79
  Darcus 75
  Derinda H. 65
  Elisha 51
  Isaac B. 40
  James 59
  John 26, 63
  Letha 78
  Marcus L. B. 67
  Nancy G. 77
  Polly 64
  Roger 2
  Samuel 4, 7, 40
  William 2
  Willie 36
Gift, William W. 40
Gilbert, Alia 2
  Frances 23
  Jane 66
  Jemima 44, 50
  John 37, 44, 46, 51, 91
  Martha 104
  Mary 45
  Samuel 2
  Thos. 22

Gilbert, (cont.)
  Willie 47
Gilbreath, Andrew 47
  Robert 47
Giles, Darcus 13
  Edward 51
  Edward S. 59
  Eli 17, 32
  Eliza 65
  Elizabeth 11
  Harriett 88
  John 8, 11, 75
  Jonah E. 6
  Josiah E. 13, 23
  Matilda 28
  Milton 36, 63
  Sally 105
  William H. 63
Gilham, Frances H. 90
Gillehand, Matthias 36
  Leah 5
Gillespie, Allen 75
  Elizabeth 51
  Elizabeth A. 42
  Elmira W. 74
  George 17, 36, 71
  Jacob 7, 59, 84
  James 40
  Jane 45
  John 47
  John D. 18
  John F. 5, 15, 20
  June 17
  Lydia 7, 43
  Mary 47
  Nancy 10, 93
  Naomi 10
  Polly 39
  Richard 23
  Richard R. 23
  Robert K. 67
  Samuel V. 52
  Thos. 10
  William 5, 59, 60
Gilliam, Frances H. 103
  J. W. 69
  James 81, 106
  Mary Jane 71
  Stephen 56
  Stephen A. 98
  Stephen R. 67
  Taylor 48
  William B. 88
Gillmore, Isable 77
Gillum, James 80
  Taylor G. 43
Gilmore, A. 36
  Abner 15
  Elizabeth 15
  Polly 53
  William 29
Gilpin, Ann 65
  ELizabeth G. 14
Gipson, Patsey 13
Givens, James 4
Givins, Betsy 35
Glasco, Polly 34
Glasgo, Sally 41
Glasgow, Isaac 47
  James 40
  Jesse 4
  Sophiah 60
  William 80
Glasser, Francis 2
Glen, Susan 71
Gloover, James 106

Glover, James 106
  William 26, 27, 29,
    38, 39, 41, 50, 61,
    78, 80
Gocey, John 99
Goff, Betsy 47
  Lucinda 88
  Malinda 88
  Moses S. 40
  Sally 57, 80
  William 25
Golden, Polly 49
Goldman, Anne 29
  Mary 38
Goldson, John M. 80
Golston, Charles 63
Goodall, Elenor D. 85
  Elizabeth 21
  John 40
  Kitty 23
  Lucy Ann 68
  Martha C.92
  Martha M. 73
  R. C. 86
  Zachariah G. 36
Goodard, Nancy 61
Goodbread, Joab 29
Goodin, Sally 17
Goodman, Jesse 106
Goodrum, John 7, 29
  Nancy 7
  Patsey 15
  Susannah 64
Gooster, Wm. 47
Goostree, Elizabeth 28
Gordan, S. B. 102
Gordon, S. B. 83
  Thomas 13
Gorley, James 77
Gossadge, Daniel 88
Gough, Catherine 57
Gourley, Eliza 106
  Hannah 107
  James 26, 94
  Jane 29
  John 15
  Mary 46
  Susanna 83
Gourly, John 88
  Samuel 103
Gowan, Amos 20
Gowen, Amos 14
  Reuben 33
Gower, Mary 51
Goyne, Amos 33
Gra---?, Nancy Ann 99
Grady, William 13
Graham, Alexander 103
  Andrew J. 98
  Delia 42
  Eliza 38, 60
  Elizabeth 7
  Evaline A. 57
  Francis R. 89
  Jane C. 50
  Jenny 5
  Jesse 26
  Lewis 21
  Mahala 106
  Margaret 45
  Margaret C. 24
  Mary L. 97
  Nellie 59
  Perry 8
  Richard 75
  Richard N. 88
  Susan A. 72

Grainger, Benjamine 13
  Henderson P. 99
  John 98
  Margaret 103
  Robert 67
  William 13, 99
Granger, John 19, 20, 59
  Mary 101
  Peggy 41
  Rebecah 12
  Susannah 7
  Thomas 8
Graves, Andrew 99
  Elizabeth 80
  Jacob 17, 49
  John 54, 62, 101
  John B. 84
  Mary Ann 102
  Michael 71
  Nelly 21
  Rachel 100
  Samuel 47
  William 20, 21
Gray, Chas. H. 88
  Clifford 80
  Frances 40
  James M. 26, 100
  Jane 82
  John 94
  Simon 33
  William 88, 97
Grayham, James 16
Grayor, James M. 40
Gready, Wm. 9
Green, Abraham 80
  Andrew J. 106
  Asa 43
  Daniel 19
  David 25
  Edmund 13, 17
  Edward 54, 84
  Elisha 21, 22, 49
  Elizabeth 22, 34, 56
  Elizabeth M. 63
  James 38
  Lewis 29, 40, 60, 75
  Littleberry 26
  Lucy Ann 98
  M. 17, 37
  Martha H. 73
  Mary H. 74
  Micahel 41
  Michael 26
  Michiel 26, 28
  Nancey 3
  Nancy 13
  Parris 75
  Peggy 24
  Sally 29
  Tabitha 32
  William 4
  Z. 73
  Zac. F. 85
  Zachariah, Jr. 84
  Zaph. 83
Greenhalgh, Israel 96
Greenhaw, Cloudsberry 6
  Elizabeth 6
  Greenberry 26
  Vloudsberry 6
Greer, John R. 92
  Lucy 103
Gregory, Archibald 94
  Boswell 24
  Daniel 54
  Dulcena 80
  Eleanor 91

Gregory, (cont.)
Elizabeth 41, 48, 59
Frances 92
Hambleton 36
Isaac 19, 24
Jacob 26, 50, 54, 66
James 59
John 20, 21, 63, 84
John W. 51
Jonathan 54
Lucinda 73
Lucy 103
Martha 33
Mary 75
Mel S. 47
Milly 52
Missouri 93
Nancy 31
Numbleton 43
Obadiah 51
Patsey 56
Polly 82
Roper 33
Ropher 33
Sally 63
Thomas 53, 67
Thomas E. 55
W. C. 106
Grey, Leathy 51
Gribble, Benjamin 97
Grider, Mary 40
Griffey, Sally 21
Griffin, Benjamine 103
Charlotte 68
Dolly 12
Humphrey 99
John L. 90
Margaret 68
Micajah 96
Sally 36
William 58, 59, 60
Griffith, Owen 45
Griggs, Daniel 98, 99
Henry 99
Joseph ·3
Permelia 99
Wm. 22
Grim, Abraham 24
Isaac 19
Grimes, Catherine 10
Eve 10
George 8
Grimm, Margaret 94
Grimsely, Fielding 19
Grimsley, Fielding 19
Grissam, Benjamine 24
Grissum, Sarah 98
Grisum, William 21
Groom, Hannah 9
James 107
Grooms, John 50, 55
Nancy 53
Sally 37
Grove, John 45
Groves, Allen 13
Ann 55
David 15, 16
Elizabeth 46
John 54
Leah 16
Lilly 13
Lucinda 75
Polly 12, 95
Thomas 12, 15
Thomas, Jr. 13
Guarrant, Elizabeth P. 75
Guestree, Watson 24

Guild, James 47
Jo. C. 62, 77
Joseph C. 60, 63
Gunn, James M. 71
Gunsaw, Jinny 14
Guthery, Joseph 63
Guthrey, Mary H. 61
Thomas 63
Guthrie, A.H. 71
Andrew H. 40, 44, 57,
90, 99
Anna M. 90
Anne 23
Charity 107
Eli 52
Elizabeth 37, 52
Eunice J. 76
James 76
L. K. 103
Robert 39, 44
Robert W. 40
Sally 39
Guthry, Sarah 58
Gwin, Catharine 64
David R. 40
E. C. 88
Edward 31, 39, 41
Elizabeth 13
Ezekiel 69
James 40, 66, 67
John 24
Margaret 36, 94
Nancy 13
Polly 11
Sally 7
Samuel 30, 33, 36, 38,
39, 60, 63
Susan 94
Thomas W. 63
William 18
Hackett, James 84
Hadley, James M. 75
John L. 80
William 34, 35, 39, 42,
43, 45, 58
Hady, Jonathan 25
Haffington, Archibald 4
William 4
Hail, Cage 17
Elizabeth 15
James 62
John 6
Haile, R. C. 99
Hails, Thomas 33
Haines, Caty 8
Edmond 30
Nancy 55
William 8
Hainey, Betsey 42
David 2
Jane 46
Margaret 34
Hains, Malinda 99
Margaret 106
Halbert, Enos 17
Hale, Cyrus B. 92
Elizabeth 18, 82
Jeremiah 6
Jeremiah W. 59
John 19
Judith 105
Milley 77
Priscilla 60
Richard 36
Sally 17, 18
William 47, 67, 105
Hales, Nancy 21

Hall, Arena 85
Cage 45
Caroline N. 83
Carter T. 80
Cerban 9
David 21
Fanny 55
George 75
Hannah D. 76
J. W. 40
James 99
Jane 23
Jesse 47
John 15, 44
Levicy 106
Lindy R. 39
M. B. 98
Mahala 71
Malvina 80
Middleton 71
Moses 24
Nancy 9, 81
Nelly 62
Patsey 67
Polly 34, 69
Rebecca 53
Richard P. 62, 63
Richard T. 63
Riden R. 71
Sally 21, 22, 66
Samuel 40
Samuel B. C. 80
Thankful, Junr. 1
Thomas T. 96
Tobias B. 84
W. H. 106
William 9, 18, 21, 34,
43, 45
Hallum, Bluford 88
Hambleton, Jenny 1
Hamblin, Milly C. 100
Hamilton, Andrew J. 99,
102
Ann 81
Anne 1
Anny 3
Betsey 18
Celia C. 93
Clabourne W. 75
Elizabeth 7
Eupha 44
Euphy 31
Fanny 2
Franklin 63
Henry 26, 29, 31
J. W. 12
James 13, 40, 94
Jane 78
Jinny 7
John 3, 6, 13
John C. 16
John O. 106
Martha 3
Mary C. 85
P. O. 106
Peggy 1, 12
Polly 6, 15
Sally M. 63
Thomas 9, 40, 63
W. F. R. 106
Wm. 13
William F.R. 106
Hamlet, Thomas 47
Hammet, Mary M. 107
Hammon, Sally 27
Hammond, Caty 4
Isiah 9

Hammond, (cont.)
  Josiah 7
  R. W. 99
  William 13
Hampton, Noah 59
  Rhodia 51
  Rhody 29
  Thomas 1
  Wade 29, 55
Hamson, Polly 41
Hamton, Adam 40
Hanes, Edmond 49
  Felix G. 75
  Harriett 55
  John D. 75
  Minor B. 101
  Robt. 11
  Thomas 59
Hankins, Fieldin 25
  Richard 6
  William 5, 6
Hanley, John M. 73
Hanna, Abner L. 103
  Agnes 83
  Elizabeth H. 72
  Elmira 84
  James B. 51
  John 80
  Lucinda 78
  Martha 51
  Polly 34
  Richard 80
  Thomas W. 51
  William 88
Hannah, Agnes 38
  Enos 7
  Izabella 104
  James 63
  John 2
  K. 106
  Martha B. 88
  Menerva 77
  Nancy 51
  Patsey 46
  Priscilla 3
  Rachael 2
  William 21, 29, 63, 80
Hanner, James B. 62
  Sally W. 97
Hannum, Jonathan 4
Hanson, John 37
  Sally 30
Hardeman, Mary 77
Harden, Elvis 103
  James 9
  Thomas S. 106
Harder, Elvis 103
  Maria A. 94
  Mary 104
Hardin, Jonathan 40
  Joseph 84
  Melinda 96
  Moses 7
  Sarah 2
Harding, Anne 16
  Gilbert 67
Hardy, Thomas A. 59
  Wm. G. 92
Harel, Reby 24
Hargrove, Nancy M. 40
  Polly 64
Hargue, William 19
Harkreader, James A. 94
Harlon, Anderson 55
Harmon, Elon 1
  Henry 63

Harper, Andrew 17
  Anna 24
  Asa 88
  Benjamine S. 59
  Elednder 85
  Elizabeth 15
  Enos 39
  Evaline 66, 74
  Ezekiel 103
  Harriet 107
  Higdon 47
  J. D. 96
  James H. 84
  Jesse 63, 94
  Joel 63
  John 33, 67
  Joseph 19, 96
  L. T. 105
  Lydia 96
  Madin D. 92
  Mary 107
  Minerva 93
  Noah 29
  Polly 67
  Rebecca 17, 57
  Riley 48
  Robert 29
  Samuel W. 55
  Summers 10
  William 15, 74
  William C. 103
Harpole,Daniel 6
  George 15
  Martin 2
  Sally 61
Harpool, Martin 2
  Ritty 99
Harrel, Elizabeth C. 54
  Henry 88
  Joseph W. 97
  Polly 97
Harrell, Anna 28
  Malinda 92
  Richard 7
  Thomas M. 94
Harrice, Elizabeth 49
Harrington, Charles 1, 3
  Rachel 3
  William 4
Harris, Aramintha Juli-
    ett 13
  Betsey 75
  Blair 7
  Bright 19, 58
  Catherine 32
  Elenor 80
  Elmore 39
  Fanny 11
  Giles C. 103
  Greenberry B. 75
  Hugh N. 67
  Isaac W. 98
  James 71
  John 29, 47
  John F. 51
  Julia Ann 88
  Mackey R. 42
  Margaret 106
  Mary 74
  Mathew 29
  Matthew 30
  Moses 88
  Rachel 62
  Rhody 13
  Robert 11, 55, 88
  Sally 7
  Sally C. 11

Harris, (cont.)
  Skelton T. 106
  Solomon H. 92
  Susannah D. 101
  Thomas 44
  Thos. L. 34, 41
  William 32
  William L. 29, 54
  William W. 75
Harrison, Betsey 50
  Betsy 31
  Cynthia 6
  Elizabeth 93
  Henry 4
  James 39, 40, 55, 69
  Jese 88
  John 6, 48
  Lowe, 59
  Lucinda 105
  Mary 88
  Masey 2
  Miram 105
  Nathaniel 106
  Polly 2, 39, 48
  Richard 24, 59, 67
  Sally 6
  Thomas 6, 33, 37
  William 82, 99
  Willis 99
Harrod, John 4
Harrold, E. 104
Harroll, Cader 33, 36
Harshaw, Hugh 44
Harshey, Hugh 44
Hart, Absolum 4
  Betsey 4
  C. 70, 74
  Cynthia 54
  Dovy 41
  Henry 20, 21
  James 24
  John 47
  Mary 89
  Mary A. 87
  W. H. 43
  William 41, 89
Harten, Betsey 15
  James 11, 15
Hartin, James 59
Harvel, Elizabeth C. 54
Harvey, C. F. 106
Hashlock, Petsey 9
Haskin, Joshua 2
Haslet, Charlotte 89
  Mary R. 103
Hassel, Catharine L. 88
  Hiddy 15
  Jesse 7
  Orphy 7
  Peggy 12
Hassell, Asa 6, 26
  Charlotte 40
  Chris---? 39
  Eliza 103
  Harriett 41
  Jesse 32
  Prescilla 15
  Sally 54
Hasten, Abel 40
Hastin, John 41
Hastings, Nancy 48
Hatch, D. T. 101
  David 80
Hatchell, Elisha 58
  Mary 58
Hatchett, Louise 35
Hatfield, John 9, 10

Haune, Patsey 16
Haw, Caty 17
  James 71
  Polly 15
  Samuel 47
Hawkins, Amy D. 78
  B. D. 100
  Benj. 45
  Elizabeth 72, 102
  Fanny H. 64
  Henry 21
  James 103
  James L. 76
  John 103
  Patsey H. 34
  Sally Alexander 45
Hay, Reuben W. 88
  Rowland 102
Haynes, Elizabeth A. 76
  F. S. 96
  James 8
  Jonathan L. 71
  Sally 3
  William 2
Haynie, Jesse 32
  John 99
Hays, Daniel 17
  Hannah 77
  James 1
  Joseph 33
  Rebecca 62
  Tilley 1
  Williams 44
Head, Alfred 99
  Beverly 96
  Fanny H. 73
  James M. 99
  Lucy 34
  Manuel 55
  Middleton 55
  Nancy 52
  Pascal 43, 63
  Penelope 89
  Tavanah 44
  Thomas 55
Heaspeth, Stasy 11
Hedgcock, Elijah 4
Heffington, Milley 39
Heffman, Michael 24
Hefner, Sarah 71
Helban, Ambrose 19
Hellartin, Peter 61
Hellmontoller, Henry 36
Helms, John 19
  Joseph 19
  Mary 48
Henderson, Bennett 22
  Bennett H. 19
  Charles 21, 45
  Daniel 19
  Elizabeth 52, 66
  James 36
  Lockey 22
  Mary 83
  Musa 39
  Patsey 29
  Polly 11
  Prudence 25
  Rebecca 15
  Samuel K. 98
  Thos. 35
  William 26, 27, 63
  William T. 9
Hendin, Polly 32
Hendirck, (See also Hen-
  drick)
  John 40

Hendrick, (See also Hen-
  dirck)
  John 40
  Polly 40
Hendricks, Abram 19
  Albert 19
  Caty 36
  Henry 19
  John 36
  Peter M. 99
  Rachael 1
  Rebecca 19
  Samuel 26
  Thomas 1
Hendrix, Susan 68
Henley, B. J. 103
  Benjamine J. 44
  John 21
  John M. 65, 68
Henly, Thomas N. 88
Henry, Elihu 73
  Elizabeth 48
  Elizabeth G. 86
  H. 80
  Hugh 8
  John 47, 68
  John H. 81
  John J. 47
  M. H. 50
  Moses 47, 60, 64
  Oney 8
  Peggy 38
  Polly 22
  Samuel 34, 38
  W. H. 48
  William 13, 14, 22,
    34, 37
Hensley, E. F. 105
Henson, Fanny 76
  John 40
  Josiah 40, 67
  Josiah (?) 69
  Martha 26
  Polly 29
  Sally 10
  Solomon 55
  William 63
Herbert, Benjamine 29
  David 29
Hereford, Charles 13
  Jesse 13
Herefore, Anny 9
Hermans, John 29
Herndon, Cornelius 2
  Frances 2
  Mary 58
  Nathaniel 84
  Nathnaiel 73
Herring, Drury 28
  Polly 13
  Sally 28
Hersley, Charles 40
Heughes, Emily 98
Hichmond, Joshua 79
Hickerson, Ezekiel 80
  John O. 84
  Leonard 75
  Martha 86
Hickison, John A. 37
  Samuel D. 37
Hickman, Joseph 17
Hicks, Abel 106
  Arthur 17
  Hannah 76
  Harry 1
  Jacob 15
  James 34

Hicks, (cont.)
  John 15
  John H. 92
  Nathaniel 96
  Polly 15, 86
  William 52
Hide, Rhody 27
Hides, Edmund 51
Hiett, Priscilla 104
Higganson, Richard 39
  Samuel 24
Higgarson, Samuel D. 61
Higgason, David 61
  Frances F. 74
  Samuel 68
  William D. 68
Higgerson, John O. 55
  Samuel 19
Higgins, Harriet 97
Higgombotham, Thos. 10
Highton, Henry 103
Hill, H. W. 103
  Hawkins 55
  Hugh B. 96
  Hugh W. 44
  John B. 84
  Polly 8
Hillburn, Ambrose 22
Hinson, Elizabeth 51
Hinton, Elizabeth 66
  John 40, 49, 50
  Samuel 19
Hire, Martin 42
Hix, Faithy 2
Hobbs, David 9
Hobday, Elizabeth 102
Hobdy, John 33, 34, 96
  Richard 40
  Tabitha 33
  Thos. 34
Hobert, Nancy 86
Hodge, Ann 27
  Asa 29
  John 5, 18, 20
  John D. 10, 16
  Joseph 99
  Katy 25
  Mary Ann 100
  Nancy 10, 11
  Robert 25, 29, 80
  Sam'l. H. 50
  W. T. 85
  William 13, 24
Hodges, Achford 21
  Asa 25, 51
  Asa W. 92
  Ashford 22
  Betsey 44
  Chloe 92
  Elizabeth C. 96
  Ezekiel C. 51, 52,
    108
  Fanny 70
  German 103
  Greed 66
  Griffin 99
  Holly 46, 70
  Isaiah 52
  Isham 40
  James 6
  M. 47
  Mariah 80
  Martha 52
  Meredith 40, 43, 44,
    51
  Nancy 46
  Polly 66

Hodges, (cont.)
R. T. 103
Ramon L. 75
Ransom 67
Roland T. 85
Sally 67
Sarah 51
Sarah A. 96
Shirley 106
William 44, 108
Hoffman, Sally 82
Hog, Samuel 4
Hogan, Edmund 15
John P. 34
Polly 34
Zachariah 9
Hogen, John P. 55
Hogg, Caty 45
Eliza 40
John 45
Hoggatt, James W. 85
Hogin, Edmund 26
Edward 5
Holand, Hizikie 55
Holaway, James 44
Sarah 86
Holcum, Julia 70
Holdman, Joseph H. 96
Nathan 4
Sally 4
Holland, Sally 8
Holliman, Elizabeth 62
Hollinsworth, Abraham
11-12
Hollis, Eliza 11, 67
J. G. 106
James 67, 103
Jesse 11, 13, 101, 105
Mary 98
Matilda 74
Nancy Ann 105
Samuel 3
Holloway, Edmund 18
Elizabeth 46, 103
Henry M. 88
Lucy 77
Mitchell 55
Nathan 29, 31
Ruth 20
Samuel 15
Thomas 34
Hollowell, Polly 50
Holly, Anna 49
Jonathan 29
Holman, Daniel 34
William C. 88
Holmes, Albert 20
Albert G. 66
James 57
Lotty 28
Margie 19
Nancy 57
Robert 59, 66
Holmon, Dred 34
Holms, John 53
Holoway, James 85
Holt, Elizabeth 44
Jesse 44
Philpeny 15
Sally C. 91
Seth 88
William 106
Hondershell, Elizabeth 80
Hondyshell, Joseph 87
Honeycut, Cauley 87
Delia 45
Wallace 88

Honeycutt, Bradlet 63
Bradley 64
Brantley 80
Elizabeth 92
Isham 52
Hood, Polly 14
Hooks, Isaac 6
Hooper, John M. 85
Judith 25
Hoover, Andrew 24
John 7
Hope, John 103
Hopkins, Margaret 4
Horn, Etheldred P. 37
Polly 44
Reddick 22
Hornsby, George 94
Horsley, Louisa E. 92
Margaret 92
Nancy 76
Rowland 75
Sally 40
Talbot 40, 77
Horsly, Susan 87
Horton, Elizabeth Ann 91
John 52
John J. 80
Robert 96
Thomas 71
William 99
Houck, Catey 8
Eve 8
Houdershell, Joseph 92
Houdeshall, Jacob 26
Houdshell, Hiram 64
Houghton, Samuel 52
Houndershell, Jacob 29
Joseph 92
Sarah A. 97
Houndeshell, Isabel 3
Jacob 3
Houndshell, Henry 1
Margaret 88
Hounshell, Hiram 64
House, Anthony M. 92
Charlotte 6
James 48, 58, 61, 75, 99
John 55
Lydia B. 94
P. M. 101
Pitt M. 71, 74
Sarah 95
Sinia 96
William 28, 29, 37
Houser, Ambrose 64
Hover, Henry 17
How, Urish 68
Howard, Benjamine R. 94
Greenberry 21
J. B. 89
James 19
John B. 34, 94
Warner 37
Howdyshell, Margaret 88
Howel, Thomas 22
Howell, Dudley 71
Eliza 65
Elizabeth 20
Mary H. 102
Philip 19
Polly 4
Sterling 37
Thomas 68
Howerton, Elizabeth 52
Hradley, Zilpha 94
Hubbard, Polly 8

Hubbard, (cont.)
William 8, 26
Hubert, John 10, 18
Huberts, John 15
Huddleston, Rutha 88
Hudson, A. G. 103
Benjamin(e) 10, 19,107
Daniel S. 85
Dawsey 10, 15
Elizabeth 24
James 44, 64
John 15, 18
Peggy 19
Polly 18
Sally 30, 107
Sarah 10
Thomas 85
William 30
Hudspeth, Amanda M. 94
Joseph 94
Huffman, Amelia 98
W. C. 68
William 21
Hughes, Benta 43
Betsey 3
Eliza 67
Geo. W. 103
James B. 37
Jane 96
John 37
Sarah 37
Tabitha 33
Thomas 79
Hughs, Crawford 103
Nancy 28
Thomas W. 71
Hugin, Richard 2
Hullett, Jerry 94
Humphrey, Charles L. 36
Sally T. 35
Hunley, John 34, 39, 40
Patsey 20
Temple 42
William 29, 32, 35, 42
Hunt, Betsey 14
Caty 23
Cloe 9
Dicy 10
H. W. 78
Hanah 34
Hanson 51
Henry 13, 71
Henry W. 77
James 46, 94
Jane 96
John 19, 37
Laverne 20
Lion 103
Lucinder 26
Lucretia 45, 61
Lutilda 30
Mary 95
Nancy 63
Penelope 19
Polly 97
S. 38, 45, 46, 47
Sally 58
Sally T. 58
Sam'l. 45
Sarah 92, 94
Sion 103
Susan 81
Thomas 20, 21, 23, 26
Hunter, Ann 106
Betsey 39, 49
Burrell 40
Burwell 28

Hunter, (cont.)
Clavin 68
Dempsey 39, 48
E. 48
Edy 92
Elizabeth 96
Fanny 85
Isaac 68
Jacob 76
John 68, 107
Josiah 2, 3
Layton 72
Lemuel S. 47
Lucinda 60
Lydia 84
Nancy 107
Needham 15
Reuben 40, 87, 88
Ruben 74
Sarah 67
Seaton H. 52
William 40, 80
Willis 68
Hurt, Absolum 4
Betsey 4
Elizabeth 93
Isaac 9
Polly 32
Thomas C. 104
Huskin, Samuel 106
Huston, Polly 95
Thomas 44
Hutchenson, Amanda 96
Hutcherson, David 40
Hutcheson, James 40
William 40
Hutchings, John 13
Hutchinson, Alexander 52
David 62
James 30, 47
John 37
Mathew 102
William 99
Hutchison, Ann 46
James 54
Hutson, Benjamine 92
Elizabeth 98
John 7, 9
Hyden, Rich'd 96
Hynes, Betsy 2
Hyronimous, Francis 47
Iacky, Mary Ann 62
Impson, Sally 6
Ing, (See also Lng)
Alfred 52, 80
Joseph 68, 90
Mathew 68
Matthew 24
Inge, Joseph 25
Patsey 25
Patsy 25
Ingram, David 59, 65, 68,
69, 72
Marmaduke 10
Patsey 25
Timothy 72
Zaddock 26
Inman, Elender 23
John 96
Nancy 37
Irby, Joseph 40
Susan 95
Irwin, Jane 5
Nathaniel 11
Polly 11
Isaacs, James 29
Iscue, Daniel 88

Isham,Arthur 85
Israel, Benjamin 68
Itson, Betsey 40
James 21
Izzard, Keziah 48
Lewis 48
Jackson, Amanda 72
Andrew 26, 59
Benjamine 44
Charles 68
Chestly 13
Elizabeth 52, 65
Francis 68
Green 75
Hugh 88
Isaac T. 106
James 15, 21, 41, 47
Jese 88
Jesse 80
John 47, 68, 72, 101,
105
John R. 89
Josiah E. 75
Jourdon 28
Larkin 15
Lemuel 40
Leroy 55
Lucy 88
Lucy A. 105
Lydia 94
Margaret 31
Martha 60
Mary 100
Mary Ann 95
Nancy 40, 59
Polly 24, 37
Richard 75
Robert 92
Sarah E. 100
Stephen 11
Susan 69
Susannah 68
Washington B. 75
William 19, 46, 49,
68
Jacobs, Edy 58, 68
Henry 17
Martha D. 101
Mary Ann 107
Moses 37
Naomah 50
Washington 100
James, Betsey 9
James 9
John 74
John J. 96
Sally 84
Thomas 58, 62, 89
Jane, Sally 37
Jarratt, John 10
Jarrett, Thomas 44
Jarritt, Sally 45
Jefferies, C. L. 69, 71
Pamelia B. H. 83
Jefferson, A. E. 103
A. G. 80
George H. 59
Judah 37
P. 80
Thomas 80
Jenkins, James P. 44
John 4
Lily 26
Nancy 4
Roderick 6
Sally 101
Thomas 26

Jenkins, (cont.)
William 6
Jennett, Hezekiah 59
John 59
Jennings, Clem 26
John 19
Sally 65
W. B. 99
Jernigan, Anna 96
Martha ? 55
Jetton, Lewis D. 99
Jewel, Robert H. 85
Sally 4
Jiams, William L. 37
Jiley, John R. 106
Jinnings, Sally 65
Joanes, Nancy 107
Job, James 15
Jocey, John 99
Johns, Benjamine 50
Ethelred H. 89
John 9
Johnson, Abner G. 94
Andrew W. 75
Archibald 15
Asa 75
Austin 75
Benjamine 51
Betsy 31
Cassandra 42
Charles 68
Charlotte 51
Daniel 89
David 50, 62, 77, 80
Elizabeth 13, 20, 45,
53
Esther 1
Frances 24
George 6, 7
Henry M. 37
Henry W. 29
James 13, 19, 27, 36,
72
Jane H. 75
John 11, 27, 52, 68
Jonathan 76
Joseph 92
Lucy Ann 61
M. C. 98
M. J. 105
Martha Ann 106
Mary G. 92
Mary L. 21
Mathew 34, 40, 62
Michael E. 75
Milly 36
Nancy 22, 95
Nancy M. 50
Nelson 104
Patsey 17
Polly 59
Priscilla 75
Rich 45
Richard 45, 46, 47, 48,
51, 52
Robert 15, 17
Sarah 85
Thomas 55, 59
Thomas A. 50
W. 48
W. B. 76
William 106
Johnston, Benjamine 26
Hugh 87
Joseph 88
Lewis 24
Milly 36

Johnston, (cont.)
  Rebeckah 43
  Reuben 64
  Thomas 26
Joiner, Absalom 64
  Dicy 50
  Eliza 25
  Hugh 64
  Jefferson 55
  John 29, 64
  Nancy 16
  Polly 67
  Robert 44, 64
  Sally 15
  Socky 106
  Susan 68
  Whitehead 5
  William 55
  Winny 32
Jones, Alfred 89
  Betsey 2, 58
  Burnice B. 94
  Casy 71
  Catharine 92
  Cintha 71
  Cinthy 56
  Clifton A. 106
  Clifton R. 79
  Cynthia 51
  Daniel 21
  David H. 89
  Edmund 99
  Edward 1
  Eliza H. 84
  Elizabeth 43, 45, 48
  Faountain P. 68
  Fiajah 106
  Hannah 9
  Henrietta B. 85
  Henry 72
  Henry L. 78
  Hezekiah 15
  Isaac 11
  James 4, 18, 89
  James B. 89, 90
  Jerusy 1
  Jinny 9
  John 13, 14, 34
  Jonathan 71
  Judithan 104
  Julias 9
  Leonard 4
  Malinda 104
  Martha 65
  Mary 48, 101
  Mary Ann 95
  Maryan 8
  Matilda 100
  Milly 1
  Minerva 91
  Moe 16
  Moses 29, 34
  Nancy 63
  Polly 7, 10, 38
  Ralph 40, 54
  Rhody 4
  Richard 7, 9
  Robert 1
  Rthua 42
  Sarah 43
  Sarah R. 89
  Stephen 1, 80
  Stephen M. 94
  Susannah Louisa 90
  Thomas 4, 52
  Thomas S. 75
  V. E. 104

Jones, (cont.)
  Walker 72, 80
  Wandy 9
  William 15, 37, 65,
    68, 75, 79, 80
  William B. 56
  Willie E. 68
Jopes, Samuel 64, 72
  Samuel H. 91
Jops, Elizabeth 70
Jordan, John W. 99
  Moses 104
  T. J. 106
  Thomas 73
Jordon, Francis A. 94
Jorey, Amanda 98
Joruth, Mary 81
Josey, Allen 11
  Amanda 98
  Betsy 30
  Martha 81
  Sally 14
Jouett, Nancy 80
Jourdan, Eliza Ann 103
  Thomas 52, 53, 70, 82
Joyce, Amos 37
Joyner, Abram 34
  Abram B. 105
  Absolom 80
  Amos 40
  Betsey 28
  Donelson 55
  Elizabeth 35
  John 49
  Martha 65
  Thomas 62
  Thomas M. 99
  Winnie 105
Judd, John W. 96
  M. E. 101
Justice, Amy 58
  Barbary 89
  Frederick 59
  Joseph 47
  Mark 58
  Sally 33
  Rebecca 82
  Susan 75
  William 44
Kaine, O. L. 99
Kean, Nancy 93
Keane, Elizabeth 93
Keefe, Thomas 23, 26, 104
Keeling, George 85
Keen, Currel 31, 56
  Currie 41
  Edmund 22, 24
  Elisha 89, 106
  James 89
  Jesse 14
  Jesse L. 56
  John 92, 99
  Mastin 72
  Mildred 104
  Nancy 31
Keergin, Melissa 76
Keese, Agnes 13
  Thomas 26
Keesee, Champness 37
  Geo. F. 42
  Jane 14
Keif, Thos. 15
Keilley, John 44
Keiser, Sally 23
Kellon, Thomas 5
Kelly, Bartholomew 96
  Charles 19

Kelly, (cont.)
  Edward 85, 100
  Harriett 55
  James 80
  Joseph 29, 78
  Lucinda 92
  Malinda 76
  Mariah 48
  Patsey 6
  Sarah 106
  Warren 50, 80
Kendrick, Jane 3
Kenedy, Eliza 95
  Emily 83
  William 104
Kennedy, Danl. 41
  Dempsey 4
  Elias 50
  Evaline 41
  John 4, 19
  Judith 72
  Rachel 48
  Samuel 15
  Samuel S. 7
  William 7, 24, 58
Kensey, Henry 19
Kent, Ann M. 106
  Joseph K. 80
  Obedience 31
  Samuel J. 85
Kerby, Edney 81
  Henry 52
  John 47
  Ruby 57
Kerley, James 80
  John 90, 104
  King 104
Kerr, Sam'l. 11
  William 34
Key, Alfred 89
  Cathron 81
  James 75, 80
  Joseph 64, 98
  Logan D. 40
  Macklin 64, 100
  Markey 21
  Nancy 104
  Nancy G. 79
  Peterson 64, 80
  Sally 43
  Solomon 40
  Strother 24
  Thomas 55
  William 44, 45, 57, 64,
    100
Keys, Charles 44, 68
Kilbrath, Polly 12
Kilbrough, Sam'l. 11
Kilpatrick, John 85
  Martha C. 83
Kimbel, Hannah 32
Kimbrough, L. 79
King, Abraham 9
  Albert 81
  Anderson 74, 80
  Ann 4
  Celia 9
  David 15, 37
  Davis 15
  Emeline 85
  Enos 25
  Henderson 100
  James B. 60, 81
  James N. 83
  Jeffery 50
  John 17, 92
  John J. 46, 49, 74

130

Lyon, John 11, 13
  Penelope 42
  William 13, 81
Lytle, James 41
  Robert 14, 16
Maberry, Evans 72
  Randolph 105
  Wm. 90
Mabry, Benjamine 41
  Elizabeth 84
  George W. 76
  Hannah 10
  James 15
  John 15
  Mildred 104
  Nancy 46
  Polly 74
  Randolph 85
  William 74, 84
Macky, Abram 89
Madding, Champ 6
Maddock, Solomon 64
Maddox, William 59
Maddry, Reddick 100
Mading, Samuel 36
Mahn, Poley (?) 54
Mahu, Reason A. 89
Main, John 100
Mains, Nancy 1
Majors, John 56
Mallard, Betsey 25
Malone, Avarilla 33
  C. B. 100
  Daniel 72
  J. N. 106
  James N. 100
  Jane 94
  John 47, 72
  Lewis 64
  Lydia 2
  Martha A. 104
  Mary 12
  Nancy 54
  S. W. 104
  Sarah 92
  Susannah 45
  Tabitha 73
  Thomas 12, 13
  Thomas F. 72
  Wesley 34
Mandrall, David 99
  Rachel 99
Mandre, Patsey 45
Mandrell, John 19
  Nancy 48
  Nathan 96
  Solomon 41
  William 41
Mandrill, Henry 100
  Leoderith 22
  Nathan 100
  Sally 69
  Solomon 69
Mankin, Jane 42
Mann, Edward 47
  Eliza A. 60
  Martha W. 61
  Newberry 76
Mansker, Archibald E. 55
  Elizabeth 61
  Jane 2
  Kasper 27
  Mary 63
  Reuben 24
  William 30
Marcum, Armstead 64
  Elisha 92

Marcum, (cont.)
  Martha 102
  Polly 17
  Sally 38
  Thomas 21
  William 106
Marcus, Porter 80
  William 72
Markham, Elizabeth M. 88
  Fanny 32
  James 47
  Mary 67
Markrum, Susanna 95
Marlen, Lewis 37
Marlin, Arch 46
  Archibald 12, 13
  Elizabeth 12
  Jemima 106
  John 38, 68
  Peggy 25
  Thomas 13
  W. G. 48
  William 11, 13
Marlow, John 9
  Stephen 52
Marquess, Nancy 102
Marquis, Thos. 11
Marrick, Henry 15
Marshall, Ann 21
  Bennett 104
  Elizabeth 13, 20
  Frances 14
  Jane B. 32
  Phoebe 95
  Richard 59, 81
  Robert 11
  William 2
  William M. 89
Martin, Abraham 47
  Abram 44, 46
  Abram, Jr. 29
  Absom 81
  Anderson 96
  Andrew 24, 26, 59, 63, 106
  Ann 79
  C. R. 96
  Eliza 85
  Elizabeth 9, 20, 51, 66
  Enoch 78
  Frances 49
  Frederick 47, 68
  Friley 92
  George 30, 37, 41, 50
  Henry 26, 37
  J. L. 83
  James 37, 41, 59, 81, 89
  James L. 41, 55
  Jasper 24
  John 64, 72
  Joseph K. 55
  Judy 42
  Lewis 13
  Lucy T. 105
  Mahala 30
  Malinda 80
  Maranda 67
  Margaret 50
  Mary 22
  Mary Jane 100
  Mathew 59
  Nancy 54
  Obediah 9
  Oliver 15
  Patsey 16, 23

Martin, (cont.)
  Peter 64
  Peter H. 47
  Peter W. 99
  Polly 30, 33
  Rhubin 3
  Sally 23
  Sam'l. 29
  Susan 102
  William 24, 30, 59
  Wooddy 100
Mason, James 100
  Little Berry 44
  Ramsey L. 43
Massey, Sally 62
Masten, Thomas 2, 4
Mastin, Thomas 1
Matherly, Levi 107
  Sally 89
Mathew, O. S. 98
Mathews, Betsey 107
  Susan 51
Mathis, Charles 98
  Nancy 92
Matthews, Charles 104
Mattocks, S. E. 101
Maupin, Ann 40
  Austin 40
Mauton, John 11
Maxey, Edward 3, 13, 32
  Walter 4
  William 3, 13
Maxwell, Peggy 3
  Thomas 22
Maxy, Eliza 89
May, Absolam 55
  Anna 80
  Baley 51
  Balie 64
  Betsey 26
  C. H. 46
  Craddock 55
  Craddock H. 22, 63
  E. J. 105
  Emily 101
  James M. 100
  Jane 99
  Jefferson 85, 100
  Katy 23
  Lemuel 49
  Major 72
  Mary 66
  Mead 52
  Milindy, 11
  Morris 55
  Nancy 21
  Pleasant 80
  Polly 53
  Richard 99
  William 30
  William , Jr. 72
Mayberry, Alexander 61
  John 100
  Nancy 96
  Polly 97
  Randal 97
  William 46, 96
Mayes, Susanna 68
Mayhew, Henry 96
  Moses 37
  Reason L. 50
  Sarah 59
  Sealy 58
Mayhue, Mary 27
Mayo, Jacob 19
Mays, James 50
  Mahaly 72

Mays, (cont.)
  Mathew 89
  Pleasant 59, 72, 81
  William 81, 89
Mayson, R. S. 45
McAdam, Polly 21
McAdams, Catharine 2, 4
  Martha 31
  Mima 29
  Polly 47
  Samuel 9
  Sarah 2
  Stanford A. 72
  Wesly 85
  William 11, 19, 24,
    29, 31, 55
McAdem, Hugh 50
McAden, Catharine 70
McAdow, Samuel 13
McAllester, Betsey 33
McAllister, Daniel 68
  James 13
McAnnis, L. P. 106
McAuley, A. 107
  Daniel 39, 43, 44, 48
McBride, Charity 10
  Elizabeth 7
  Hugh 14
  James 36, 100, 107
  John 7
  Nathaniel 7
McCaffry, John 47
McCall, Maria 93
  Rhoda 86
  S. L. 75
  William 7, 25, 49, 68,
    81
McCalley, Elizabeth 96
McCallon, Wm. P. 81
McCann, Samuel 84
McCarther, Amos 28
McCarthney, John 11
McCarthy, Amos 30
McCartney, John 11
McCarty, Ann R. 70
  Annie 34
  Peggy 5, 10
  Pollard W. 68
  Polly 37
  William 16
McClain, John T. 98
  Polly 69
McClarey, Robert 34
McClary, Emily T. 103
McClelan, John 41, 44
McClendon, Jesse 11
McClenon, John 90
McClothlin, (See also
    McGlothlin)
  James 85
McClung, William 76
McCollaster, James 13
McCollester, Nancy 33
McCollock, James 78
McConahay, William 41
McConnel, Susan 61
McConneley, Wm. 47
McConnell, Andrew 104
  Jane 48
  John 9
  Latitia 79
  M. 10
  Peggy 10
  Winfrey 85
McCorcle, Sam. 38
McCorkle, George 89
  Miles 47

McCorkle, (cont.)
  William 3, 5
McCormack, Andrew 22
  Mahala 93
  Mariah 71
  Mary Ann 80
  Meridy 107
  Narcissa 77
  Ritty 107
McCormick, Amarilla 95
  Andrew 25
  Eliza 90
McCoy, James 24
McCrady, Jonathan 92
McCrary, Elizabeth 80
McCrory, Robert 2
McCullock, Wm. 57
  Wm. B. 47
McDaniel, Allen 34
  Betsey 102
  C. P. 87
  Christian 30
  Elizabeth 39
  Fountain 72
  Fountain L. 76
  James 85
  Jane 24
  John 9
  Joseph 24
  Mathias 41
  Sally 40
  Samuel 81
  Winston S. 65
McDole, Henry 47
  Martha 67
McDonald, A. 1
  Elsy 2
  Francis 9
  James 1
McDougal, Duncan 37
McDowell, Betsey 17
  John 17
  Polly 24
McElarath, Jenny 6
  John 96
  Joseph 6
McElroy, Alexander 13
McElruath, Wm. 78
McElurath, Abby Ann 95
  John 28, 37, 42
  Joseph 31, 35, 37,
    38
  Polly 22
  William 37, 99
McElwrath, David 89
  John 16
  Rebecca 20
McFadden, William 1
McFarland, Alexander 37
McFerson, A. N. 89
McGaha, Elvira 106
McGammon, William 81
McGavock, James R. 89
McGee, Hugh 76
  James 26
  John 13
  Sam'l. 79
  William 4
McGlothlin, (See also
    McClothlin)
  Alexander 81, 85
  Andrew 44, 50
  Elizabeth 24
  Isaac 96
  James 100
  John 41, 42
  Joseph 12, 44, 82,

McGlothlin, (cont.)
  Joseph (cont.) 85,
    100
  William 44, 73, 81,
    100
McGloughlin, Hannah 21
  Joseph 24
McGoodwin, James K. 85
McGowen, James 68
McGreggor, Flower 3
McGuary, William 30
McGuire, George 43, 72
  Polly 51
  Sally 27
  Thomas 9
McGundy, Margarett F. 27
McHenry, Fanny 8
McIlmore, Charles 56
  Harvel 56
McInger, Wm. H. 87
McIntosh, Sally 12
McKain, E. G. 86
  Eli G. 89
  James 7, 10, 14, 17,
    28
  Jenny 4
  Prudy 7
McKee, Catharine 13
  Jacob 7
  Nancy 12
  William 13
McKelbury, Stephen 50
McKendre, John 42
  Polly 30
McKendree, F. E. 99
  John A. 70
  M. W. 106
  Rebecca 53
McKennie, John 30
McKenny, Archibald 17
McKethen, Robert 41
McKindrey, Margaret A. T.
    84
McKinley, Robert 3
McKinly, James 61
McKinney, Harriett 52
  James 22
  Nancy 22
McKinnie, William 26
McKinsey, Betsey 44
  James 11, 30
  John 24
  Nancy 11
  Peggy 27
  William 24
McKinzy, Jas. 3
McKisick, Robert 17
McKissack, John 20
McKissick, Arch. 17
McKithen, Catherine 21
McKnight, Patsey 49
McKoin, Eli G. 89
  James 86
  James L. 87, 90, 97
McKorkle, Elizabeth 16
McKoun, Isaac 22
McLaffey, Henry 59
McLain, Jacob 68
McLean, John 37
  Murdock 96
McLin, John 13
  Nancy C. 93
McMane, John 68
McMillan, John 30
  Peggy 41
McMillen, John 4
  William 48

McMinn, Joseph 47
   William 16
McMullin, Thomas 1
McMurry, Betsey 23
   Elenor 17
   Elizabeth M. 69
   J. M. 104
   James 23
   John 59
McMurtry, Eveline 47
   Henry 7
   James 37
   Jane 13
   Jenny 7
   John 13, 15, 18, 39,
     41, 44, 45, 47, 52,
     56
   John, Jr. 17
   Polly 33
   Thomas W. 87
McMury, S. M. 45
McNealy, Betsey 48
McNeely, Asa 84, 89
   Mary 63
   Sarah 89
McNeil, John 85
   Joseph 101
McNeill, Elizabeth 45
   John 45
McNutt, William 14
McQuay, William 33
McReynolds, James 59
   Joseph 30, 45, 67
   Joseph, Jr. 37
   Joseph A. 72, 76
   Leonard 68
   Nancy 31, 71
   Samuel 9
   Tabitha 30
McRunnel, Rottey 20
McWhirter, Wm. 11
McWrath, John 96
Meader, Arrey 30
   Jobe 37
   Joseph 52
Meaders, Christiana 44
Meador, Annanias 72
   Archibald A. 81
   Bennett 48
   Bluford 100
   Catharine 103
   Isaac 72
   James 76
   Jesse 60
   Joel 57
   John 81
   Joseph G. 64
   Judith 48
   Locky 73
   Lucinda S. 93
   Mahalia 96
   Malvina82
   Martha 80
   Mary 43, 103
   Nathaniel 104
   Perlina 100
   Thomas 82, 88, 89
   Wm. C. 100
Meadors, Jesse 44
   Lewis N. 104
Meadow, Thomas 87
   William 104
Meadows, Janny 19
   Valentine 64
   William 104
Meallias, Priscilla 73
Measles, Martha 61

Meek, Adam 60
   John 37
Meens, M. L. 82
Meggs, Loving 64
Meirs, Allen 33
   Thomas 32
Melton, Celia 24
   Daniel 19
   Marian 27
   Mary 29
   Nancy 17
   Patty 7
   William 7, 38
Mercer, Nancy 3
Mercum, George 34
   Jonathan 26
Meredith, Armstead 59
   Sam'l. 23
Merell, Jinny 14
Merley, Nancy 21
Merryman, Nancy 104
Mertin, Vina 55
Michel, Robert 68
Mickelbury, James 50
Middleton, Samuel 50
Miers, Benjamine F. 81
   Daniel 26, 62
   Hannah 22
   Humphrey 29
   John 22
   Martha 78
   Mildred A. 85
   Miles 26
   Milley 38
   Patsey 33
   Peter 77
   Priscilla 62
   Thomas 24, 35, 53
Mifflin, Matilda 77
   Niona 48
   Pleasant 89
   Stewart 48
Miflin, Stuart 77
Milam, Adam 11
   Elerna 17
Milan, Drury 7 , 11
Milburn, Rhody 22
Miles, Elizabeth G. 56
   Thomas 26
Millar, Simon 67
Miller, Ann 82
   Barbary 84
   Beverly 88
   Elizabeth 10
   F. 22
   Frederick 10, 20, 24,
     35
   Henry 16
   Jacob 56
   James 68
   Jesse 76
   Michael 64
   Milley 15
   Morris 22
   Nancy 80
   Sally 27
   Sarah 78
   William 2, 50, 100
Million, George 62
Mills, A. 84
   B. W. 99
   Elizabeth 37
   George 52
   James 44, 63
   James L. 48
   Martha A. 101
   Moses 45

Mills, (cont.)
   P. C. 48
   Pinkey C. 48
   Pollyanna 66
   Robert S. 64
   Samuel H. 81
   Sarah G. 52
Milton, Lucy 66
   Nancy 90
   Thomas 30
   Wm. 44
Ming, Robert W. 94
Mingion, John F. 13
Minnick, John 64
Minor, Daniel 11
Minsey, Peter 48
Minter, Henrietta 81
   Jane 76
Mires, David 76
   Humphrey 76
Mitchell, Addison 100
   Alfred 81
   Beky M. 47
   Betsey 34
   David 16
   Delia 95
   Elizabeth 38, 79, 84
   Frances 62
   James 37, 48
   John 12, 13, 16, 17,
     18, 20, 39, 41, 42,
     46, 48, 58, 60, 81,
     85
   Louisa 56
   Lovy 72
   Mary G. 53
   Nancy 12, 48
   Patsey 76
   Pleasant 92
   Robert 17
   Sally 29
   Solomon 24
   Turner 90, 101
Mitchener, William 16
Mitchenor, Clarissa 73
   Thomas 104
Mitchner, Clarissa 73
Mock, Elizabeth 22
Moffit, Robert 7
Montero, Frances J. 89
Montgomery, Daniel 23,
     33, 50
   Elizabeth 85
   Jane 42
   Jefferson 81
   Margaret 41
   Nancy 25
   Polley 24
   Robert 69
   William 24, 30, 40,
     41, 43, 47, 48, 51,
     74, 75, 76, 80
Moodey, Bricey 66
Moody, Anne 21
   Dinnon 22
   John 41, 68, 72
   Maclin 104
   Nancy 28
   Peggy 19
   Robert 19
   Sally 17
   Spencer 68
   Vineny 34
   William 13, 14
Mooney, John 12
   Sally 12
Moor, Amariah 41

Moor, (cont.)
Edward 60
Elizabeth P. 59
Joseph 59
Moore, A. 47
Alfred 34, 55
Ann 66
Austin 48
Betsey 4
Edwin A. 102
Edwin L. 5
Edwin S. 6
Elizabeth 73, 86
Elizabeth M. 77
Emily 97
Frances 34
Granville 74
Isaac W. 48
Isarael 16
Isham L. 64
Israel 24, 60
Isreal 4
J. 36, 64
John 4, 19, 33, 50
Joseph 4
Leona 74
Loucissa 68
Marcus 52
Martha 4
Mary 50, 106
Mary Ann 86
Mathew 107
Milley 31
Nancy 37, 53
Peggy 40
Peter 48
Richard 13, 16, 30, 36
Robert 13, 17, 18, 24, 102
Robert T. 98
Sally Ann 55
Samuel 9, 10, 11
Sara 45
William 11, 59
Ziga 41
Morgan, Amaziah 96
Armistead 1
Charles 41, 51, 54, 56
Elizabeth 49, 52
James 4
Jeremiah 1, 3
John Frederick 1
Joseph 3
Mary 1, 81
Mathew 101
Nancy 2, 99
Nathan 34
Palsey 93
Polly 5
Wm. 4
Mornington, Abraham W. 69
Morris, Betsey 21, 34
Catey 45
Cinthia A. 104
Claiborn 48
Elijah 48
Elinor 17
Elizabeth 100
Esther 37
G. R. 89
George 10
Granville P. 75
Granville R. 66
Hannah 64
Henry 4

Morris, (cont.)
Isaac 24, 48
Jacob 48, 56
James S. 85
Jesse 24, 47
Joel 60
John 48, 52, 53, 57, 81, 87, 89, 98
Joseph 37
Joseph R. 76
Lithey 87
Martha 33
Moses 21, 48
Mourning 32
Nancy 36, 48, 99
Peggy 32
Polly 25, 53
Rachel 57
Sally 21
Samuel 50
Tilford 107
Walter B. 60, 66
William 50, 89, 104
Willie 107
Morrison, Caty 4
Eliza 8
Hugh 26
Jane 38
John 26
Josiah 8
Lucy 24
Sally 4
Sarah 107
William 4, 5, 6
Morrow, Cyntha 36
Rebecca 20
William 20
Morton, B. T. 107
Jonathan 17
Thomas 30
Mosby, James C. 89, 90
Moseley, F. G. 76
Moser, A. H. 104
Moss, Carter 32
Cato 88
Eliza 68
John 11, 17
Joseph 26
Polly 70
Ransom 30
Sara Ann 102
Sophia G. 77
Wm. 30, 32
Motheral, Anna 18
James 81
Jane 22
Joseph 22, 26
Sarah 44
Motherall, Betsey 26
Mary 38
Mouch, Mathias 17
Mounton, John 92
Mouser, Caty 21
Muce, Abraham 97
Murden, Mary Ann 52
Murdin, Annis 54
Murdock, Sarah 107
Murnan, Polly 15
Murphey, Tabitha 18
William 17, 26
Murphy, Jeremiah 7
John 69, 100
Margaret 19
Mary Ann 75
Sally 17
William 19
Murrah, Jeremiah L. 96

Murray, Synthia 16
Murrel, William 37
Murrell, Maria 65
Wm. 14
Murrey, Joseph 41
Thos. 39
Murry, Daniel H. 100
Elizabeth 89, 90
H. I. 107
Nancy 80
Rachel 76
Sophia J. 62
Thos. 37
Wm. 58
Muse, Daniel 44
Myars, Charles 2
Myers, David 107
Nancarro, John 2
Nanney, John H. 37
Nanny, James 68
Rebecca 68
Uriah 37
Napier, Ashford 56
John 44
Susanna 44
Neal, Andrew 38
Britton J. 48
James 38, 52
Lurena 57
Mathew 19, 44
Matthew 34
Nancy 38
Sally 85
William 18, 59
Neale, Henry 56
M. 52
Polly Ann 66
Nealy, John A. 96
Neece, Abraham 100
Neel, Aron S. 98
Mathew 16
Nancy 52
Samuel 104
Sarah 104
Thomas 104
Neeley, Robert 11
Neely, Ann 4
Anthony B. 30
John 2
L. 105
Margaret D. 74
Massey 5
Polly 37
Robert 26
William 1, 3, 4
Neighbors, John 104
Neill, Nancey 6
Neilly, Alexander 42
Nelson, George 19
Peggy 3
Polly 14
Stephen 81
Thomas 56
Nemo, Elizabeth 28
Mary Ann G. 73
Nancy 104
Peggy 22
Sally 22
Nest, Hollen 70
Nevill, Sally 42
New, Mary 56
Newby, Nathan 41
Newlin, Henry M. 16
John 30
Newman, Edward 76
George 72
Henry 96

Newton, Amanda 92
·Benjamine 76
Henry 24
John G. 94
Mary 107
William 13
Nicholl, Sterling 44
Nichols, James 52
Nicholson, Thos. 20
Nickens, Elizabeth 96
Nickins, William 22, 38
Night, Elizabeth 99
Nimmo, Henry 30
Nipper, Polly 11
Nix, Andrew 89
Christian 104
Sally 99
Noble, Elizabeth 11
Henrietta 19
Henry 12
Nancy 20
Noel, Henry P. 44
Nelly 10
Reubin 10
Nolen, Sally 18
Nolin, C. 32
Crisia 32
Norman, Ezekiel 20
James 85
Joseph 9
Reuben 16
Thos. I. 92
Normant, William S. 89
Norris, James 5
Milly 25
Polly 14
Sally 5
Stephen 22
William 44
Northam, Harriett 83
Norton, Stephen 48, 71
Norvel, Peggy 19
William 19
Norvell, Aynthia 76
Dolly Ann 84
James 56
John 69
John D. 101
Katherine 71
Norwell, Nancy 47
Norwood, Andrew 11
Novell, Wm. 13
Nowell, Reuben 12
Nowlen, Bird 44
Nowlin, Nancy 18
Nathaniel 34, 38
Null, Jacob 7
Louisa 73
Margaret 70
Nancey 6
Nunaly, Jacob 70
Nuner, William M. 64
Nye, Shadrack 9, 15, 17
O'Bryan, Dennis 3
Odam, Eli 52
Odle, Martha J. 106
Odom, James 25, 41
Sally 14
Ogburn, Catherine 52
Ogle, Margaret 36
Ogles, John 60
Minerva 75
William 7, 23, 24
Oglesby, Daniel 9, 13
Elisha 69
Hannah 11, 13
James 10, 97

Oglesby, (cont.)
John 92
Lina 15
Polly 11
Wesley 59
Old, Charlotte E. 95
Olivis, Shadrack 9
Oneal, Austin 60
Hezekiah 94
Oneil, James 41
Oneill, Thomas 100
Oniell, Alsey 107
Orean, William 56
Organ, Holly 19
Ormand, David 21, 89
Ormond, David 6
Orr, Adaline 66
David 6, 25
Elizabeth 35
Green B. 41
Greenberry 13, 34
James 5, 16
John 6, 7
Peggy 7
William 17
Osbourn, Lurany 62
Matilda 67
Osbrooks, Sterling 9
Osburn, Bartholemeu 11
Bartholemus 38
Daniel 81
John 44
Robert A. 41
Overall, Jacob 34
Overby, Archibald 44
Louise 20
Polly 27
Overstreet, Patsey 55
Overton, John 42
Mariah 17
Owen, James M. 100
Laurence 12
William 26
Owens, Randel 11
Rebecca 22
Owings, James H. 30
Owins, Peter 81
Oxford, Daniel 74
Ozborn, Thomas 17
Ozbrooks, Nancy 30
William W. 44
Ozburn, Bartholemew 24
John 19
Peggy 20
Pack, Jannet 36
Samuel 36
Smith 41
Padget, Nancy 101
Padgett, David 73, 77, 84
Fanny 48
Pagitt, Harriett 54
Palmer, Elizabeth 102
Henry 7
William 7
Pankey, Betsey 4
John 4, 10, 11, 31
Nancy 11
Polly 10
Panky, Lewis 34
Nancy 21, 92
Paradice, Phanny 15
William 15, 16
Pardue, John 94
Nancy 104
Parham, James H. 73
Parish, Priscilla 69

Parker, Andrew 11
Anna 15
Benjamine 24
Betsey 23
Britton 76
Cherry 79
Cloe 7
E. C. 101
Elizabeth 21, 73, 78, 105
George W. 81
Isaac 84
Isaac N. 56, 89
Jailey 65
John 7, 57, 61, 87
Lucindy 73
Malinda 70
Margaret 57
Marian 43
Mary 47, 72, 96
Mary I. 103
Mary T. 61
Milton 47, 81
Nancy 19, 22
Nancy R. 84
Nathan, Jr. 17
Nathaniel 2, 3, 34
Nelson 96
Noah 16, 18
Pamelia 54, 92
Peter 19
Polly 6
R. 85
Rhoda 16
Richard 34, 55
Robert 16, 20
S. N. 41
Sally 18
Susan 96
Susannah 76
Thomas 16
William 48, 54, 59, 66
Parks, Hamilton 81
Jacob 13, 19, 63
John 7
M. 76
Margaret 19
Robert 13, 21, 30, 32, 42
Robert H. 94
Parmer, Henry 9
William 3
Parnel, Gilley 44
Henderson 22
Nancy 84
Parnell, Betsey 50
Henderson 41
Patsey 48
Polly 15
Tabitha 90
Parr, Elizabeth 48
Jane A. 22
Parrish, Benj. 48, 49
Claiborne 81
David 26, 30
David W. 68
E. S. 107
Henry 56
James 48
Joe 14
Joel 24, 30, 31, 32, 37, 38, 42, 44
Lewis 38
Paterson 22
Peterson 22
Priscilla 77

Reed, (cont.)
  Catherine 38
  Clarissa B. 97
  Elenor 80
  Elizabeth 20
  F. B. 74
  Gardner 20
  George 36
  James 11
  John 4
  Joseph 20
  Martha L. 85
  Nancy 8
  Peggy 43
  Peggy D. 30
  Peter 24
  Samuel 20
  Samuel D. 91
  William 2, 3, 8
  Wm. Jr. 34
Reeder, William 22
Reese, A. M. 56
  A. W. 46, 47, 49, 50,
    72, 77
  Ashel W. 39
  Catharine 86
  Flavia 8
  George 27
  Georges 8
  Jacob 68, 75
  James 1, 8
  Joel 11
  John W. 107
  Thomas 3
  William 18
Reeves, ---- 16
  Adam 11
  Elizabeth 27
  John 18, 35
  Prudence 19
  William 19
Reid, Anthony B. 56
  Hezekiah 42
  Thomas 7
  William 7
Reiley, John 6
  Rachael 6
Reir, Geo. 40
Renfro, Bartlett 7
Renser, Mary 103
Reyley, Barney 27
Reyman, Philip 16
Reynolds, Aly 52
  Betsey 67
  E. R. M. 99, 101
  Jacob 66
  James 18
Rhodes, James 38
  Louisa G. 54
  Milley 5
  Moses 14
Rice, Amy 40
  Elizabeth 31
  Elizabeth L. 23
  Harriett 18
  Henry 51, 65
  James 85, 90
  James C. 38, 45
  Jeremiah 56
  John 40, 45, 94
  John M. 35
  Joseph 53, 69
  Joshua 15
  King 34
  Malinda 88
  Martha 51
  Mary O. 60

Rice, (cont.)
  Mathew 43, 52
  Nancy C. 56
  Nathaniel 55
  Polly 13
  Sam'l. 4
  Susannah 18
  William 69, 98
Richard, Nathaniel 20
Richardson, Catherine 99
  David 79, 90
  Elizabeth 89
  James 11, 90
  Jane 23
  Jemime 101
  Joel 105
  Polly 19
  Susan 49
  Tabitha 69
  William 56
  Winnie 8
Richmond, A. 104
  Betsey 24
  George 17, 24
  John 69, 96
  Levi 97
  Rachel 71
Rickman, Ann T. 73
  Betsey 27
  David H. 38, 101
  Frances 41
  J. A. 104
  James 48
  Jane H. 82
  John 82
  Malinda E. 94
  Malvina 105
  Margaret 60
  Mary Ann 105
  Nancy 49
  Nancy W. 92
  Rebeckah 45
  Robert 31, 38
  S. A. 104
  Sally H. 61
  Samuel 82
  Thomas 22
Rickmond, Caty 21
  James 48
Rider, Caty 58
  George 56
  John 48, 56, 81
  William 107
Ridley, Elsy 12
  George 1
Rieff, Joseph 38
Riggs, Elijah 6
  John 36
Right, Berry 104
  Nancy 46
Rigsby, Daniel 50
  Henry 60
  James 65
Riley, Polly 20
Rimmer, Benjamine 64
  Pheobe 64
Rimmers, Betsey 45
Ring, Delia 80
  Murrell 82
  William 7, 26
Riper, James R. 52
Rippey, Abigail 51
  Eli 65
  John 50, 60
  Josiah 50
  Polly 23
Rippie, Malinda 106

Rippy, Elvis 107
  Henry 85
  Hetty 87
  Jesse 73
  Jinny 36
  John 67
  Josiah 69
  Martha 79
  Nancy 67
  Polly 64
  Samuel 101
  Susan 43, 64
  William 69, 73
Ritchey, L. H. 82, 101
  Robert 41
Ritter, Betsey 28
  Elizabeth 45
  William 41
Robb, Charlotte 75
  Eliza M. 82
  James 30, 36, 63
  Joseph 18
  Samuel 20
  Sarah 98
Roberson, Caty 4
  Elisha 44
  John 3, 58
Roberts, George 31
  James 11
  John 2, 47
  Pamelia 92
  Stephen R. 43, 65
  Thos. 75
Robertson, Allen 34
  Anna 39
  Charles 31
  David 74
  Elijah R. 22
  Eliza 77
  Elizabeth 41
  Frances H. 74
  Isaac 88
  Jacob 11
  James 92
  Jane 26, 51
  John 19, 20
  Marcus 92
  Michael 8
  Polly 39, 85
  Susannah 24
  William 11, 20, 35
Robeson, John A. 96
  S. W. 103
Robinson, Andrew 4, 20
  Betsey 50
  Elijah 34
  Isaac A. 56
  James 41
  John 17, 78, 82
  Margaret 9
  Martha 103
  Mary 2
  Micheil 31
  Nancy 78
  Nathaniel 101
  Polly 69
  Robert 72
  Sally 53
  Thomas 4
  William 7, 50
  William L. 35
Robison, Elizabeth 72
Rock, Page 11
Rodgers, Patsy 55
Rogan, Frances 85
  James 14
  Peggy 24

Rogers, Armstead 7, 44,
  64
  Barbara 13
  Bediah 64
  Betsy 31
  Britton 41
  Creasy 34
  Eliza 21
  Elizabeth 13
  James 13, 92
  Jefferson 85
  Jonathan 20
  Lucinda 50
  Lucresia 15
  Margaret 50
  Mary 58
  Nancy 44, 49
  Polly 27
  Priscella 5
  Robert F. 35
  Sally 16
  Samuel 20, 48
  Sarah 88
Roister, George R. 52
Rolin, Elizabeth 36
Romkins, R. A. 65
Roney, Benjamine 94
  Betsy 10
  Dovey A. M. 77
  George W. 96
  James 77, 94
  James, Jr. 16
  John 72, 94
  Lydia 20
  Malinda 68, 69, 98
  Sally 105
  Sam'l. 10
  Samuel 11, 13, 55, 71
  Sinai 57
  Susan 107
  Susanna 15
  Thomas G. 104
  William 16, 101
Rooney, Samuel 16, 29,
  36
Roper, Polly 50
  Sally 19
  William 60
Rork, Barnet 11
Rose, Richard 35
  Robert 52
Roseton, William 82
Ross, Allen 96
  Ezekiel 18
  John 38, 50, 52
  Polly 26
  Reuben 11, 38
  Robert 72
  Sally 70
  Thomas 72
Roulston, Samuel 14
Rousey, William 38
Rowe, Laurence 38
Rowland, Rebecca 50
Rowling, Matilda 67
Roykin, Deliah 35
Royster, Thomas W. 54
Rucker, Edmund 65
Rule, Abel 56
  Albert G. 72
  Betsey 2
  Catharine 63
  Caty 1
  John 1, 2, 65
  Magdaleen 1
  Mary 91
  Peggy 2

Rullage, Sally 45
Rumby, Stenley 35
Ruminger, Christian 35
Rumley, Shadrick 32
  William 85
Runnells, Jacob 48
Ruse, James 1
Rush, John 92
  Nancy 95
Russell, Albert 22
  Elijah 27
  Haley 35
  Margaret M. 56
  Seth 24
Rutherford, A. J. 99
  B. L. 69
  Benj. 77
  Betsey 37
  Elizabeth 4
  Griffeth 5
  Griffith W. 6-7
  J. 37, 38, 39
  James 12
  John 29, 36, 37, 38
  Manerva 86
  Mary 54
  Pemmy 52
  Thomas 77
  William 82
Rutland, Clarissa 46
Rutledge, Abraham 11
  Fanny 76
  Susan 84
  William W. 77
Ruyle, Aaron 31
  Alfred 65
  Elizabeth 18
  Frankey 18
  Henry 18, 35
  Henry, Jr. 31
  John 18, 38
  Moses 18, 38, 65
  Moses, Jr. 38
  Tiney 34
Ryan, Pleasant 94
Ryner, Sally 22
Rynes, Sally 22
Ryons, Patrick 35
Sacra, James F. 92
Sadler, Alexander 46
  Alexander S. 48
  Benjamine 72
  Jincy 70
  John 102
  Susan 96
  William F. 53
Saffarns, Daniel 50
  David 77
Saffarrns, Elizabeth 75
Saffarson, Cecilia 21
Safferan, Daniel 97
Sails, Cornelius W. 82
Sample, Daniel 74, 81
  Elizabeth 50
  Jared 52
  Nancy 52
  William 9, 11
Sanders, Abraham 3
  Betsey 35
  Catharine Mary Jane
    83
  Charles G. 48
  Cloe R. 58
  D. M. 86
  Daniel T. 90
  David M. 62, 72
  E. 106

Sanders, (cont.)
  Edward 6, 9, 14
  Edward B. 82
  Emily 106
  Ethelbert 46
  Ethelbert M. 52
  Ethelbert N. 43
  Fanny 12
  Frances 62
  Gail 104
  Goldsberry 7
  Green B. 69
  Harriet 24, 105
  Harriett 80
  Hubbard H. 100
  Jacob 2
  James 14, 27, 50, 60
  John 48, 82
  Lastitia 5
  Lorenzo 101
  Martha 16, 78
  Mary 38
  N. 41, 45
  Nath. 47
  Nathan 48
  Nathaniel 24
  Nath'l. 40
  Peter T. 101
  Polly 17
  Richard 9
  Robert 14
  Sarah Ann 59
  William 50, 77
Sanderson, Edward 74
  Elizabeth M. 42
  Fanny 22
  John 92
  Mary M. 74
  Robert 52
  William 25
Sanford, Henrietta 56
  Maria E. 98
  Mary 23
  Mary Ann 89
  Robt. W. 51
Sarver, Calvin 80
  Casten 65
  Caston 69
  Catharine 19
  George 20, 40
  Henry 54, 60, 69
  Jeremiah 20, 64, 67,
    71
  Kisiah 51
Satterfield, Henry 82
  Margaret 96
  Mary 107
  Reuben 35
  Reubin 82
Saunders, Adaline 103
  Ann 103
  D. M. 79
  David 69
  David M. 84
  Elizabeth H. 38
  Maria 26
  Mary 94
  Mary Ann 84, 85
  Mildred B. 99
  Parlie 102
  Reubin 81
  Sally 67, 81
  Sally E. 33
  Thomas 85
  William A. 85
  William R. 89, 94
  William T. 82

141

Savely, Betsey 44
  Karen 58
  Rosey 57
  Samuel 50
  Wesley 107
  William 45, 48
Savley, John 4
Schabell, Sarah 101, 107
Schluter, James F. 94
Schubert, John F. 41
Schulter, Lewis 39
Sciva, Jacob 31
Scobey, Harvey L. 48
  Joseph 9
Scoby, David W. 90
  Elizabeth 4
  John 20
  Joseph 30, 38
  Matthew 20
Scoggins, James 104
  John 84
  William 77
Scott, Abner 20
  Elizabeth 67
  James 104
  John 16, 82
  Randel 25
  Robert 65
  Sally 72
  Samuel 4, 10
Scruggs, Edward 35
  Harriette 69
  Jane 44
  Jemima Ann 59
  John B. 72
  Nancy 65
  Willie W. 69
Scurry, Clarissa B. 93
  Thomas 20, 27, 28,
    29, 31, 32, 33, 34,
    35, 36, 41, 43, 45
Searcy, Harriett 34
  John 4
  Nancy 50
  Patsey 25
  Penelope 10
  Reuben 37, 57
  William P. 90
Sears, Lydia 39
Seat, Herod 14
  Penny 7
  Sarah 50
Seaves, Jacob 12
Seawell, Benjamin(e) 26,
    38, 60, 75
  Eliza B. F. 100
  Hardy 60
  J. P. 107
  Jacob 29, 33
  Joseph 11
  M. T. 104
  Margaret 94
  Mary B. 76
  Robert 73
  Susan C. 99
  W. N. 104
  Wylie B. 94
Seay, William 52
  William W. 60
Sebastain, Priscilla 18
Sebastan, Joseph 6
  Polly 14
  Sarah 3
Sedgley, John 7
Seffaran, Cecilia 21
Seffason, Cecilia 21
Senter, Bathshelia 9

Senter, (cont.)
  James 90
  John 31
  Luke 101
  Mark 90, 106
  Mary 106
  Milly 27
  Samuel 69
  Wm. 9
Settle, Nancy 96
  Rebecca 41
Settles, John 48
Sevier, Joseph 107
Shabel, John F. 63
Shackleford, James 50
  Thomas 9
Shaddis, Susanna 15
Shaifer, A. K. 19
  Abraham 22
Shall, William 35
Shane, Wm. 89
Shannon, Harvy 69
  Michael 4
  Robert 2
Shapell, John F. 56
Sharlock, John 61
  Rebecca 52
Sharp, Anthony 3
  Elizabeth C. 93
  James H. 101
  Nancy 19
Shaver, Daniel 11
  Elizabeth 75
  James 65
  James C. 63, 82
  John W. 82
  Matilda 50
  Michael 22
  Nicy 72
  Polly 39
  Susan 94
Shaw, Betsey 17
  Betsy 12
  Elizabeth 12, 14, 41
  Joseph 86
  Nancy 59
  R. S. 104
  Robert 7, 17, 18, 35,
    42
  Sarah 35
  Susannah 7
  Thomas 25, 28, 29, 31
  William 38, 63, 64, 74,
    76, 78, 81
Shaws, Ann 103
Sheeke, C. 75
Shelby, A. B. 30, 33
  Albert 73
  Anthony B. 22, 36
  D. 34
  David 2
  David, Esq. 5, 6, 8
  Henry 18
  John 8, 19, 24, 28
  Lucinda 19
  Orville 60
  Priscilla 21
  Sally B. D. 77
Shell, Wm. 42
Shelton, David 35
  John 43
  Martin 50, 52
  Rebeccah 50
  William 6
Shepherd, Catherine 86
  Cynthia 92
  John 22

Shepherd, (cont.)
  Rachel Caroline 83
  Susan 93
Shepley, Rachel 69
Sheppard, James 2
  John 21
  William 6
Sherlock, Elizabeth 61
Sherry, Nancy 52
Shields, Enoch 56
  John 52
Shoals, Thomas 26
Shoat, Valentine 2
Shoecraft, Simon 19
Shoemaker, Leather 87
Shook, Elizabeth 26
Short, Betsy 76
  Edmund 77
  Isaac 27, 44
  Jenny 11
  Jessia 25
  Joseph 16
  M. 70
  Martha 21
  Polly 70
  Thomas 60, 77
  William 17
Shoulders, Abner 11, 14
  Alfred 65, 71
  Solomon 8, 24, 26, 38,
    41, 44, 45, 49, 50,
    57, 58, 62, 69, 73,
    79, 85, 86, 88, 90,
    97, 101, 107
  William 10, 11
Shoulers, Solomon 20
Shreve, George W. 60
Shrum, Carrol 100
Shy, Amelia 57
  Eli 56
  Levi 57
  Levy C. 42
Sibles, Sarah 25
Sikes, Polly 91
Silber, Hardy 101
Silbur, Hardy 101
Sillers, Samuel 38
Silliman, Thomas 7
Simmons, Charles 65, 96
  Edward 77
  George 59
  Isaiah 33
  James 101
  Joel 101
  Josiah 41
  Lucinda 97
  Marget 59
  Matilda 92
  Solomon 69
Simons, Amelia 61
  Fanny 66
  Joseph 45
  Mary 54
Simpson, Benjamine F. 65
  Benjamine T. 65
  Betty 16
  Charles 7, 11
  E. 37
  Elijah 11, 37
  Elizabeth 94
  Enoch 88
  Isaac 15
  John 9, 16
  John W. 42
  Margaret 84
  Margaret L. 79
  Patsey 7

Stalcup, (cont.)
 Pleasant 77
 Ruth 20
 Sally 23, 25
 Saml. 35
 Stephen 27
 Thomas 25
 William 35
Staley, Christopher 107
 Elizabeth 100
 John M: 65
 Oscar 88
Stallcup, George 14
Staly, Eli 65
Stamp, John 39
Stamps, Angelina 65
 Clarinda 101
 Luther 101
 Nancy 27
 Volney 63
Stams, Telitha 39
Standfield, Ashley 42
Stanfield, Ann 52, 60
 Ashley 27, 42, 43, 46,
  56, 59, 62, 75
 Cinderilla 58
 Elizabeth P. 70
 H. B. 83
 Josiah 70
 Mary 49
 Sarah 51
Stanford, Jemima 37
 John 56, 58
Standley, David 65
 Jonathan 65
Standly, Hutchinson 56
Stanley, Cynthia 74
 Isaac 4
 Raney 79
Stanly, John 69, 82
Stapleton, John 25
 Solo. 101
 Solomon 101
Stark, Adah 67
 Coleman 77
 Elizabeth 87
 Jeremiah 50
 Mariah 82
 Mehetelen 90
 Thomas 16, 67, 77
Starke, Mariah D. 101
Starkey, Lydia 96
Starks, Barry R. 27
 Sophia 49
Starnes, Adam 24
 David 40
Starr, Mariah 42
Starret, Wm. A. 95
Stealy, Amanda 73
 Theodore B. 73
Steel, George 16, 20, 50
 James 90
 James M. 87
 Joseph 4
 Mary 101
 Mary P. 74
 Rebeccah 13
 Robert 60
 Robert, Jr. 13
Steele, Joseph 3
 Martha 107
 Nancy 79
Stephens, Abraham 50
 Eliza 84
 Esther 68
 Irena 63
 James 52

Stephens, (cont.)
 John 22
 Joseph 90
 Rebecca 78
 Sally 95
Stephenson, Wm. 97
Sterns, David 45
Stevens, Mary 24
 Vatchel 9
 William 18, 20
Stevenson, Edward 60
 Joseph 11
 Josiah 11
 Polly 11
Stewart, Alexander 48
 Anny 107
 Asa 52
 Barnet 90
 Daniel 24
 Elizabeth 65
 Frances 98
 Hamblin 95
 Hannah 20
 Harbert 101
 Harriett M. 89
 James 65, 73
 Jane C. 102
 Jeremiah 90
 Jese 90
 John 33, 34, 41, 42,
  50
 Malinda 90
 Mary 52, 93, 102
 Milus 48
 Reuella 45
 Sally 45
 Tenesy 41
 Thomas 42, 107
 William 85, 101
 Woody 77
Stills, John 38
Stilts, Rachel 41
Stiner, Barnabas 7
 Nathan 7, 9
Stinson, Alsey 35
 John L. 107
Stockard, John 4
Stone, Anderson 72
 Anny 54, 76
 Barton W. 22
 Daniel 35
 Dolly 13
 Dotia 33
 Eusebius 7, 13
 Eusebues 16, 43
 Eusibus 48
 Fanny 10
 Francis 55
 Greenville P. 65
 James 95, 107
 John 31
 Keziah 57
 Kisiah 44
 Kitty 23, 39
 Levi 95
 Malinda 103
 Maranda 82
 Mariah 97
 Mary S. 97
 Nancy 84, 102
 Nicholas 16
 Polly 72
 Richard 32, 35
 Sarah 66, 104
 Sidney 63
 Sophia 91
 Stephen 7, 101, 107

Stone, (cont.)
 Thomas 82
 William 16, 47, 48,
  66, 101
 Z. A. 105
Stoode, Catharine 53
Storey, Sally 9
Storm, Polly 100
Story, Ann 6
 James 16, 50, 105
 James, Jr. 104
Stout, George 6
Stoval, Joel 40
 Nancy 40
 Patsey 14
Stovall, America C. 69
 Bartholomus 107
 Byard 31
 Byrd 47
 George 27, 64
 James 31
 Joel 45
 Louisa 80
 Lucinda 40
 Polly 40
 Sarah 18
 Thomas 14, 35, 82
 W. R. 105
 William 18, 27, 28
 William B. 60, 87
Stovell, Robert 107
Stower, Jane 100
Stowers, William S. 107
Strader, Ruth 40
Strain, James 4
 Thomas 4
Straiter, Jacob 27
Strange, Elias 80
 Henry 70
Strate, Rody 91
Strather, Jacob 69
Straton, Malvina 105
Strator, Benjamine 45
Stratton, Edward 66, 71,
  77, 86, 101
 James 28, 33, 35, 41,
  50, 60, 89, 99, 101
 John L. 90
 Rozena 94
 Synthia 98
 William 42, 88
Street, Fanny 12
 James 20
 Judith 22
 Lalinda 35
Strictlen, Henry 45
Strode, Catharine 53
 Margaret 66
Strong, John 20
 Lyman J. 73
Strother, Betsey 9
 Elizabeth 40
 Ira 90
 James 45
 John 79
 Malinda 102
 Nancy 3
 Patsey 48
 Richard 3, 90
 Robert 7
 Susannah 16
Stroud, Dixon 43, 45
Stuart, David 7, 8, 10,
  24
 Elizabeth 16
 Hugh 35
 James 6

144

Stuart, (cont.)
James B. 45
John 7, 50
Minerva 81
Nancy S. 2
Peggy 33
Rebeckah 15
Rebekah 36
Salley 14, 50
Sam'l. 14
William 7, 11
Stubbins, Chas.B. 26
Stubblefield, Betsey 6
Garrison 53
Lemuel 15
Nancy 20, 86
Peter 77, 101
Robert 60
Sally 42
Sarah 87
Stublefield, Cina 82
George 80
Sturgeon, John B. 61
Subtle, Sandy 101
Subttle, Sandy 101, 105
Suddarth, James 35
Suiter, Benjamin 9
Benjamine 7
James 7
Rebeckah 9
Susanna 7
Sulivan, Elizabeth 17
Peter 20
Sarah 79
Sullinger, James 7
Sullivan, Caroline M. 81
Fletcher 11
Isaac 90
James 92
Joseph D. 85
Samuel 9, 36
Summerman, L. 100
Summers, Alexander 35
Betsey 19
Celia 9
Cornelias 35
Cornelius 90
Edward 61
Esther 26
James 14
John 31, 63, 69, 90
Levi 31, 35, 45
Nancy 67, 95
Noah 69
Peter 35
Polly 6, 69
Rebecca 29
Robert 61
Sally 42
Sarah 68
Thomaas 69
Thomas 9, 19, 38, 57,
90
William 9, 26
Suttle, Polly 59
Strother P. 52
Sutton, Benjamine B. 97
Colby 97
Delila 102
Oneida 102
Wilkerson 95
Swain, William M. 69
Swan, John 61
Swaney, ---- 82
Betsey 25
George 97
J. L. 45, 80

Swaney, (cont.)
James M. 77
James N. 65
John 46
John L. 12, 14, 40,
42, 43, 77
John Lea 44
Mariah E. 96
Swann, Thomas 20, 24
Swayney, Caroline 84
Sweringer, Thomas 61
Swift, George A. 101
Harriet H. 100
Sidney C. 101
Swiney, Joel 31
Sypert, Hardy S. 65
Taite, Richard 45
Talbot, Elizabeth 91
Shadrick 77
Talbott, J. H. 48
Thomas 48
Talley, Reuben 42
Zach., Jr. 39
Tally, Augustus N. 69
Eliza W. 86
Lucy 39
Mary 60
Reuben 60
Reubin 61
Sally 61
Tarpley, Hubert 35
Tarver, Benjamine 14
Eliza O. 65
Tatum, Anna 51
Tavenor, Nancy 59
Taylor, Alexander 86
Amelia 45
Andrew 58
Andrew F. P. 73
Benjamine 21, 22, 65
C. I. 107
Catherine 47
Charity 100
Charlotte 14
Chrislly 77
David 86
Eliza P. 92
Elizabeth 5, 6, 42,
56, 71
George 20
Hugh 82
Jacob 70
James 42, 48, 58
James P. 97
Jane 94
Jarratt 53
John 6, 12, 14, 23,
48, 52, 61, 66
John K. 52, 86
John M. 22
Jordan 70
Joseph 18
M. A. 105
M. M. 107
Margaret 96
Mary 81, 97
Monoah 6
Nancy 6
Pleasant 107
Poley 58
Polly 14
Richard 11, 52
Robert 6, 44, 52, 82,
102
Sarah 105
Stephen 70
Turner 86

Taylor, (cont.)
William 16, 105
Teasly, William 31
Templeton, John 45
Terry, Champion 35
Granderson 107
Polly 42
Teysdale, Louisa 46
Thacker, Ann 77
Thomas, Archibald 65
Arioch 20, 67
Berkly 61
Daniel L. 65
Elisha 24
Eliza A. 43
Elizabeth 71
Enoch 95
Jacob 4
Jesse 64
Maria 24
Milly 52
Nancy 53
Polly 11
Sally M. 27
Susannah 14
Wayne 49
William 9
Thompson, Anne 4
B. W. 73
Betsy 41
Burrell 9
Catherine 28
Charles 18
China 17
David 92
Elizabeth 51, 107
George 49, 51
George W. 75
James 22
John 11
Joseph 103
Joyce 50
Margaret 3
Mariah 73
Mary 1
Nancy 41
Nicholas 20, 50, 86
Richard 86
Richard G. 87
Richard J. 86
Robert 101
Sally 1, 10
William 6, 25, 42
Willis 82
Thomson, Jacob 17
Richard J. 76
Thorn, Betsey 14
Thornhill, Epperson 95
James B. 40, 45
Judy 28
Reuben 52
William 92
Thornton, Elizabeth 23
Thrower, William 73
Thurman, George D. 82
Goalsberry 19
Goldsberry 23
Goolsby 14
Hastin D. 82
Thomas 38
Thurmand, Lucinda 80
Thurmond, Geo. C. 79
John 31
Nancy 71
Thurmonde, S. G. 106
Tiller, Thomas 98
Tilley, Allen 101

145

Tilley, (cont.)
Ann 61
Dicy 45
Polly 46
Tilly, Tennessee 82
Wily 53
Tinnell, Henr_t_ 77
James 77
Tinner, Susan 38
William A. 38
Tinnin, Azariah 24
Elizabeth 23
Hugh 26
James A. 77
Jane 24
Lawrence 48
Mary 48
William 23
Tinnon, John 4
Lemuel 20
Samuel 17
Tinsley, Absolum 90
Cornelius 10
Elizabeth 32
Francis 11
Isaac T. 90
Jane L. 55
Jane Lee 34
Kitty 30
Mildred B. 69
Moses 20
Nancy 59
Patsey 47
Paul 27
Polly 60
Sally 31
Spicey 65
Sterling 16
Tire, Polly 13
Tisdale, Barrel 78
Orren 97
Todd, Anney 29
Asa 10
John A. 69
L. 9
Nancy 51
Penelope 9
Polly 54
Samuel 10
Tomblin, Elizabeth 80
Tombs, Archibald L. 82
Tomkins, Eliza 76
J. R. A. 73
R. A. 65
Richard A. 66
Tomkkins, John 24
Tomlinson, Polly 63
Tompkins, E. S. 107
John 52
Tomson, William C. 95
Tonville, Sally 41
Took, Milly 70
Tooley, Joseph G. 107
Toombs, Mary A. S. 93
William 52
Topp, John D. 92
Tops, Elizabeth 70
Totwine, Cretia 5
William 1
Towel, Isaac, Jr. 86
Towell, Catharin 69
Henry 65
Isaac 12, 73
Margaret 73
Nancy 40
Samuel 69, 86
Townsend, Elizabeth 86

Townsend, (cont.)
Elizabeth H. 95
Geo. 99
Henry 61
Jane 61
John 42, 61
Joseph 31, 42
Joseph W. H. 73
Lucretia 62
Mary A. 61
Mary Ann 94
Peter 31
Richard 42, 55
Sary Anne 57
Towpence (See also Two-
pence)
Nancy 55
William 67, 89
Tracey, Mary 28
Michael 28, 66
Tracy, Darham 66
Elizabeth 49
Michael 56
Rebecca 57
Trago, Peggy 15
Trail, Friar 102
William 27
Tramell, Daniel 35
Trap, James 26
Trasey, Isiah 26
Travelstreet, Frederick
42
William 22
Traylor, Edmund 35
Treadwell, Betsey 32
Tribble, Abram 14
Benjamine 82
Rebeccah 13
Trible, Abraham 13
Abram 26, 39
Dicy 14
Lucinda 27
Nancy 21
Polly 26
Rebeccah 13
Stephen 27, 28
Trice, Dolly 16
Eliza 44
John 13
Patsey 18
Trigg, Abraham 16, 17,
31, 32
Abram 17, 20, 21, 23,
24
Abram, Jr. 11
Daniel 6, 7, 11
Dotia 17
Haden S. 95
Jane 80
John H. 86
Juliet 9
Locky 6
Nancy Ann 62
P. W. 17
Sally 72
Sukey 6
Theodotia 52
Will 6, 16, 26, 31
Will, Jr. 7, 15, 23,
32, 38
Wm. 10
William, Jr. 30
Trimble, Walter 53
Troffilsted, Lucinda 50
Troudale, Sally 95
Trousdale, James 5, 10,
11, 34

Trousdale, (cont.)
Jonathan 12, 14, 38
Katy 5
Robert 10, 11, 16, 18
Sally 16
W. 76
William 36, 43, 56, 69
Trout, Elizabeth 71
George 49
Henry 69
John 49
Malinda 96
Samuel 71, 73
Troutt, George 69
Jacob 69
John 48
Margaret 69
Trusty, Biddy 46
David 57
John Giles 77
John J. 81
William 86
Tucker, Amey 38
Dickson 59
Dixon 61
Garrett 82
Jesse 101
John S. 105
Mary 101
William 73
Tuner, Nicy D. 94
Tunnage, George W. 90
Tupner, Jacob 2
Turnage, Alexander 77
Turner, Adam 13, 20, 46
Bartlett 103, 107
Betsey 39
Boyd M. 42
Charles W. 102
Edmund 40
Eliza B. 65
Elizabeth 2, 35, 56
Frances 51, 78
Frederick 10
J. H. 105
Jacob 2, 22, 42
James 7
James B. 86
Jemima 88
John 7, 16, 18, 27,
80, 81, 82
John E. 91
John G. 61
John H. 50, 76, 85,
86, 89, 90
Lavinia 25
Letha 83
M. B. 97
Martin 20
Mary 90, 94
Mary Ann 68, 90
Margaret 86
Martha Ann 81
Mathew 89
Matthew 69
Milly 51, 68
Nelson 45
Philip 25, 33, 35
Polly 7, 13
Sally 10
Sally W. 51
Samuel R. 82
Samuel S. 92
Seaton H. 82
Senith 105
Stephen 50
Stephen H. 45, 57

146

Turner, (cont.)
  Sumpter 51, 57
  Teriha 31
  Terisha 77
  Terrisha 69
  Thos. H. 88
  Verdela 47
  W. 28
  William 42, 54, 61,
    70, 77, 102
  Wm. H. 78
  William L. 27
  Wilson 86
Turney, Mary 4
  Peter 2
Turpin, Averilla 88
  Edmond 10
  Elizabeth 95
  Evelina 96
  Lucy 30
  Patsey 69
  Polly 33
Tuttle, Betsey 44
  Jesse 45, 64
  Polly 95
  Robert 57
  Sally 58
Twopence (See also Tow-
    pence)
  David 70, 86
  Nelly 48
  William 70, 98, 105
Tyler, Roxey 28
Tyomas, Matilda 68
Tyre, Richmond C. 101
Tyree, Fanny 26
  George M. 91
  Jacob 91
  Jane M. 102
  John P. 79
  Pleasant 30, 44
  Sam'l. 53
  Samuel C. 38
  Sarah C. 77
  William 54
  Y. E. 106
Underwood, Harriett 76
  J. J. 97
  Jane 103
  John 42, 49
  Joseph 14
  Nathan 42, 99
  Virginia 102
  Winifred 104
Uzzell, Jordon 25
  Polley 13
Vaden, Burell 73
Valentine,---- 38
  Isaac 19
  Lotey 46, 49
  Prudence 23
  Sarah 61
  Thomas 38
Vallentine, Polly 19
Vanable, John 61
Vance, Abraham 83
  David 45, 56
  Joseph 97
  Nancy 50
  Philip 97
  Phillip 49
  Rachel 83
Vane, Catherine 70
Vanover, Frances 95
Varvel, Katherine 71
Vaughan, Henry B. 42
Vaughn, Edmund W. 38

Vaughn, (cont.)
  Henry 62
  John S. 42
  Lavica 81
  Leticia 97
  Mathew 38
  Polly 51
  Turner 72
Vaugn, James 102
Vaun, Mathew 38
Velentine, Betsy 36
Verdin, William 37
Vinly, Permelia 63
Vinson, B. 22
  Bental 7
  Delilah 7
  Edmund 31
  Elias E. 95
  Elizabeth 18
  Enos 25, 28, 31, 49
  Eoline 73
  George 25
  Henry 13, 24
  I. B. 105
  James 5, 68, 72
  Louisiana 53
  Lucky 38
  Mary 35
  R. A. 99
  Rhody 17, 24
  S. E. 107
  Stokely, 77
  Stokley, 31
  Susannah 13
  Wiley 64
  Willie 98
Virgin, Henry 31
Volentine, Catherine 55
  Henry 107
  Henry M. 97
  Solomon H. 64
  William 50
Volner, William 35
Wade, Walter 38
Wadkins, Fanny 27
Waggoner, Elmore 27
  Ephraim 50
  Martha 83
Wagnor, John P. 59
Wagnore, John P. 38
Wagoner, Edmond 27
Waide, Kitty Ann 78
Wainscott, Caty 37
Wakefield, John 49
Walch, James F. 102
Walker, A. 22
  Alexander 1
  Elizabeth 103
  Erasmus D. 102
  James 22
  James M. 86
  Joel 107
  John P. 38
  Lucinda L. 84
  Malinda H. 82
  Moses 97
  Pleasant 61
  Rhody 105
  Sally 74
  Sally P. 99
  Thomas 3
  William 3
Wall, Millinton 14
  Pearce 4
  Peter 89
Wallace, A. E. 107
  Adam 14, 20

Wallace, (cont.)
  Archibald 20
  Betsey 4
  David 25
  E. E. 83, 84
  Elizabeth 30
  Felisa 64
  Harbard 53 ⸱
  James 5, 7, 49
  Jenny 5
  John 27, 41, 82
  Jonathan 45
  Joseph 26
  Joseph B. 38
  Magdalene 64
  Mary 87
  Mary I. 91
  Matilda 26
  S. S. 107
  Samuel 49, 64, 82
  Sarah M. 85
  William 37, 53
Waller, Joseph 2, 10
  Lydia 7
  Richard 6
  Thomas 3
Wallington, H. L. 81
Wallis, Polly 24
Walsh, Baker 70
  Thomas 105
Walters, John 23, 51
  Mary Ann 51
Walton, Caroline 26
  Douglas 91
  Douglass 49
  Elizabeth 20
  George 42
  Gray 61
  Harris 53, 81
  Isaac 61
  James 22, 76
  John 66, 73, 92
  Josiah 45, 61, 71
  Kitty 57
  Lavinia 101
  Mabry 18
  Nancy 23
  Ollivia 62
  Patsey 33
  Polly 26
  Sally 19
  Sebella C. 89
  William 4, 39, 57, 81
  William P. 102
Ward, Betsy 41
  James 10
  John 72, 73
  Mary Ann 93
  Nancy 90
  William 35, 50, 59
Warner, David 105
  J. L. 79
  John 77
  Levi 77
  R. L. 74
  R. T. 100
  Reubin T. 77
Warren, Cinthia 87
  Hardy 14
  Isaac 53
  J. L. 91
  John 27
  Margaret 67
  Mary D. 81
  Seathmead 95
Watkins, B. 64
  Bartholomua 82

148

Will, Matthew T. 61
Willard, Henry 35
Willcomb, Nathaniel 7
Willerford, Mary 75
William, James 5
Williams, Abisha 32
  Alexander 86
  Alisha 41
  Anthony 30, 61
  Betsey 33
  Celia 64
  Charles Wesly 83
  Chesley 61
  Chipley 57
  Daniel 27
  Davis 83
  Dusty 12
  Edward 2, 5, 25
  Elijah 66
  Elizabeth 30, 58, 91, 104
  Elizabeth E. 104
  Francis 82, 97
  Green B. 66
  Grissim 45
  Henry 12, 37, 44, 73, 82
  Henry C. 47
  James 4, 61
  Jenny 10
  Job 10
  John 2, 20, 32, 53, 83
  John H. 61, 86
  John L. 83, 102
  John V. 42
  John W. 70
  Jonathan 57
  Joseph 42
  Lewis 70
  Malinda 53, 80
  Marguritt 67
  Mary E. 47
  Matilda 28
  Nancy 63
  Patsey 47
  Peggy 25
  Pheby 83
  Polly 63, 85
  Rebecca 70
  Robert 12, 97
  Sally 57, 97
  Samuel A. 97
  Stewart 86
  Thomas 57, 70
  William 45, 57, 66
Williamson, George 2
  George P. 91
  John 107
  Robert 14
  Sarah 26
  Thomas 1
  W. G. 50
Williford, Alfred 93
  Green 16
  Lucy 29
Willis, Cabel 10
  Caleb 58
  Daniel 10, 18
  Elender 24
  Elenor 97
  Francis A. 94
  Harvey R. 18
  Henry Richard 10
  Jesse 61
  John 14, 24
  Lena 53

Willis, (cont.)
  Malchi 25
  Mary 7
  Merrell 10
  Meshack 14
  Minerva 79
  Thomas 8
Willmott, Robert P. 102
Willoughby, William 57
Wills, George 1, 58
  James 27
  Jane 1
  Nancy 11
  Wyat 11
Willson, Selah 50
Wilson, Addision 87
  Addison 66, 70, 78, 87
  Anna 25
  Anne 21, 35
  Annes 60
  Ashby 83
  Benjamin(e) 58, 60, 67, 83, 88
  Betsy 10
  Charity 27
  Cynthia W. 26
  Darcus 3
  David 1, 2, 3, 10, 24, 65
  Ebenezer 16
  Elenor 6, 17
  Elizabeth 2, 3, 37, 89, 95
  Fannie 30
  Fanny 24
  George 25
  H. L. 105
  Hannah 6
  James 1, 3, 4, 6, 10, 24, 35, 71
  James A. 7, 8
  James C. 16
  Jas. R. 61
  James T. 26, 35, 57
  Jane 23, 37
  Jeremiah H. 91
  John 1, 66, 80, 84, 86, 89, 90, 97
  John B. 91
  Jonathan 11, 86
  Joseph 17, 32
  Joseph T. 27
  Josiah 76
  M. W. 37
  Malissa 38
  Mary 1, 26
  Matilda 27
  Montetion W. 23
  Montilion W. 78
  Montitian 22
  Montition 61
  Moses 20, 22, 38
  Nancy M. 73
  Patsey 21
  Pleasant 66
  Polly 12, 23
  Prudence 15
  Richard 9
  Robert 25, 73
  Sally 16, 60
  Samuel 38, 45, 53, 66, 68
  Sarah E. 102
  Sealah 50
  Stephen 22
  Thomas 32

Wilson, (cont.)
  Violet 26
  William 3, 70, 73
  Zacheus 2, 7, 78
  Zacheus R. 57
  Zack 17
Wimbelly, Susan 46
Wimberley, Lewis 39
Wimberly, Edy 10
  Levi 18
Wims, James 102
  Nancy 92
  William 102
  William H. 86
Winbane, William 35
Winbourn, Betsey 50
Winburn, Mary 63
Winchester, Almira 61
  Ann 81
  Elizabeth Caroline 60
  Emily 94
  G. 5, 6
  James 12
  Louisa 65
  Lucileus 83
  Lucilius 51, 65, 67
  M. 31
  Mary Hall 76
  Maryann 22
  Selina 35
  V. P. 81, 85
Windle, George 55
Winham, Permelia 32
  Robert 50
  Stephen 91
  William 53, 56, 81
Winn, James F. 32
  Jane 45
  Louisa I. 91
  Martha 32
  Peter 20, 32
  Polly 23
  R. S. 105
  William J. 70
  Willis 61
  Woodson 49
Winnberry, Levi 17
Winns, Joseph B. 53
Winston, Eliza B. 36
  Joseph B. 82
  William L. 86
Winters, Betsey 4
Wirt, Logan D. 25
  Sally 25
Wise, Frederick 80
  Hannah 43
  Joseph H. 42
  Susan 63
Wiseman, Evelina D. 96
  John 42, 43, 47
  Sarah 86
Witcher, Savory 6
Withers, Hugh H. 32
Withrey, Sally 35
Witt, Marthena 90
Witte, Georgett C. 91
Wolf, Martha 97
Womack, Hartey 7
  Harty 9
  Hiram 13
  James 3
  Rebeccah 13
  Wm. 78
Womberdurf, Daniel 20
Wombledorff, Betsey 24
Wood, Benj. 4
  Charles 27